DELMORE SCHWARTZ
AND JAMES LAUGHLIN

ALSO IN THE SERIES

William Carlos Williams and James Laughlin:
Selected Letters

Kenneth Rexroth and James Laughlin:
Selected Letters

Delmore Schwartz

AND

James Laughlin

/ · /

SELECTED LETTERS

EDITED BY ROBERT PHILLIPS

W·W·NORTON & COMPANY

NEW YORK   LONDON

First Edition

The text of this book is composed in 11.5/13 Bembo,
with the display set in ITC Garamond Book Condensed.
Composition and manufacturing by The Maple-Vail Book
Manufacturing Group.

Library of Congress Cataloging-in-Publication Data
Schwartz, Delmore, 1913–1966.
Delmore Schwartz and James Laughlin : selected letters / edited by
Robert Phillips.
p.   cm.
Includes bibliographical references and index.
1. Schwartz, Delmore, 1913–1966—Correspondence.   2. Laughlin,
James, 1914–   —Correspondence.   3. Poets, American—20th
century—Correspondence.   I. Laughlin, James, 1914–   .
II. Phillips, Robert S., 1938–   III. Title.
PS3537.C79Z485   1993
811'.52—dc20
[B]   92–25154

ISBN 0-393-03471-2

W.W. Norton & Company, Inc.
500 Fifth Avenue, New York, N.Y. 10110
W.W. Norton & Company Ltd.
10 Coptic Street, London WC1A 1PU

1 2 3 4 5 6 7 8 9 0

FOR
SOPHIE WILKINS
AND
KARL SHAPIRO

I don't like to hear that I have not fulfilled the promise of my youth, but almost everyone else is too polite to tell me and left to myself, I tend to put all new poems and stories in my filing cabinet and forget about them. Hence, in view of the fact that we have now been friends for some fifteen years, it is, I think, your duty as well as your privilege to say what you really think. I would prefer that you say it in a pleasant tone, but I'd rather have the tone unpleasant than be left in ignorance and self-delusion.

DS to JL, January 16, 1953

CONTENTS

INTRODUCTION

This book gathers the best of the extant correspondence between Delmore Schwartz (1913–1966) and James Laughlin (b. 1914). The correspondence began in July 1937, when Schwartz posted an unsolicited submission to Laughlin for the latter's newly established annual anthology, *New Directions in Prose and Poetry*. Laughlin was in his fifth year at Harvard (he had taken a leave of absence in 1934 to travel to Europe, visit Gertrude Stein and Alice B. Toklas at their summer home in Bilignin in the South of France, and study with Ezra Pound in Rapallo). He already was writing his free-verse poems and had established his small publishing company in 1936, financed largely by family gifts. One of America's most literary presses was thus kept alive in its formative years by the income from the Jones & Laughlin Steel Corporation of Pittsburgh, Pennsylvania.[1]

Schwartz, on the other hand, was an impoverished twenty-four-year-old Harvard dropout. At Harvard he had been a Briggs-Copland Instructor, together with Wallace Stegner, Mark Schorer, and John Berryman—a group of great promise.[2] But he had left in March 1937 without taking a degree. His father was dead and his mother was unable or refused to support him any longer. (He had attended the University of Wisconsin in 1931–32, New York University from February 1933 to June 1935, and would begin graduate studies in September 1937.)

The backgrounds of the two men obviously were quite different. Laughlin grew up in Pittsburgh, went to the Arnold School there, then on to Le Rosey near Geneva, Switzerland; Eaglebrook School in Deerfield, Massachusetts; and Choate School in Wallingford, Connecticut. At Choate he studied with Dudley Fitts, and it was Fitts who arranged for him to study with Pound abroad.[3] There was Laughlin family money and support for his literary ambitions. He had no brother. Schwartz was the eldest of two sons of Romanian immigrants who had settled in New York's Lower East Side. After a time his father made a considerable sum in real estate speculation—but most of it was later lost, due to the Depression and indifferent investment management by bankers.[4] Schwartz was to spend most of his life resenting the fact that he was poor.

At the time of his first letter to Laughlin, Schwartz was a "promising young poet": a play in verse and prose had been published in *The New Caravan* anthology, and his poetry reviews appeared in *Poetry* magazine in both 1936 and 1937.

Laughlin had already established a solid base for his fledgling publishing house when he enlisted William Carlos Williams, whose publisher—The Macaulay Company—had become defunct. Laughlin published his first Williams title in 1937, and by 1938 he had three Williams books in print. He added Ezra Pound to his list, and would remain Pound's publisher for the rest of the poet's life.

Publishing the young Delmore Schwartz was much more of a gamble. Yet Laughlin recognized genius in Schwartz's early poetry and prose, and published some of both in his 1937 *New Directions* annual. Next, he asked to see a collection of poems. Schwartz submitted the manuscript of *In Dreams Begin Responsibilities* (the title comes from an epigraph used by Yeats) in January 1938.[5] Laughlin was taken with the manuscript, and soon was calling the poet "the American Auden," citing a comparable fluency. He offered a contract for the book, which was to make Schwartz famous at age twenty-five—and the success of which he could never live down.

These early letters between the two are charming. Laughlin can never remember to put an "h" in Schwartz's name, and Schwartz is puzzled how one should pronounce "Laughlin" (it's "Lockland"). Laughlin told him simply to call him "J"—but Schwartz thereafter usually wrote him as "Jay." As Patricia C. Willis, Curator of American Literature at Yale's Beinecke Library, has remarked, "Laughlin is one of his generation's better letter-writers, and when inspired by a stimulating correspondent, he produces wonderful mail!"[6] Schwartz was to produce such stimulation. Even as a young man, he was deep in his anecdotage. He loved to be slightly naughty, as when recounting William Carlos Williams's immortal first words to him ("Where's the can?"). But when it came to maliciousness, Laughlin was no slouch either, describing his mentor Dudley Fitts as "A kind of algae."

In Dreams Begin Responsibilities was an immediate critical success, and the two men felt quite comfortable with their relationship. Laughlin even made Schwartz an employee who, along with his wife Gertrude, worked in a room of the house they rented on Memorial Drive in Cambridge. (Schwartz had married Gertrude Buckman—his high school sweetheart—in 1938.) Gertrude kept the financial records, and Schwartz solicited and read manuscripts and often carted packages of books to the post office. Laughlin and Schwartz became best friends. Then the relationship began to change. From the letters it is evident that Schwartz came to resent Laughlin's absences from the office and his easy life style—trips to Europe, skiing in Utah—while the poet was often nearly destitute and stuck in Cambridge, New York, or New Jersey.

Further, Schwartz's next two books—a translation of Rimbaud's *A Season in Hell* and the first volume of his magnum opus, *Genesis, Book One*—were panned by critics. Laughlin had recognized the weakness of *Genesis*, but reluctantly published it out of loyalty. Thereafter there was a barrage of mail from Schwartz, much of it accusing Laughlin of no longer believing in him or his work. After four years, Schwartz delivered a collection of short stories entitled *The World Is a Wedding*. Laughlin published it in 1948, and it was universally well received. Both writer and publisher were reunited in their feelings of mutual regard.

But other difficulties ensued. Successive Schwartz manuscripts reached Laughlin only after "the famous Schwartz delay," to quote one letter. *The World Is a Wedding* had been announced years before delivery. Schwartz was always out of money, and tried to obtain advances for projects that often never materialized, such as a book of criticism on T. S. Eliot, for which Laughlin paid the largest sum his firm had advanced to any writer. There was to be a collection of Schwartz's literary essays, entitled *The Imitation of Life,* also not delivered. Through these delays and disappointments, Laughlin in his letters reveals himself to be patient and supportive.

Like all of us, James Laughlin was not without faults. He expected the Schwartzes to provide hospitality for his good friends in his absence, and according to Schwartz he revealed his parsimonious nature by urging Gertrude Schwartz to steam uncanceled three-cent stamps off envelopes. He could not account for one of Schwartz's book-length manuscripts for several months. Schwartz claimed it was found under the floorboards of Laughlin's station wagon in Utah; Laughlin states it was found in a mail truck. The latter's has proven to be the more reliable memory.

But there is no doubt Laughlin was more sinned against than sinning. It became clear after a time that Schwartz was not rooted in reality. This can explain why some of his letters are so uncommonly fascinating. In Laughlin's words, "He was so witty and such a magnificent confabulator";[7] he loved to make up stories about Laughlin and the Harvard critic Harry Levin and other friends, as well as about himself. These are wonderfully funny, but it is sometimes difficult to tell where reality ends and fantasy begins. Schwartz also loved to tell fabrications about his literary idol, T. S. Eliot. The most hilarious involved Eliot's courtship of his first wife, Vivienne. According to the tale, the pair were punting on the Cherwell when Vivienne suddenly wanted to pause and called out, "Put your pole in, Tom!" Schwartz maintained that the poet mistook her words for a sexual advance, took action, and then felt the only honorable thing to do was to marry her.

All this is fun. But as Schwartz began to ride what his first biographer, James Atlas, called "the manic-depressive roller coaster,"[8] his fantasies became paranoid and his letters developed into dark and obsessive harangues. Gertrude left, and divorced him in 1943. He accused Laughlin of disaffection, even of cheating him on his royalty statements. The saddest accusation was when he maintained that both Laughlin and Nelson Rockefeller were having an affair with his second wife, Elizabeth Pollet, whom Schwartz had met in the spring of 1944. (She was the daughter of the painter Joseph Pollet, and had been educated at Black Mountain College and the University of Chicago.) Despite such outbursts, some of Schwartz's friends took his paranoia lightly. In Dwight Macdonald's view, for instance, it was never "self-aggrandizing or deadly (except to himself)," and "His aggressions against old friends always seemed to me more a despairing cry than an accusation."[9] Still, it must have been extremely painful to Laughlin to receive such attacks. It was he who had helped Schwartz finance the down payment on a farmhouse in New Jersey. Even as late as 1955, he was offering Schwartz guest editorships and book review assignments in an effort to bolster the poet's morale and bank account.

These letters reveal Schwartz's early *joie de vivre* and later despair. They also show the two men's shared interests: literature above all, both classic and modern; but also music, pretty women, baseball, and politics. They afford glimpses of other writers as well: William Carlos Williams, Kenneth Rexroth, Kenneth Patchen, José Garcia Villa, W. H. Auden, Jean Garrigue, Alfred Kazin, Harry Levin, Ezra Pound, John Berryman, Allen Tate, Kay Boyle, Philip Rahv, Philip Horton, Mary McCarthy, Louise Bogan, William Barrett, John Crowe Ransom, Horace Gregory, Marguerite Young, Katherine Anne Porter, and Dwight Macdonald are just a few of the figures involved in their exchange. In a way, the correspondence reads like a fever chart of American literary activities over several decades. It also provides our best source for Laughlin's philosophy of publishing:

I don't care what Belitt or anybody else says.[10] I am not in the business to have little cat fights with literary ladies. I shall turn the cheek until the neck-joints give out. I know what is in the book. There is some crap, some good stuff, some middling. Furthermore, everything is relative. Plenty of people liked what B— didn't like.

The thing is to get the non-conforming stuff in print when it is written and not fifteen years after. That is my job. I hope I don't make a mess of it. (Letter 6, October 24, 1937)

And:

There is no beating the game that I can see. It takes money to run a press like New Directions, and although the books might conceivably come to pay their way, you cannot count on that. The minute I began to count on making money, I would drift into printing crap. The only thing I can see to do is to focus on the quality of the stuff and take the gain or loss as it comes—keeping the two kinds of value rigidly separated. (Letter 42, April 27, 1939)

And again:

Business has been worse in the past year than anyone can remember and all except those who have had at least three best sellers or Books-of-the-Month are preparing to shoot themselves. As for me, I shall simply retire to the country, eliminate all overhead, and practice the pure essentials—printing books, selling them to the really interested by mail, and by-pass the prodigious waste of advertising-promotion-sales pressure, all of which is now revealing its complete futility to even the great minds who invented it. A book of poetry, after all, is in its essence not the same as a bottle of mouthwash. (Letter 163, June 30, 1951)

Laughlin was no longer Schwartz's publisher after the poetry collection *Vaudeville for a Princess* (1950)— another critical disappointment. But this was at Schwartz's insistence. He took his new and selected volume of poems, *Summer Knowledge* (1959), to Doubleday. It was awarded both the Bollingen Prize in Poetry and the Shelley Memorial Prize, restoring to Schwartz much of the luster his reputation had lost in the prior decade. The last book published in his lifetime, *Successful Love and Other Stories* (1961), was issued by Corinth Books. Yet Schwartz wanted to repair his relationship with Laughlin. His last communication to his friend was a telegram from Syracuse, in February 1963, hoping to smoke "the peace pipe." But the two came together only after Schwartz's death in 1966, recounted in the Coda to this edition. Laughlin published three posthumous volumes: *In Dreams Begin Responsibilities and Other Stories* (1978), edited by James Atlas; and *The Ego Is Always at the Wheel: Bagatelles* (1986) and *Last & Lost Poems* (1989), both edited by Robert Phillips. These went into several printings, proving that Schwartz was being read once again, decades after his brilliant debut.

NOTES

1. For biographical facts about JL, I am indebted to Hugh Witemeyer's introduction to *William Carlos Williams & James Laughlin: Selected Letters* (New York: Norton, 1989), and Lee Bartlett's introduction to *Kenneth Rexroth & James Laughlin: Selected Letters* (New York: Norton, 1991).

2. Note from JL to RP, January 1992.

3. Bartlett, ed., *Kenneth Rexroth*, pp. xvii–xviii.

4. Richard McDougall, *Delmore Schwartz* (New York: Twayne Publishers, 1974), p. 16.

5. Schwartz appended a note to his first volume: "The title of this book is derived from the quotation which heads *Responsibilities,* a book of poems by William Butler Yeats, published in 1914. There the quotation reads, 'In dreams begins responsibility,' and is attributed to an 'Old Play.' " *In Dreams Begin Responsibilities* (New York: New Directions, 1938), p. 172.

6. Letter to RP, January 22, 1990.

7. Letter to RP, August 19, 1989.

8. James Atlas, *Delmore Schwartz: The Life of an American Poet* (New York: Farrar, Straus & Giroux, 1977), pp. 253–54.

9. Ibid., p. 345.

10. Ben Belitt's highly critical review of *New Directions in Prose and Poetry 1936* appeared in *Poetry,* LVI (October 1937), 45–48.

NOTES ON THE TEXT

Only a few of the 204 letters in the present text have
already been published. My edition of *Letters of Delmore Schwartz* (Princeton: Ontario Review Press,
1984) contains complete versions of sixteen letters to
Laughlin, of which a number but not all are reprinted
here. For that edition I was limited to letters selected
by Mr. Laughlin from the New Directions Archive
at his home in Norfolk, Connecticut. He chose spar-
ingly, perhaps saving letters for his personal use in
the future. Since that time an entire carton of additional Schwartz / Laughlin correspondence has been
found in Norfolk, to which I was given complete
access. This considerably facilitated the selection and
editing of this volume.

In addition to the New Directions Archive, additional letters from both sides of the correspondence
were located in the Delmore Schwartz Papers at the
Beinecke Rare Book and Manuscript Library, Yale
University. Special thanks to Patricia C. Willis,
Curator of American Literature at the Beinecke, and
to Daria Ague and Stephen Jones, Public Services.

I have selected 151 letters from Schwartz to
Laughlin and members of his staff, and 53 from
Laughlin or staff members to Schwartz. I have tried

to select correspondence that contains information about the writing or publication of the two men's writings, their relationship as author / publisher, their friendship and personal lives, their opinions of contemporaries and other writers, and the early years of New Directions and the vision of its founder.

While preparing the letters for publication, I employed the guidelines set forth in Hugh Witemeyer's *William Carlos Williams and James Laughlin: Selected Letters,* inasmuch as that volume was the first of the series to be published by W. W. Norton. The series will include both sides of correspondence between Laughlin and various other New Directions authors. It is an ambitious project which, when completed, may give us the most revealing portrait of the publisher / writer relationship ever attempted. It will also give us a history of New Directions publishing.

On editing principles, I quote Witemeyer: "Every letter is preceded by a headnote which gives its number in the present edition, its form, and the number of its pages. To designate epistolary forms, I have used the following abbreviations: TLS (typed letter signed), TL (typed letter unsigned), ALS (autograph letter signed), AL (autograph letter unsigned), TCS (typed card signed), and ACS (autograph card signed)." When letters from either correspondence were written on official letterhead (e.g., New Directions' New York office or Alta Lodge, Utah, for Laughlin; Princeton University or *The New Republic* for Schwartz), but clearly emanated from their homes, the latter address is cited.

As Witemeyer established, positions of dates, salutations, closings, and signatures have been standardized. Salutations and signatures appear in capitals and small capitals. Letters dictated in offices appear without typists' initials. Typed names following autograph signatures are omitted. Titles of book-length works are italicized, while quotation marks are given to titles of shorter works. Typographical errors and misspellings have been corrected, including those of proper names. For instance, Schwartz habitually misspelled Karl Shapiro's surname as if it were the same as that of his friend Meyer Schapiro, and always added a "u" to Chandler Brossard's last name.

Also in accordance with Witemeyer's practices, editorial insertions appear within square brackets. As in previous volumes, when a person, place, or work is not identified in the notes on a given page, the index provides a cross-reference where information about the same subject can be found.

Whenever poems or doggerel accompany a letter, I have included them to recreate the spirit of the correspondence. In a couple such instances, interesting new work appears for the first time.

My editorial practice differs in one respect from that of my first predecessor. Not every letter is reproduced in its entirety. In a few instances I have made editorial abridgements in the interest of avoiding repetition, maintaining liveliness, or protecting an individual's privacy. Deletions are indicated by ellipses, sometimes explained by editorial brackets.

In preparing the annotations for the present volume, I have benefited from the work of several scholars. In addition to Professors Witemeyer and Bartlett, I wish to cite James Atlas for his *Delmore Schwartz: The Life of an American Poet* (already noted); Richard McDougall, for his study, *Delmore Schwartz* (New York: Twayne Publishers, 1974); Elizabeth Pollet, who edited *Portrait of Delmore: Journals and Notes of Delmore Schwartz, 1939–1959* (New York: Farrar, Straus & Giroux, 1986); Bruce Bawer, *The Middle Generation: The Lives and Poetry of Delmore*

Schwartz, Randall Jarrell, John Berryman and Robert Lowell (Hamden, Conn.: Archon Books, 1986); and David H. Zucker and the late Donald A. Dike, editors of *Selected Essays of Delmore Schwartz* (Chicago: University of Chicago Press, 1970). Professor Zucker's bibliography is invaluable.

Other sources consulted include Ian Hamilton's *Robert Lowell: A Biography* (New York: Random House, 1982); John Haffenden's *The Life of John Berryman* (Boston: Routledge & Kegan Paul, 1982); Russell Fraser's *A Mingled Yarn: The Life of R. P. Blackmur* (New York: Harcourt Brace Jovanovich, 1981); Eileen Simpson's *Poets in Their Youth. A Memoir* (New York: Random House, 1982); and Daniel Bismuth's *Delmore Schwartz ou le démon de l'origine* (Paris: Editions du Rocher, 1991).

Other recent Schwartz scholarship includes William Barrett's *The Truants: Adventures Among the Intellectuals* (Garden City, N.Y.: Anchor Books, 1982); B. Bernard Cohen's "Delmore Schwartz," *Encyclopedia of World Literature in the 20th Century*, Vol. 4, Leonard S. Klein, general editor (New York: Frederick Ungar, 1984); Lawrence S. Friedman's "Delmore Schwartz," *Critical Survey of Poetry, English Language Studies*, Vol. 6, Frank N. Magell, editor (Englewood Cliffs, N.J.: Salem Press, 1982); Mark I. Goldman's "Delmore Schwartz," *Dictionary of Literary Biography*, Vol. 28, Daniel Waldman, editor (Detroit: Gale Research Co., 1984); Robert Phillips's "Delmore David Schwartz," *Dictionary of American Biography, Supplement 8* (New York: Charles Scribner's Sons, 1988); Bryan Read's "Delmore (David) Schwartz, 1913–1966," *Major 20th-Century Writers*, Vol. 4, Bryan Read, editor (Detroit: Gale Research Co., 1991); Craig Tapping's "Delmore Schwartz," *Dictionary of Literary Biography*, Vol. 48, second series

(Detroit: Gale Research Co., 1986); and David Zucker's " 'Alien to Myself': Jewishness in the Poetry of Delmore Schwartz," *Studies in American Jewish Literature,* IX, 2 (1990).

I have incurred debts to others as well. My principal obligation is to James Laughlin, for asking me to undertake this project, for making his files available, and for patiently correcting and adding to my annotations. His letters appear with his permission. He was unfailingly courteous in answering my many queries by post, phone, and cassette tape, and in making identifications—such as which Theodore (Morrison or Spencer?), which Philip (Rahv or Horton?), which William (Barrett or Phillips?), which Gertrude (Buckman or Huston?), even which Elena (Levin or Wilson?) was which. There were a number of such problems to solve.

The letters of Delmore Schwartz appear by permission of his heirs, the late Kenneth Schwartz and Wayne Schwartz, and also by permission of the Beinecke Rare Book and Manuscript Library, Yale University. I thank Dr. David Stam and Mr. Mark F. Weimer, Bird Library, Syracuse University, for their help and courtesy. I especially thank Kathleen Manwaring, Archives / Manuscripts Supervisor, The George Arents Research Library at Syracuse University; Professor Walter Sutton, Syracuse University; Griselda Ohannessian, at the New York office of New Directions; Betty Fussell of New York City; Edwin Gallaher, University of Houston; and Alexandra Eylie of Syracuse. All responded to queries; Ms. Eylie did additional bibliographical research.

My wife, Judith Bloomingdale, helped to locate and check poetic quotes as well as to decipher Schwartz's handwriting. (In these letters, Laughlin's hand is always clear—a contrast perhaps indicative of the differences between the two personalities.) All these friends and individuals have aided me, and none is responsible for omissions or errors.

A portion of this book was serialized in *The Paris Review*, 123 (Summer 1992), pp. 137–188. Thanks to the editor George Plimpton for permission to reprint.

LETTERS

1. TLS-1
700 West 180 St.
New York City,
July 22, 1937

DEAR MR. LAUGHLIN:

I do not know if you intend to pay any attention to unsolicited contributions to *New Directions,* but I think the enclosed pieces are the kind of work you want for your anthology. If I am wrong, forgive me, and thanks for looking at them.

Yours,
DELMORE SCHWARTZ

/ · /

Mr. Laughlin: Still a Harvard undergraduate, JL was already a respected publisher. He had begun New Directions in the fall of 1936 in Norfolk, Connecticut. His first title was Montagu O'Reilly's *Pianos of Sympathy,* followed by *New Directions in Prose and Poetry 1936* (the first annual), Dudley Fitts's *Poems,* and Robert McAlmon's *Not Alone Lost.*

the enclosed pieces: Schwartz submitted five poems and two short stories ("In Dreams Begin Responsibilities" and "The Commencement Day Address").

2. TLS-1

700 W. 180 St.
N.Y.C.
Sept. 6, 1937

DEAR LAUGHLIN:

Will you return to me the manuscripts which you are not using. I'd like to try to dispose of some more of them and can't until I know which pieces you have and which pieces you are using. Thanks.

Yours,
DELMORE SCHWARTZ

3. TLS-1

October 11, 1937

DEAR MR. SCHWARTZ:

As an editor, in defense of editors, of our time & our sanity, I must *give you hell* for disposing of a manuscript which you had offered to me. You simply must not do things like that. It raises no end of trouble.

"In Dreams" is the piece that I want most and I must insist on your making an effort to have it released for me. I'm sorry about this, but it is the right thing to do.

The other manuscript which I have is "Commencement Day Address." I like this one too, but not as much as the other.

Please let me hear from you at once. Perhaps there is some reasonable explanation for what you did. I repeat, it is, in principle, a serious thing.

Sincerely,
JAMES LAUGHLIN IV

/ · /

offered to me: Not having heard from JL since his submission in July, Schwartz sent "In Dreams Begin Responsibilities" to the editors of the new *Partisan Review*. His letter informing Laughlin of this has been lost. The story appeared in *PR,* 4 (December 1937), 5–11, and created a sensation.

4. TL-1   October 18, 1937

DEAR SCHWARTZ:

No I didn't actually think you were wicked, but I just wanted to make enough of a stink so that you would realize that it was a serious thing.

When you didn't hear from me you should have sent a follow-up card. If there were no response to that you would *then* have been justified in sending the things elsewhere.

So we will use both the pieces and make acknowledgement to the *Partisan Review*. Where, I wonder, are they getting so much money from? It is many a day since anybody has payed [sic] me $40. I congratulate you.

Perhaps then *you* are the author of several poems [on my desk] that have been causing me some worry—since they seemed to have no owner. Here are the titles: "The Discourse Concerning Santa Claus," "Poem Imitating a Fugue," "At This Moment of Time," "Metro-Goldwyn-Mayer," "Song." Are any of those yours?

Let me know.
Sincerely,
[UNSIGNED CARBON]

/ · /

Partisan Review: JL in fact published "The Commencement Day Address" and three poems in *New Directions in Prose and Poetry* (New York: New Directions, 1937). The *Partisan Review* story was to become the title piece of Schwartz's first collection of poetry and prose, which Laughlin would later publish.

5. TLS-1   700 W. 180 St.
                                  NYC
                                  Oct. 19, 1937

DEAR LAUGHLIN:

I am glad that everything is straightened out so amiably. Perhaps I can give you something really good next year.

Those are my poems, all right, and I'd like to have them back. If I can get paid again for some piece, I'll begin to regard myself as a professional. The *Partisan Review* has a backer now, who is not only well-heeled, but also, it seems, very intelligent: That explains the handsome rewards.

I hope you were not annoyed by the review in this month's *Poetry:* Belitt is a fool and everyone knows it. Meanwhile I see that *kudos* is again bestowed upon you for the second straight issue in *The Criterion.* And I hope, by the way, that you see my long piece on Yvor Winters in *The Southern Review.*

                              Yours,
                              DELMORE SCHWARTZ

/ · /

Belitt: Ben Belitt, American poet (b. 1911).

The Criterion: T. S. Eliot (1888–1965), poet and critic, published this magazine. Reviews of a Henry Miller novel and several new *Cantos* by Ezra Pound appeared in the magazine in 1937, as well as a full-page advertisement for *ND 37*. Pound (1885–1972) and Miller (1891–1980) were to be important ND authors.

The Southern Review: Schwartz's review of Winters's *Primitivism and Decadence* did not appear until 1938 (*SR,* III, 3, 597–619).

6. TL-1   October 24, 1937

DEAR SCHWARTZ:

I hate to part with these poems of yours because they are so damn much better than a lot of the stuff that I have already had set up for the book. However, there just isn't the space, so I'm only using the three short ones—"At This Moment of Time," "Metro-Goldwyn-Mayer," and "Song."

I want to use the verse as well as the prose, because people must get an eyeful of you. I think you are good. Maybe just beginning, maybe will not turn out, but something real to go on. This is not just schmiklery, I don't have to get anything out of you.

I don't care what Belitt or anybody else says. I am not in the business to have little cat fights with literary ladies. I shall turn the cheek until the neck-joints give out. I know what is in the book. There is some crap, some good stuff, some middling. Furthermore, everything is relative. Plenty of people liked what B— didn't like.

The thing is to get the non-conforming stuff in print when it is written and not fifteen years after. That is my job. I hope I don't make a mess of it.

Yours,
[UNSIGNED CARBON]

/ · /

The book: *New Directions in Prose and Poetry 1937.*
schmiklery: From the German *Schmeichelei*—flattery.
B— : Nickname for Ben Belitt.

7. **TLS-1**   73 Washington Pl.
                                NYC
                                Jan. 6, 1938

DEAR LAUGHLIN,

   Thanks for writing to me so soon and speaking so generously of me. I will look forward to seeing you here or wherever you would like to meet me any time next week. Unfortunately this rooming house has no phone, but you can send me a card setting the time or you can walk in on me if you like—I'd prefer the card, but you can be sure of finding me at home; I'm somewhat of a recluse, a state of affairs which it seems you are going to help me to continue, much to my satisfaction. The whole business has become complicated, but I can tell you about that when I see you. This address is two blocks south of 8th St. and one block west of Washington Square Park. Until some time next week then,

                                Yours,
                                DELMORE SCHWARTZ

/ · /

73 Washington Pl.: The address to which Schwartz moved, with his brother Kenneth, on his twenty-fourth birthday, December 8, 1937. According to James Atlas, the room was an attic loft, with a low ceiling, which could be reached only by climbing a ladder.

somewhat of a recluse: "He soon fell into a routine of sleeping until noon, working until dinner, and then walking to Times Square to take in a movie" (Atlas, p. 104).

become complicated: Schwartz had discussed the possibility of a book contract—for a novel—with Clifton Fadiman (b. 1904), then editor-in-chief of Simon & Schuster, and subsequently an influential editor at the Book-of-the-Month Club. Schwartz later sent the book to W. W. Norton. Neither had made a concrete offer at this time.

8. TLS-2   73 Washington Place
                             New York City
                             Jan. 13, 1938

DEAR LAUGHLIN:

I am sending you my volume of poems by express. I hope you will forgive me for the untidy and provisional way in which I have thrown the whole book together, but there is, as you know, a need for haste. I have stalled off Fadiman for a week and he finds it difficult to understand my delay, although I explained to him that I wanted a publisher who would print my written poems, rather than one who would finance an unwritten novel. You were, by the way, quite helpful in mentioning Saroyan's case, for by taking money I would merely be getting into debt; I was actually unaware of this.

The book you're going to read is only in a tentative state of organization, as you will soon see. I have another play which might be, for all I know, better than the one which is enclosed in the book, and is certainly of a less disreputable plot. Of the eighty-eight lyric poems which are in the volume, some of course will eventually be excluded. There is also the possibility of revision and of a few better poems before September, or whenever you would send the book off to the printers.

On the whole, however, I am sure there is enough evidence for you to make a decision. Please let me hear from you as soon as possible.

                             Sincerely yours,
                             DELMORE SCHWARTZ

P.S. If the play is the only barrier, it could be simply excluded without substituting another one.

/ · /

poems by express: The typescript of *In Dreams Begin Responsibilities.*

Saroyan's case: William Saroyan (1908–1981), American fiction writer and playwright, who had apparently accepted an advance for an undelivered manuscript and found himself in debt to his publisher.

another play: Choosing Company, Shenandoah, and *Paris and Helen* had all been written by this time.

less disreputable: The plot of *Dr. Bergen's Belief* involved suicide and pathological disease.

eighty-eight lyric poems: The published book contains thirty-five lyrics, plus the long narrative poem "Coriolanus and His Mother," and the verse play *Dr. Bergen's Belief.*

9. TL-1   January 15, 1938

DEAR SCHWARTZ:

I have studied your manuscript and it confirms my belief that your work is very well worth publishing.

If you don't mind being labelled, I think you are going to be the American Auden. Without being in any way derivative from him, you have a fluency that is comparable to his.

I should like very much to do the book. My plan would be an edition of five hundred in September. Your royalty would be fifteen cents a book until costs were paid, thereafter half of the net take. I would want an option on your next five books.

The play seems to me good, though perhaps it could profitably be cut a bit in the mid-section. It lags there a little as drama, though it remains interesting as poetry.

What would you think of putting the play in *New Directions 1938*? That is just a hunch of mine. What do you think of it. The prose piece and the poems would make a book of 120 pages, which is about right for a book of poems. I figure the play at about 55 pages.

But all these matters can be worked out. The important thing is for you to decide whom you want for your publisher.

I repeat, if you want to make money, Fadiman can do the best for you, but if you want to serve God and not the Devil, I can do best for you.

I'm returning the manuscript right away. As I am obliged to send it collect, I am enclosing some stamps to make up that charge.

Let me hear from you as soon as you know.

/ · /

in New Directions 1938: The play first appeared there.

a book of 120 pages: The actual book totaled 174 pages.

the American Auden: W. H. Auden (1907–1973), influential poet and critic.

10. TL-1   January 23, 1938

DEAR SCHWARTZ:

I seem unable to get the "h" into your name at the first shot. I can't tell you how glad I am that you have decided to cast your lot with New Directions. I realize the sacrifice that you make but it is one which I think worthwhile in view of your understanding of what the art of writing really can be. If, like your Noah Luft, you are trying to build a life that will satisfy you, I think that your piety will mean more to you than the immediate financial success. I think you will get the financial success in time, but by publishing the plays and poems you will get an artistic standing. There is always the danger that the young writer will go after the money first and in so doing imperil his ability to do real creative work. I think you have made the right choice and I shall do everything I can to prove it to you.

I'll make up some sort of simple agreement. I suggest that you give me the option on three books at the royalty I outlined (15 cents a book until costs are paid, then half the take), and then the right to revise the royalty against a further three-book option. Let me explain that. I would like to be able to subsidize you right now, but I simply haven't the cash. It is likely however that in a few years I will have the cash, if business conditions improve. Then I would like to give you the same sort of advances which the larger houses give, though for a higher type of work.

An agreement such as I suggest would leave you entirely free after three books, as you would be at liberty to reject the new options if my new terms weren't satisfactory, but it would have the advantage of preserving the idea of continuity. I can only do my best work for you if I feel that you are going to be loyal. Such an agreement would facilitate that loyalty without tying you down to it.

Please let me have your reactions to this proposal. We must find the balance that will make our interests one.

[UNSIGHED CARBON]

/ · /

your Noah Luft: Character in Schwartz's play, *Venus in the Back Room;* an idealistic young writer.

11. TL-1   January 30, 1938

DEAR SCHWARTZ:

I enclose a contract in duplicate which I trust will prove acceptable to you. If it is, please date and sign it and return the carbon to me.

Don't misunderstand the formality of the document. I hope our relationship will be a friendly and not a business one, but I thought it best to put everything in proper legal form.

As you know, I am planning to sail from New York on the 12th. I hope that I'll have an opportunity then to see you again, but if I don't manage it, please take this letter for a temporary goodbye.

I expect to be back, as I told you, in June or July. I have your book all designed and hope that we can put it to press the minute I get back. I guess I'll have Little & Ives print it. They are good, but not expensive. I am planning to use Bodoni, a slightly cream-toned paper, and a black natural finish cloth binding; in general the style will follow that of the Faber & Faber poetry books. Have you any special mark or device that you would like to have incorporated in the design that might serve as your personal trademark?

All of the reviews which I have seen so far of *New Directions 37* have praised your work; you seem to be the star. I hope that when I get back, perhaps at the time when we read proof, you and your girl can come and visit me at Norfolk.

With every good wish,

/ · /

to sail from New York: Laughlin was going to Europe to visit Ezra Pound.
Little & Ives: The book in fact was printed for New Directions at the Walpole Printing Office in an edition of 1,000 copies.

Bodoni: A style of typeface invented by Giambattista Bodoni (1740–1813), Italian printers.

Faber & Faber: The British publishing house.

New Directions 37: The anthology included Schwartz's story, "The Commencement Day Address" (since uncollected) and "Three Poems."

your girl: Gertrude Buckman, a classmate of Schwartz's at George Washington High School in New York, whom he later courted and married.

12. TLS-2   73 Washington Place
                                              New York City
                                              February 1, 1938

DEAR LAUGHLIN:

I am enclosing the signed contract with a few misgivings about being Quixotic, with much relief that I am finished with publishers for, I hope, the next twenty years, but really with the strong feeling that everything is going to come out well for both you and myself. I had better explain the misgivings, even if it means repeating myself: the offer I am turning down to go with you would free me from the parental grip once and for all and also get me a little more of the world, flesh, and devil than I have at present.

There are several things which are not quite right in the contract, but I am letting them go because I think that our interests are one, that though we scarcely know each other we have a friendly unity about the way things should be, or to put it pompously, that we both want to realize the same values. There is, however, one thing that I am going to insist upon—twenty free copies, which is the least an author is entitled to and which is, as you know, what he gets from everyone else. I need twenty copies because I want to keep my friends feeling that I am interested in their being interested in what I write—but seri-

ously, I have to have them and can't afford to buy
them; and I'm taking the liberty of changing the
number in the contract.

The book will be ready in July when you get back
from Europe, unless I have another spell of sickness
of the sort I had last year. After that's done, I'll revise
the play you want to print in *New Directions 1938*.
Printing it there may sell a few more copies of the
book of poems. The cover, print and paper are hard
for me to see, since I don't know what Bodoni is,
nor cream-toned paper, but if it is going to be like
the Faber & Faber poetry books, it will be fine. I'll
have a device ready too before you send the book to
the printer's.

I'd like very much to write ballet scenarios for
Kirstein, and have two ideas, one involving comic-
strip motifs, the other a baseball game. From all that
I hear it would be a chance to make some money,
which I badly need, badly in the sense that a few
luxuries are sometimes a necessity. I'd be grateful to
you if you sent me Kirstein's address and told him
that I was going to submit a short scenario to him—
or perhaps it's enough to mention your name.

All these fine reviews and all the rest of the things
that I've been getting during the last few months are
accumulating to the point where I am going to be
terrified—because it can't last, I can't be being praised
for the right reasons by so many people, it is much
too soon, and it is taking my mind away from
working. I hope that it does not make you expect
me to be afraid that you will have such expectations.
The latest salutation, by the way, is from Wallace
Stevens, who sent *The Partisan Review* a letter, which
they're printing, saying that my review of *The Man
with the Blue Guitar* was the "most invigorating
review" that he had ever had. On the one hand, this,
all of this, is going to help you get rid of my books,

and on the other hand you don't have to be afraid that I will take this praise too seriously, forget how much one has to do to be a good writer, or rest on the laurels.

If I do not see you before you sail, goodbye, thanks for all your generosity, and I hope that old Pagany starts you writing again.

Yours,
DELMORE SCHWARTZ

/ · /

the parental grip: Schwartz still accepted sums of money from his mother.

spell of sickness: "For most of his life," according to Atlas, Schwartz complained of "a mysterious illness that beset him in February and March, although he never specified its symptoms" (p. 168). This letter was written on the first day of February.

Kirstein: Lincoln Kirstein (b. 1907), founder and editor of *Hound & Horn,* and later general director of the New York City Ballet. No collaboration between Schwartz and Kirstein was produced.

my review: Schwartz's review of the Stevens volume appeared in *Partisan Review,* 4 (February 1938), 351–67.

Wallace Stevens: (1879–1955), American poet.

old Pagany: Reference to William Carlos Williams's novel, *A Voyage to Pagany* (1938). *Pagany* also was an important little magazine of the 1920s, edited by Williams and Richard Johns.

13. TL-1   February 3, 1938

DEAR SCHWARTZ:

What the hell do your friends call you? They call me J.

Thanks for the contract. I know what you're giving up and I'll try to make it up to you just as soon as I can. Right now I'm working by candlelight as the steel business is not paying any dividends. If it

does get going again, things will be different. I hope
you aren't too devout a Leftist to object to sharing
the fruits of sin.

Twenty copies is all right. I just put in six because
that, I think, is the customary number. That's how
many Fitts got free from Harcourt.

I have changed my plans somewhat and may not
go abroad till March. So perhaps I'll be able to see
you again on my next visit to New York.

I am sending a note to Kirstein and suggest that
you telephone him and make an appointment to see
him, for, unless he is a hypocrite, he is readily acces-
sible to "young talent" as they call it. His address
is—damn it, I can't find his address, the card is missing from the files. Will you look it up in the telephone book and let me know what it is? If you can't
find his own, look for American School of Ballet, or
School of American Ballet.

I think the comic-strip ballet sounds good. You
could use the stock figures and have them play out
an action that would be more than mere parody—
something with social meaning in it. A damn good
idea.

I hope that you can get access to all the nice things
that are being said about you so that we can use them
for the publicity for your book. I want to give you
the right sort of sendoff with advance blurbs and
pictures and advts. and all that. Will you ask the boys
at the *PR* if we may have their permission to write
to the big shots who wrote the letters for their permission to use the quotes? Also, how are you fixed
for a picture of yourself, preferably in tights or other
art pose?

Send me K's address and I'll write him right away.

Best,

/ · /

Fitts: Dudley Fitts (1903–1968), who was Laughlin's English master at Choate. It was he who arranged for JL to study with Ezra Pound in Italy. Laughlin published his poems, and later the *Poems from the Palatine Anthology,* an English-language paraphrase. The book was so called because the manuscript of this version was found in a monastery library in the Rhenish Palatinate.

the boys at the PR: The founding editors of the new *Partisan Review* were William Phillips (b. 1907), F. W. Dupee (1912–1987), Dwight Macdonald (1906–1982), and Mary McCarthy (1912–1989).

14. TLS-1   73 Washington Place
                                                    New York City
                                                    February 8, 1938

DEAR JAY,

My friends use my first name as I hope and expect you will. Difficult at first, it soon slips right off the tongue. Contractions have been tried without success, and I will have to tell you some day the riotous story of how I came to get the name and the magical effect it had upon my childhood. In fact, the subject of names fascinates me and I have given it no little thought, the shift from formal surname to first name being itself, as I need not say, productive of the finest psychological shades between one and another. The kind of self-consciousness which comes up when you say, "May I call you by your first name?" to a girl is worth diamonds. You can recognize the extrovert and the introvert by this. The one assenting with ease and a joke, the other being moved and suddenly shy.

Your mention of the fruits of sin is piquant, since I have been supported and educated by the fruits of real estate speculation. I am not a "devout Leftist"; merely devout would be the word, if I can pretend to so much, and nourishing and being led by a sense of ineluctable evil and the endless bureaucracy involved in existence (Herr Kafka's obsession) and with a profound disgust and hatred of all churches, all parties, which debase always the divine, if only by attempting to give a name and a local habitation to it. When I was an undergraduate I studied for two years with Sidney Hook and James Burnham and thus the best brand of Marxism was pressed upon me, and the only result was a long thesis for Burnham on the relationship of religion and Communism which seemed to perplex Burnham exceedingly. It does seem to me, however, that Marxism illuminates very well the inseparable tie-up of social and intellectual elements at any given moment of time, and it is also valuable negatively as a judgement of the present. Only the most naive actually think that any kind of salvation can come from a political party, and everyone worth speaking to in N.Y. now has seen the moral bankruptcy of Marxism in the Moscow trials.—Now you know what kind of an author you have on your team; you know, at least, as much as he does about it. But I hope that we will be able to discuss these matters many times hereafter, and as you imply in your fine essay in *N.D.*, in speaking and finding words one finds out what one really means.

We can arrange the various matters having to do with my book later on, perhaps in June. Kirstein's address is 637 Madison Avenue, but I should think, from all that I have heard of him, that not too much can be expected—the American Ballet is really very poor. I have read most of *N.D.* and agree with you about Henry Miller, although I'd like to see what it all comes to in an extended book, and I like especially the pieces by O'Donnell and Mary Barnard, probably because they show a feeling for thought,

tough-mindedness, I mean. Only if you have a sensibility as perfect and pure as Williams can you get
along without thinking.

Yours,
DELMORE

/ · /

how I came to get the name: "Delmore Schwartz had a particular fondness
for stories about the origin of his first name. Sometimes he would
insist he had been named after a delicatessen across the street from the
house where he was born, sometimes that his mother had been fond of
an actor who was named Frank Delmore. In still other versions, the
name was taken from a Tammany Hall club, a Pullman railroad car,
or a Riverside Drive apartment house" (Atlas, p. 3). In *Shenandoah,*
Schwartz examines the forces and events which molded his essential
identity. Instead of "Delmore Schwartz," the protagonist in the drama
is named, just as incongruously, "Shenandoah Fish." Other such com-
binations were to follow in his work: Cornelius Schmidt, Marquis Fane,
and Hershey Green among them.

real estate speculation: Schwartz's father, Harry Schwartz, dealt in real
estate, first with his brothers Phil and Louis, then on his own.

Herr Kafka's obsession: Reference to subject matter of novels and stories
by Franz Kafka (1883–1924), Austrian writer born in Prague.

a name and a local habitation: Schwartz is paraphrasing Shakespeare's *A
Midsummer-Night's Dream,* Act V, sc. 1, line 17.

Sidney Hook and James Burnham: Two of Schwartz's professors in the
Washington Square College of New York University, where he enrolled
as a philosophy major, 1932–35. Burnham, co-editor of *Symposium,*
gave Schwartz A's. Hook's seminar in contemporary philosophy was
one of Schwartz's favorite courses.

the Moscow trials: Reference to the great purges, when Joseph Stalin
launched a campaign of political terror against the Communist Party
members who had brought him to power. In August 1936, Zinoviev
and Kamenev were sentenced to death and shot, and in June 1937,
Tukhachevsky was court-martialed and executed. More followed.

your fine essay in N.D.: Laughlin had published "Language and the
Experimental Writer" in *New Directions 1937.*

O'Donnell and Mary Barnard: George Marion O'Donnell and Mary
Barnard were two poets published by Laughlin in *Five Young American
Poets* (Norfolk, Conn.: New Directions, 1940).

Williams: William Carlos Williams (1883–1963), poet and fiction writer,
a friend of Laughlin's and an ND author for many decades.

15. TLS-2   February 26, 1938

DEAR DELMORE:

I don't have your last letter at hand as I write, but I recall that you asked in it for more time. I certainly want you to have all you can for making it a fine job, but I must urge on you the importance of having your dates fit into the general plan.

You see, the books and the catalog must be all done by the end of August so that I can go on the road with them during September. I plan to visit every store in the area lying between Washington, Portland, Chicago, and Cincinnati. This is the only way to sell books. Personal visits do the trick. And you must have the book right there in your fist for them to look at it and see that they are getting something.

That's why I hope that you can be ready to print at the very latest by the first of July. I would like to have it ready much sooner, so that literary tycoons could read it and hand out blurbs for ballyhoo. But since you have some pretty good blurbs already—or so you tell me—we can do without that in this case.

Try to have it in shape by mid-June. That gives you quite a bit of time.

The next matter is the offer of Emily Sweetser, whom I think you met with Polly Forbes-Johnson, to bring your play to the attention of the Bennington Theatre Group.

This seems to me a possibility of the greatest value. The Bennington group is recognized as one of the leading experimental theatres of the country and there is a good deal of prestige connected with their productions. Sweetser is in very close with the director and it is not impossible that, if she liked the play, she could get it staged.

I might point out that such a production would be a helpful stepping stone, and not a hindrance, to a Broadway showing. As you know, a great many plays are picked for Broadway from the small and summer theatres.

I think that this is something that you should think about right away. I know that you want to make revisions, but Sweetser will only be at Bennington this spring. I suggest that you send the present draft to her right away and have her start the ball rolling. Then if they like it you can revise in rehearsal. I could arrange to have you go up there and really work the thing out as a stage piece.

Sweetser says that if you will lend her your ms., she will copy it in a few days and return the original to you. I can say that she is absolutely reliable and that you need have no hesitation about letting her use the script.

Please let me hear right away what you think about this. Emily Sweetser, Bennington College, Bennington, VT., is her address. You might get directly in touch with her.

I suggest that you let her get under way before you tackle Orson Welles. He is going to be a hard nut to crack. My feeling is that your play is a good deal better than he is.

Best,
JAY

/ · /

Emily Sweetser: After Ms. Sweetser graduated from Bennington in 1942, she worked in the Cambridge office of New Directions, located in the basement of the Schwartzes' house on Memorial Drive. Eventually Schwartz's erratic behavior caused her to flee to New York City. According to Atlas, Schwartz was upset by delays in publication of *Shenandoah,* insomniac at night and incommunicative by day. He did very little work for New Directions at this time (Atlas, p. 197).

Polly Forbes-Johnson: Later known as Mrs. Forbes Johnson-Storey. Laughlin engaged her to take Schwartz's jacket photos. She took the famous photograph of Schwartz gazing, Narcissus-like, into a mirror, reproduced most recently on the jacket of *Portrait of Delmore: Journals and Notes of Delmore Schwartz, 1939–1959*, edited and introduced by Schwartz's second wife, Elizabeth Pollet (1986).

your play: Dr. *Bergen's Belief,* a late addition to the manuscript of his first book.

Orson Welles: (George) Orson Welles (1915–1985), American motion picture actor, director, producer, and writer, who—like Schwartz—was declared a prodigy and had a difficult time in later life living up to his early notices.

16. TLS-1   Monday, Feb. 28, 1938

DEAR JAY:

I will devote myself to nothing but the book from now until the first of July, and if I escape the numbness which always afflicts me in April and May, we ought to have everything finished by the time you have set.

Thanks for writing the letter to K., which I am returning. As I said, nothing will come of it in all probability.

The Bennington College thing is out of the question for this year. The play is not genuinely finished, putting it on will only get me completely stupid about it, and besides, it is not a play for a girls' college, no matter how bright the girls are, and with due respect to E. Sweetser whom I liked when she came to help take my picture.

I suppose Polly Forbes-Johnson has sent you the pictures. Please use the conventional one, not the mirror one, not the one with the Picasso in it, or I will have my head handed to me by Gertrude, my girl, who paints and therefore considers herself authoritative in all matters related to portraits.

I have seen copies of your new book by Williams, and if it could possibly be arranged without trouble to you, I would like my book to have the same cover and jacket, although perhaps in a different color. It is certainly a beautiful thing and so was *White Mule*. I've read the book itself and apart from that wonderful story, "The Venus," I think it is far below the novel and suffers very much from Williams' vice of incompleteness.

> Yours,
> DELMORE

/ · /

the letter to K: Lincoln Kirstein.

your new book by Williams: Nineteen stories by William Carlos Williams, *Life Along the Passaic River* (1938).

17. TLS-1   73 Washington Place
                                    Saturday, March 5, 1938

DEAR JAY,

I have been thinking of the deadline which I promised to meet (July 1st) and working on the fairly extended poem which I want to include in my volume and which I would like to dedicate to you (if you don't mind too much) for the good reason that I probably would not have written the poem if you had not decided to print my book.

But what troubles me now is this: the deadline. This is the first year in eighteen that I have not been in school (or kindergarten) and in all of those years I was tortured by a time-schedule imposed from without. "Tortured" is too strong, but I was, at any rate, upset and annoyed by examinations, term papers, classes which had to be attended, etc. This year, on the other hand, I have been working as I please and it is not only very enjoyable but it purifies the spirit. I would like to feel the same way about getting the book to you; although I will probably have it done by July 1st, anyway, and certainly have it done then, if you insist, still I would benefit very much by being told that you would give me more time if I wanted it. All I want, childishly enough, I suppose, is the idea of leisure. What you want, as you said, is to fit the book into the general plan so that it can be sold when you go on your trip; but I think this may not be so important when one remembers that what will probably sell the book, if at all, is good reviews, and later, possibly, the overflow of an interest in my fiction.

But you're the boss, as they say, and you know, I am sure, much more about what is needed than I do, so that I am going to do what you tell me to do, about making haste or not. Let me know how you feel about this.

DELMORE

/ · /

the fairly extended poem: At this time Schwartz was writing what became "Coriolanus and His Mother: The Dream of One Performance," which when published was dedicated to Laughlin. Schwartz dropped the dedication when the poem was reprinted in *Summer Knowledge* (1959).

18. TL-1   March 6, 1938

DEAR DELMORE:

Thanks for your letter. That's fine; get the book ready just as soon as you can.

If . . . [words deleted] Kirstein doesn't get in touch with you I'll know he's a fake. He made a particular squawk about wanting young poets, etc. etc.

I'm sorry about your decision on the Bennington matter. Them little girls have strong stomachs, and could have swallowed the play all right. Perhaps you'll change your mind.

I like the pictures very much, especially the mirror one. That is the one I would like to use, and I hope you'll agree to that. It will catch people's eye and editors will be more likely to print it along with the reviews than the plain one. It is not a freak, just good modern photography. It is just what I wanted, and fits in with the character I wish to build for you—a poet in the tradition of poets—Symbolist, one foot in the other world. That is the way to sell books. Dramatize the author.

I'm coming down to New York next week, I think, about Tuesday, and will see Forbes-Johnson. Also you, I hope. Would you like some of the pictures for your own use? I don't think she soaks one much for them; she'd better not.

I would rather not use the white linen on your books. Two reasons. a) it "belongs" to Williams b) gets dirty too easily. I had planned black for you. That's part of the character. I think you'll like it when you see it. Have you worked out a design to represent yourself? I spoke about that before.

This letter seems to be full of argument. Sorry. You will find that I have ideas of my own, but that I am not stubborn. You can talk me out of anything you really object to.

/ · /

19. TL-1 March 7, 1938

DEAR DELMORE:

Just got your note about the time element. Don't worry too much about that.

I *must* have the book to take with me on my sales trip if we are going to make you "take," but we can get you a week or two by setting the book in pieces. That is, get the bulk of it finished and while they're setting that you can finish the rest.

We'd have to wait until 1939 if the book missed the selling trip, and I know you wouldn't want that. You see, there are only about thirty stores in the whole country that will order a book of good poetry of their own accord. But if you go and shove it on them, many others will at least try to sell it for you. That's the story.

But don't think about it.

As to your dedicating a poem to me that would make me very happy; I am thoroughly sentimental and enjoy all such pleasures to the full.

All the reviewers continue to speak well of you.

/ · /

All the reviewers: Of New Directions 1937.

20. TLS-1 c / o Overlea Inn
North Bennington, Vermont
June 22, 1938

DEAR JAY:

I don't know whether or not you received the letter I sent to London, but, at any rate, in brief recapitulation, a million thanks for being so decent about the finishing-line, and here I am or rather, we are, in Mrs. Stanwood's white cottage, and I have been trying very hard to get something finished. I should guess that you must be more or less familiar with this neighborhood and I hope you'll be coming up here during the summer. You're welcome at any hour of the day or night, Chez Schwartz. I would take my bride by the hand and come down to see you, except that we did not get that second-hand car which I expected to get.

I'll send you the reviews I've had and you can fix them as you see fit—I think it would be a good idea to print one loud razz amid the chorus. I suppose you will need this in a week or two in order to get the jacket printed and the dummy made up. I met Paul Rosenfeld one night after midnight before I left New York and he asked me to let him know when the book was coming out so that he could review it. We might do so, although it is a little too close to a scheme for me, since I know exactly what he will say and that he'll be getting the review from *The Nation*.

I hope you find the enclosed portion of one of Tate's letters useful. All I said was that you were curious about his judgement of O'Donnell, and the reference to "scout" is unwarranted, although I can think of a more dignified occupation. Will you send me back the clipping and will you let me hear from you soon or better still, come up here and pay us a visit.

Yours,
DELMORE

/ · /

or rather, we are: Schwartz had married his high school sweetheart, Gertrude Buckman, on June 14. She held various editorial jobs. The marriage ended in divorce in 1943. Today Ms. Buckman is an editor in London.

Mrs. Stanwood's white cottage: The Schwartzes honeymooned in a summer rental. The arrangements were made by Schwartz's *Partisan Review* associate, F. W. Dupee.

Paul Rosenfeld (1890–1946), American music and art critic, and co-editor of *The New Caravan* anthology, which published Schwartz's early play, *Choosing Company*.

the review from The Nation: Rosenfeld did not review the book for *The Nation;* rather, this assignment went to Louise Bogan, who gave it perhaps its most unfavorable review. See letters following.

one of Tate's letters: Allen Tate (1899–1979), American poet and critic.

21. TLS-1   June 23, 1938

DEAR DELMORE:

Yes, I got your letter to London, but didn't answer it, as I thought I might be seeing you in New York.

Glad to know where you are. That's a fine place.

I'll drive up there sometime soon and we can get down to business. Have to write up your blurbs and also figure probable number of pages in the book.

Things are busy as hell here. The manuscript of the Williams poems is here and big as a house. That will be some book. I feel pretty good about doing that.

I'm also getting *New Directions* into shape. What do you think? Would it help sales to have you in it? I should think it would. I had hoped to have a play, but I think now there isn't enough room.

What about a poem or two or a story? I leave that to you. Send what you judge best.

I'm not at all sorry to be home. This is a lot of fun this work. You'll have to come down here for a weekend this summer and see the shop and the works.

Could you and Heliodora help me read some proof? *New Directions* gets printed in Brandon Vermont near Middlebury—and I usually have to go there for the page proofs. We might do them in Bennington. It is quite a labour, but rather fun when done en masse.

We'll have fun up there. Have you met that Sweetser girl again? She is at Bennington you know. I really think she knows something about staging plays and might come in handy to you later. Fergusson is a good egg too.

Best,

J

/ · /

the Williams poems: Complete Collected Poems, the definitive edition, which ND published in 1939. It was named one of the "Fifty Books" of the year.

getting New Directions into shape: The annual which Laughlin began publishing in 1936.

Heliodora: Made-up name for Theodora Sedgwick, daughter of Ellery Sedgwick, editor of *The Atlantic.*

Fergusson: Francis Fergusson (1904–1986), drama professor at Bennington College.

22. TLS-1   Thursday

DEAR JAY:

We looked for you briefly in Bennington last night. We'd be delighted to visit you and see Williams, especially now that we have our 1931 Ford, known in the family as "Black Mule." I met the old boy in 1934, when I asked him to come to speak to our

Poetry Club at NYU, and his opening remark to me was classic, if not Shelleyan: "Where's the can?" says he. There's another thing. Tate is at Cornwall, Conn. and has invited me to come down and stay for a few days. I don't want to do that, but I would like to go over there with you. You never can tell when he might be handy for something, and besides, he's a good poet . . .

Let us know about the visit and whether there's anyone there who will mind the fact that I have not had a haircut since May Day.

Yours,
DELMORE

/ · /

"*Black Mule*": Take-off on William Carlos Williams's novel, *White Mule*. *Tate:* Allen Tate at the time was an editor at Henry Holt, the publishers.

23. TLS-2

Thursday,
the 28th of July 1938

DEAR JAY:

We were delighted to see you and sorry to have you go so soon and will be offended if you do not return. I finished that play the other day, and if you will forgive me for saying so and discount my present state of well-being, it is remarkable. Suppose then, instead of sending you the specimens you are asking for, I send the whole manuscript in two weeks? Will that be all right? It will take two weeks for us to bat out the whole thing on the typewriter. I give you my word that I will make no changes in any poem except the long one, "Coriolanus and His Mother," which I intend to keep correcting until the printer cuts my throat. It is going to be a big book as volumes of poetry go, but then it is not all verse, and besides let us not be coerced by precedent. What do you think of this for a subtitle: *IDBR, then, A Story, Poems, and A Play In Verse,* by D.S. This is the page division, which can't be exact because some is single-space, some double-space, some handwriting:

In DBResponsibilties	10⅓ typewritten double-space
CORIOLANUS A.H.M.	70 handwritten
T. R. HEART (11 fugues)	11 typewritten single-space and some of the poems will surely take two pages
LYRICS	23 typewritten single-space, and here again some will need two pages, but in these poems I'd like you to print one after another, not each separate on a page, and this will make it less than 23
DR. BERLIN'S BELIEF (the play)	31 handwritten pages, probably less when typed out 145 pages, perhaps 10 pages on either side

This is no longer than Winters' anthology and the whole thing really constitutes a unity, a consistent way of regarding the world and the flesh. In two weeks then, unless I hear otherwise from you.

We are touched by your desire to give us a wedding present, and somewhat embarrassed; not so embarrassed, however, as not to say that the Bach records would delight us very much. I did not recognize the strange beast whose photograph arrived and no one else will, which is just as well. We were reading Kay Boyle's *365 Days* and very pleased to find your pieces there and would like to know how you found out so much about breaking out of jail. The Cardinals won the pennant that year and that crook could not even get the pennant races straight. Once more, for the last time in a perfectly disinterested way, I offer my wholly unasked opinion that if you could write like that, all this publishing, wonderful as it is for everyone else, such as myself, is liable to hold you back. We met D. Fitts the other day, a curious fish indeed, but I suppose I must have seemed so to many in my time.

Send me a card as to your reception of the plan in this letter. Jack Johnson tells me that my soft-boiled egg is becoming hard. She sends her regard.

Yours Indeed
DELMORE

P.S. For God's sakes, how do you pronounce your last name? I have tried every alternative in the last six months and was on the wrong one with Fergusson the other night. Is it as in "lock" or as in the British "laugh"?

/ · /

that play: Dr. Berlin's Belief, later retitled *Dr. Bergen's Belief.*

IDBR: In Dreams Begin Responsibilities.

T. R. Heart: "The Repetitive Heart, Eleven Poems in Imitation of the Fugue Form."

Winters' anthology: Twelve Poets of the Pacific, which ND published in 1937, edited by Arthur Yvor Winters (1900–1968). American literary critic and poet.

Kay Boyle's 365 Days: Anthology of stories made up of one-page tales, one for each day of the year. JL contributed four. Boyle is the Ameri-

can novelist, short-story writer, and poet (1903–1992), published early
on by JL.

the Cardinals: Saint Louis, Missouri, baseball team.

Jack Johnson: Reference to Gertrude Buckman, Schwartz's wife, whom
the poet claimed was always "battling" him. She is here likened to a
prizefighter named Jack Johnson who fought Jack Dempsey.

24. TL-1   Friday

DEAR DELMORE:

Yes, I think that's a fine idea that you should send
down the manuscript in two weeks. That will be
fine and solve many problems.

But as I understand it, you want to go on fussing
with "Coriolanus" until sometime in November.
Right? Or perhaps fussing is not the right word.

The table of contents looks fine.

Yes, Fitts is a funny guy. A kind of algae. But
very rewarding when you get used to him. Soul of
a poet and kindly school-children-crossing police-
man. Etc. Also a bit of a snob. Mixture. Admixture.
Oh what the hell—character eludes me.

I'll be coming up with the Bach sometime soon.
And the name is "Locklin," though I don't know
why.

25. TLS-1   Overlea Cottage
                                              N. Bennington, Vt.
                                              Aug. 4, 1938

DEAR JAY:

I am sending you the typescript today. Please let
me hear from you as soon as you get it. After work-

ing over it day and night for the last 2 weeks and looking at it in practically every state of being, I am sure, for the time being, at least, that it is very good in all of its parts—it is just barely possible that I may be prejudiced in the matter.

You can send the whole thing to the printer's as soon as you want, the sooner the better for me because of the Guggenheim business. I am pretty exhausted right now and the revisions I might make in a month or so would certainly expand the long poem, and God knows the book is big enough as it stands. Let me know when the printer does get it. If I do happen to decide that I can't do without corrections, I am going to pay the printer's charges; there's no point in taking advantage of you and having you pay for my changes of mind.

There may be a minor question of censorship in a few places and if you have to, go ahead and abbreviate, such as f- - -, a dash for every vacated syllable. But no omissions, abbreviations is the minimum; you will see that I need the obscenity when you read the play.

I hope you read the play and the long poem very soon and let me know how they hit you. You can fire away with questions about the script by mail and I'll answer them immediately.

If it is not too late, will you make these minor changes in the poem in *ND '38* called "Socrates' Ghost Must Haunt Me Now": 1. 13 should read, "from the topless sky to the bottomless floor," not "Seek the diamond, search manure," which was an early version; also, 1. 12, which may be correct: "But grasp it all, there may be more!"

We hope to see you soon.

Yours indeed,
DELMORE

/ · /

the Guggenheim business: Schwartz had applied for a Guggenheim Fellowship, which he was awarded in 1940 and again in 1941.

26. TLS-1   August 4, 1938

DEAR DELMORE:

About those two last changes that you suggested for the French poem—I am against both of them, and thought I would express my feelings before ordering the changes.

1) I may be a sucker for off-rhymes, but that last line, as first written, was a real delight to me. I like it very much and would hate to see it replaced by one that I don't find as strong. But after all it isn't up to me to tell you how to finish off a poem!

   If you really want the change, please avail yourself of the enclosed order to the printer right away. If not, tear up the order, after first having Joe Jacobson soak off the 3¢ stamp for future use.

2) About the note on the French:

   a) There isn't room for it on the page—however, if you want it much we could shift poems around and make room for it.

   b) I have a sense that such a note would detract from the impact of the poem.

   Again, you make the decision.

I disapprove of meddling like this with authors, but I just happened to get right fond of that poem and take a personal interest in it.

Just to show you what a hot printer I am going to be, I enclose a sample of my initial labour. This impression is made without make-ready or lock-up. Imagine what it will be when fixed up!

                                                  Yrs,

                                                  J

/ · /

the French poem: "Parlez-vous Français?"

Joe Jacobson: Another version of "Jack Johnson." The reference again is
to Gertrude.

about the note: It was placed in the Acknowledgments at the rear of the
book.

27. TLS-1   Wednesday

DEAR JAY:

   Will you substitute the enclosed version for the
earlier one in my manuscript? You will find it in the
part entitled "Poems of Experiment and Imitation."
Please send me back the early version.

   Also, I think we had better change Dr. Berlin's
name to Dr. Bergen. "Berlin" suggests Nazi too
much and I did not intend either that symbol, nor
any kind of direct allegory, but merely one of the
activities of the so-called middle-class.

   Our visit last week was very pleasant, especially
seeing Williams and except that we seem to have
disturbed you. We will be returning to New York
this time next week.

Yours,
DELMORE

Ode on the Study of Philosophy

It was late in the evening when K. arrived. The village was
deep in snow. The Castle hill was hidden, veiled in darkness,
nor was there even a glimmer of light to show that a castle
was there.

—Kafka

Heard autos' muffled trekking in the snow,
Under the window, on the quiet street,
The low sky over the driven chimney smoke,

The shovel's fresh scrape and the stamping feet,
All these beneath my gazing mind I keep,
Learning of definitions and of principles
Equally true in Asia, June, and sleep.

The reading lamp is lit, and dark December's
Pale afternoon and black dusk descend;
The snug room sleeps, the frosted pane shuts out
The wind-turned shrouding host, the year's pure end,
And I have separated every white page,
Black print, refluent breath, my body's tone,
From the mind's noumenal act alone.

In the house next door, behind the curtains,
The firelight leaps; its orange glassy horns
Acutely stain the shadow of warmth and being
Upon my turning feeling which returns
Seeking for signs and angels in that snow
Infinitely extended, possible, and neutral,
Yet stuff of all stuffs, the stuff of all we know!

Tact of the blind most learned in introspection!
Shall I not fear to have but a bitten page,
Its colorless shapes, its pinched and tiny dots,
Instead of pleasure's cash, the certain wage?
Love is historical, that is, of time,
It is itself the stillest point, and yet
All its sweet lines and forms flow with the age
As whirling spokes about a hub are set.

I risk all things! not even narrow sleep
(Whose beauty is death's shadow, as you knew
Kneeling in childhood, that God might be true)
Subtracts the moving actual like this
—Its opposite immediate in the kiss—
Here where no flesh can breathe, where no moist lip
Is bitten in pride and fear, where verbal play,
Mere syllables, mere repetition, rote,
Erects, essence by essence in the abstract light,
Monad and entity, the metaphysical day.

What dog of the mind seeks for the secret bone
Not hidden by him, not hidden, nothing at all?

Does desperate wish call nothing the unknown
As every heaven painted past the tomb
Derives its country house from pain and June?
Old Nobodaddy has deceived all men,
Kant has exiled the transcendental host:
Doubt questions, guilt offends, I ask

What income and dividend provide the room,
And what prestige extolls the studying soul
Dependant on the owner and his tool?
In the turning world men organize to kill, the while
I seek ecstatic stillness, theory's jewel.

As in the lunch room, in the present hour,
Men warm their hands about a coffee cup,
Murder and fornicate in tabloid power,
Revenge their foolishness in the cartoon,
Warm their indifference in the coffee's noon,
And hope in utter vagueness, which I know,
For the new life fashioned *ex nihilo*.

O part of them, as they are part of me,
How can I turn my head, what can I find
But the self-sensuality of the mind?
A girl becomes a shadow in the south
Distant two hundred miles from me, apart
From her picture on the wall in black and white:
Memory alone sees one in both and my
Belief alone can cross the pure abyss,
Shadow and substance!
                              as I try,

I see the light within my nothingness!
I hold my hope, which is self-consciousness!
Belief brings me that girl, my memory
Renders her richness, lost in time, to me,
O memory restores the false and true,
I hold the past, I know myself anew,

I know the mind! its true identity.
The mind alone can grasp the moving world,
Instruct all voices and correct the sea,
The mind examines hearts, the mind unseen

Responds, creates, judges the unjust, shows
The working process and the secret scene,
The beauty, ghost, and surd where process sews
All lives in history or private dream:
Nor power, nor belief ruins him who knows
And studies the light in which all things seem.

/ · /

the enclosed version: The "Ode" was later withdrawn from the typescript. Its appearance here marks first publication.
Williams: William Carlos Williams.

28. TLS-1   Friday

DEAR JAY:

Thanks for making those changes. I wish you
would make two more, if it is not too much trouble
to that printer:
Let the last line read, "The foreigner's preposter-
ous excited fear," and the following footnote might
be added: "The French of this poem is unidiomatic,
an English French: why should it be good French?"
That will puzzle them.

As ever,
DELMORE

/ · /

Let the last line read: Schwartz refers to a revision of the last line of the
poem "Parlez-vous Français?" He later revised it again. In the book,
the last two lines read,

> He stands there speaking and they laugh to hear
> Rage and excitement from the foreigner.

good French: In the section of notes at the end of the book, the note reads: "In this poem, the French is unidiomatic, an English French. Why ought it to be an idiomatic French?"

29. TLS-1   8 West 105 St.
New York City
September 29, 1938

DEAR JAY:

Enclosed is the final version of my play. If you have the time, you might read the last few pages once more to see if I have eliminated the abruptness you observed and mentioned to me. I have re-written the whole piece so that the discussion of the Jewish problem and the obscenity became unnecessary.

I want to omit two of the poems also, "Father and Son" and the "Ode on the Study of Philosophy." Both of them are academic exercises and have nothing to do with the main burden of the book.

If you send me copies of your catalogue, I may be able to pass them about among the few I know who will be interested in buying your books. I hope that your tour was a great success and that you will be coming to Babylon soon.

Yours as ever,
DELMORE SCHWARTZ

P.S. I want my manuscript back when the printer gets done with it, and I would like to have the first version of my play soon.

/ · /

8 West 105 St.: The Schwartzs had left Bennington and moved into an apartment not far from Columbia University.

"Father and Son": This poem was not deleted and appears in the collection.

30. TLS-1   Tuesday

DEAR JAY:

I am afraid that I can't get a good story finished for you. I gave up the trip to Pittsburgh in order to give myself every chance to write it, but my mind just won't issue the necessary words, let alone ideas. It is very difficult for me to understand why I can write with ease for awhile, and then not at all, but perhaps I will rid myself of this alternation in the future. Your idea was a good one and perhaps you can save it for my next book or for some other flowering Judas.

It was good of you to get your mother to ask us and the Macdonalds to call on her in Pittsburgh, and also good of you to offer to speak to my mother, but I am afraid it would do no good at all. All the tenacious bourgeois virtues—prudence, a savings account, and a steady job—prevent my mother from seeing any meaning in my supposed profession, and she seems to think that if she removes her support, I will alter my ways. But we will manage, or God, in fact, will provide.

I am glad that you feel as you do about publishing all my books, and it was merely a desire to be practical that made me consider Warren's offer. If you really are going to spend a thousand dollars advertising my book, you ought to be sure to get separate notices for me in *Poetry, The Southern Review, Partisan Review, The Nation,* and *The New Republic.* I think that it is in these magazines that a separate announcement really impresses other readers. Another thing: I wish you would get T. Spencer to include my book in his omnibus review in the next *Southern Review*. My guess is that the reviewers are going to be hostile this time and that I am due for some large-scale knocking. This guess is based not on the uneasiness of pre-publication, but on remarks brought back to me by the ubiquitous boys of the *Partisan Review*.

As ever,

Delmore

/ · /

story finished for you: Laughlin had written on October 29, 1938, asking Schwartz if he had a very good unpublished story which he could publish separately in pamphlet form and distribute at the better bookstores and to reviewers as a publicity tie-in with publication of *In Dreams Begin Responsibilities*. Such limited editions become collectors' items.

flowering Judas: Allusion to Katherine Anne Porter's short story of that title.

your mother: Mrs. Henry Hughart Laughlin (Marjory Rea).

the Macdonalds: Dwight and Nancy Macdonald.

my mother: Rose Nathanson Schwartz.

Warren's offer: Robert Penn Warren (1905–1989), poet, fiction writer, critic, and editor, had suggested some other publisher to Schwartz.

T. Spencer: Theodore Spencer, critic and professor, and director of the Breadloaf Writers' Colony.

31. TLS-1   November 25, 1938

DEAR DELMORE:

I'm sorry that you didn't manage with the story, but I understand how at times a person just can't coax a good word out. It was a good stunt. Well, it would be just about as good next year.

The book is now at the bindery and should be ready in about a week. I think you'll like it. I saw the sheets, and think it is about the best book I have ever designed. I am sorry that I had to cross you in a few things, but I take myself seriously as a typographer and that is part of my fun. I think when you see the finished product you won't feel so badly about things. I refer to the left flush setting, spaces between paragraphs, and titles on two lines. That had to be. The style would have been ruined by a title sticking into the margins or in smaller type than the others.

Mother was very sorry that you didn't get out to Pittsburgh. She was very much looking forward to meeting you.

I am going to start the advertising campaign in January. I don't want you to get lost in the pre-Christmas rush. In the weeks before Christmas there is so much space taken that our small ads would be completely lost. In January they will show much better. I plan to use the *Tribune, Times, Nation, Saturday Review, New Republic,* etc. In fact, all the ones you mentioned as well as a few more.

Then there arc circulars going to all the stores that ordered the book. They will use these—we hope— in their packages and bills, etc. I'll have Higgins send you a few for personal distribution.

Don't listen to what those boys down there tell you. They are nice guys but a bit spooky. I mean they take it all too seriously. Breathe deeply and get some sleep.

Best,

J

/ · /

Higgins: James Higgins, member of Laughlin's ND staff in charge of publicity and promotion.

32. TLS-1
8 West 105 St.
New York City
December 14, 1938

DEAR JAY:

My book arrived in time for my 25th birthday. I will not trouble you with my feelings except to say with the formality due on such an occasion: Thank you for printing it. I hope now that you are going to believe in me for several more books and not expect too much and not pay attention to the reviewers. It takes time to get really good, as I don't have to say, and it is sad but true that even the best writer has to write a good deal that is no good. What annoys me most is the flood of criticism which I have to write because I need the money: Five unwritten articles await me and there is liable to be another in every mail. What I would like to do is to get obsessed with my unfinished long poem for the next six months.

Speaking of criticism, your article on Pound was excellent, much better than mine because it was full of concrete analysis. You ought to write more criticism, if only because the better your taste, the more honor involved in getting printed by you. Your Latinity dumbfounded me: One does not take you for the Latin scholar.

Will you see that Symons of *Twentieth Century Verse* gets a review copy? He promised a review in his last issue. And also, as a troublesome favor, can you get Higgins to send me a postcard whenever a review appears? There are papers very difficult to get in New York. I did, by the way, inscribe the five copies for Penn State and re-ship them. I wish also that you would keep all the orders you get: There are persons to whom I will never again speak if they do not buy copies of my book. May the Old Pervert who directs all things smile on New Directions.

Yours,
DELMORE

/ · /

for my 25th birthday: Schwartz's birthday was December 8.

long poem: He was writing *Genesis, Book I.*

your article on Pound: Laughlin had published "Ezra Pound's Propertius" in *Sewanee Review,* 46 (October–December 1938), 380–91.

much better than mine: "Ezra Pound's Very Useful Labors," a review of Pound's *Fifth Decade of Cantos,* which appeared in *Poetry,* LI (March 1938), 324–29.

Symons: Arthur Symons (1865–1945), English poet, critic, editor, and anthologist.

---

33. TLS-1   December 16, 1938

DEAR DELMORE:

Well, here we are underway and as far as I know, everything is all right.

I was disappointed that Fadiman didn't do more; he seemed to miss the quality of the poems. But after all, he did say some pretty nice things about you.

I haven't seen any other reviews. I'll send the clippings down to you as they come along, but please send them back, as we need them for our permanent scrapbook. I am sending out nearly a hundred review copies as it is good advertising. Will send to Symons and all the other English johnnies.

It's hard to trace sales of books because so many people buy through stores, but a record is kept for all direct orders and you can scrutinize same the next time you come to Norfolk.

Very glad you have some lucrative articles. One has to eat. I have been making some money writing bilge about skiing. Glad you liked the Pound article. I felt it was pretty shallow.

Best to all,

J

/ · /

Fadiman: Clifton Fadiman's short review appeared in *The New Yorker,* December 17, 1938, pp. 90–91. He called Schwartz "the most interesting experimental writer I've noted in the last season or two."

34. TLS-2   [N.D.]

DEAR JAY:

Louise Bogan's review in *The Nation* is favorable enough, I suppose, but from beginning to end it is full of mistakes which show how poorly she read the book. I think some good might be done if you wrote to *The Nation* just listing her errors. It would probably look much more disinterested coming from you. Here is the kind of letter which might be right:

L. Bogan's review of D. S. *IDBR* is full of unwarranted mistakes of fact which indicate the most careless and irresponsible reviewing. Miss Bogan leaves out the punctuation and changes the word "disease" to "desire" in one of her quotations, radically altering the meaning; and in the second quotation, she alters another word. She says that the story of the book is about childhood, while the story is not at all about anyone's childhood, but about the protagonist's view of his parents' courtship at the age of 21. She incorrectly names one of the poems which she mentions, she names Kant as one of the characters in the long poem of the book, although he is merely invoked once by the hero. And above all, she fails utterly to see the simplicity and directness of style which characterize Mr. S's long poem and which has been recognized and praised by such disinguished poets and critics as Allen Tate, Wallace Stevens, Mark Van Doren, and others. This is not a question of taste, but of an incompetent reading by your reviewer which is exhibited beyond dispute in the inaccuracies which are questions of fact. Surely *The Nation* owes it to its readers to provide the reviews of important books in which the reviewer finds it possible to quote from the book under review without changing the meaning and re-writing the words of the author.

As an advertiser, you could insist on the publication of this letter, and besides being free advertisement, it would serve to make the critics more careful with the books they get from you. They have no business writing as Bogan did. Let me know what you do.

Tally-ho!
DELMORE

/ · /

Louise Bogan: (1897–1970), American poet, critic, and poetry reviewer for *The New Yorker.* Her "Young Modern" appeared in *The Nation,* March 25, 1939, 353–54.

the story of the book: The title story, "In Dreams Begin Responsibilities."

Mark Van Doren: (1894–1972), poet, critic, and Columbia University professor, who was awarded the Pulitzer Prize for his *Collected Poems* in 1940. New Directions published his *Our Lady Peace* in 1942.

what you do: A rebuttal, written by a ND editor, was published in *The Nation* in 1939.

35. TLS-2   229 Perkins Street
                                            Jamaica Plain, Mass.
                                            January 16, 1939

DEAR DELMORE:

Here is a copy of Tate's statement, of which we
are using the first part in our advertising.

Schwartz's poetic style is the only genuine innovation
we've had since Pound and Eliot came upon the scene
twenty-five years ago. In his verse there is a wholly new
feeling for language and in the regular versification a new
metrical system of great subtlety and originality. I wish
he had chosen instead of Coriolanus some less arbitrary
frame of reference; he doubtless will in his next work;
and that will be the real test of his capacity.

The first part of that makes a pretty strong blud-
geon. I am holding up on some of the ads in the
hope we'll get something equally good from some
other big gun.

That's a good review of the Williams. I hope you
will do a really extended study of him. No good one
has been done that I have seen. If you could get it
into the *Southern* or some place like that it would be
a fine thing. Then into the book. And later into the
"Homage to Williams" collection which I plan for
some future year. I want, when I get some money
to pay for them, to have all the guys like Blackmur
and Ransom and the *PR*s to do essays on various
aspects of Williams' genius, and put them in a book
along with various photographs and personalia. There
seems to be no way to establish Williams except to
have all the writers make a racket about him. The
stores refuse to cooperate. A matter of timing, I guess.

Yes, that is OK about the long poem. "Helpless
Judges" also sounds fine. You are damn good on

titles and conceptions. I think that is really the essential factor of your creative talent—as I shall get around to declaring in print when God further enlightens me—that you create in concepts. So very different from Williams, who creates in sort of emotional flashes or something. I'm not very clear on it yet, but I begin to see what it is.

The plan for the dialogue also sounds excellent. I would certainly do that. We need a little spreading about in this thin age. Write it in that rich, smoky prose that you used for the interludes of "Coriolanus"—a very powerful instrument—full of fables and stories and symbols. That will fix 'em.

I wish you would tell the *PR* boys to get a decent typographer. Their layout on our ad was atrocious. I insist on their fixing it up before they go to press. Tell them that.

So *Criterion* is gefinisht? I wondered. They returned our last batch of review copies with no explanation. That is bad, that is really bad. I suppose the backer got tired of backing.

Will send out copies of *IDBR* as you suggest. Who to get on the *PR* and what are the addresses? I have no addresses here. Let me know. Also what is Read's address? We have never had any contact with him.

Did Rodman pan you? What is Gregory doing? Has Dos Passos been sent a copy? Let me know.

Not much new here. Higgins reports that we sold two copies of your book last week. Whee! It makes you wonder, don't it?

About a deadline on the essays. Just remember that I will not publish anything earlier than September or later than December and will not again go through such fires of hell as we went through this time, trying to get that book done right when I was busy with other things. I expect to die a year sooner than otherwise from the sleep I lost driving up to the printer's in the middle of the night after a terrific day selling in the stores.

Whatever we do next year we must have the ms. in August at the latest, or it must wait till the next year. So please plan to work hard this winter and spring, which is a good time to work anyway.

I think we would be selling twice as many books if we could have published you in October. I dope it out this way. You were the tag end of the list and the stores were exhausted by the time you came along and bored with the whole idea of good literchoor in general and new directions in particular. So next year let's have the ms. by August and the book out in October.

Cheerfully,
JAY

/ · /

Jamaica Plain, Mass.: JL was still a student at Harvard University, but living off campus with the Charles Storey family in Brookline.

a good review: Schwartz's review of William Carlos Williams's *Collected Poems, 1906–1938,* which appeared in *Common Sense,* 8 (February 1939), 24. Presumably Schwartz shared the typescript with Laughlin in January.

into the book: Schwartz had proposed a collection of his essays and reviews, to be titled *The Imitation of Life.* It was never published.

"Helpless Judges": No poem by this title was ever published.

the dialogue: Unidentified.

Read's address: Sir Herbert Read (1893–1968), British poet, critic, and editor.

Did Rodman pan you?: Selden Rodman (b. 1909), American poet and anthologist.

What is Gregory doing?: Horace Gregory (1898–1982), American poet, critic, biographer, anthologist, and classicist.

Dos Passos: John Roderigo Dos Passos (1896–1970), American novelist. Schwartz had published a review of his trilogy, *U.S.A.:* "John Dos Passos and the Whole Truth," *Southern Review,* IV, 2 (1938), 351–67.

36. TLS-2   8 W. 105 St.
                                         New York City
                                         Jan. 18, 1939

DEAR JAY:

Everything gets better all the time, except that no
copies are being bought. But what do you expect
before the reviews and the ads come out? If my present luck holds, I bet you get paid for every copy in
two years.

As for the August deadline, I will do my best, but
my mind just stops working now and then, and the
following parts have to be written: 1) Essay for the
S.R., 2) essay for *P.R.,* 3) review of Eliot's new play
for *The Nation,* 4) review for *K.R.,* 5) dialogue, 6)
essay on Williams, 7) comprehensive title essay.
Meanwhile I would also like to write a few poems
and stories, entertain my young wife, study and
memorize all the favorable reviews, and get in trim
for the next pennant race. Another idea is an essay
on *The Criterion,* which would end by passing the
buck to Warren, Ransom, and you. You admit: This
is no minor chore. But I will go fast once I get started
and perhaps I will manage it. As to getting the piece
on Williams printed, I will try again, but have failed
before—Eliot really blocks W.C.W. for some readers; they expect everyone to write like Eliot because
they like him so much. Another thing: I admit I was
a dreadful nuisance about getting the book finished,
but the fact is that you did have the book in your
hands by August 6. And I doubt that it would have
made much difference to have published the book in
October.

Will you send copies to William Phillips, 166 Second Ave., N.Y.C., Philip Rahv, 9 Bank St., N.Y.C.,
F. W. Dupee, 408 W. 20th St., N.Y.C.? I gave Mac-

donald a copy and swore him to eternal silence, and
Morris will buy one. Read can be reached care of
Faber and Faber. Gregory is a deadly enemy: send
him nothing but a time bomb. Dos Passos could only
be offended by getting one, but it might help to get
one to Hemingway, if you can reach him before
Franco arrives in Barcelona, and cuts out his black
heart—maybe he is still in N.Y. though. The essay
I wrote on him was a pretty insidious compliment
and he may be interested.

Probably all this maneuvering is not very good
for our souls, but it is very pleasant. Tate's praise is
perfect, especially for places like the *S.R.* and *K.R.*
where Tate is the leader. Try to use the whole thing
when it does not cost you more money—the last
sentence makes it sound more judicious, because of
the qualifying tone. If you can't use the whole thing,
please try to get in as much as "originality"; the
technical remarks relieve the strain on the reader's
credulity imposed by the first sentence. I hope you
realize what a sacrifice Tate was making by going
out on a limb in this way for me. He had nothing to
gain except the suspicion that he was trying to get
me to praise him in my essay, and he knew well
enough how much I respect him beforehand.

Gertrude says she is some company. She is.

Tally-ho,
DELMORE

/ · /

Essay for the S.R.: "Poetry and Belief in Thomas Hardy," *Southern
Review,* VI, 1 (1940), 64–77.

essay for P.R.: "The Poet as Poet" (on W. B. Yeats, 1866–1939, Irish
poet), *Partisan Review,* 6 (Spring 1939), 52–59.

review of Eliot's new play: "The Family Reunion," *The Nation,* 148 (June
1939), 676–77. This item is not listed in David H. Zucker's bibliography in *Selected Essays.*

review for K.R.: "The Two Audens," *Kenyon Review,* 1 (Winter 1939), 34–45.

comprehensive title essay: No essay entitled "The Imitation of Life" was published.

an essay on The Criterion: "The Criterion, 1922–1939," *Kenyon Review,* I (Autumn 1939), 435–39.

Macdonald: Dwight Macdonald (1906–1982), American author and critic.

Morris will buy one: Wright Morris, American novelist (b. 1910).

before Franco arrives: Francisco Franco (1892–1975), Spanish dictator and general, who ended the Spanish Civil War in March 1939, with German and Italian assistance.

Hemingway: Ernest Hemingway (1899–1961), American fiction writer.

The essay I wrote on him: "Ernest Hemingway's Literary Situation," *Southern Review,* III, 4 (1938), 769–82.

37. TL-2

229 Perkins St.
Jamaica Plain, Mass.
Thursday

DEAR DELMORE:

. . . I am currently engaged upon a course paper for Professor Rand entitled "Coriolanus Old and New." It is a comparison of the classical accounts of the gent with your and Bill's versions.

Quite a lot of fun. I have been ploughing through such Johnnies as Livy, Florus, Dio Cassius, Plutarch, Dionysius of Halicarnassus, und so weiter. If you are interested I'll let you see my conclusions. Some of them have to do with the political and constitutional struggle of which Cory was the symbol and victim, part with such details as the fact that Menenius died a year before your action takes place, etc.

By the way, would you object to clearing up for me the sentence of some of your ghosts? I get what Marx and Freud and Beethoven (syph) are driving at, but Harry Stottle and Kant elude me. What does Harry say? It's too subtile for me. And you don't have Kant say anything at all.

However, there are several unidentified ghostly utterances, some of which may be his.

Would it be an intrusion on your poeticated privities to advise your servant who is, are, the speakers in the following passages: pages 26, 28, 29, 33, 43, 66.

Another matter: Shouldn't your mystery man be referred to as the 6th ghost? You've got five in that box besides him. What about that?

I read over the thing line for line with Old Bill and it really stands up excellent well under such competition. You have some really swell lines scattered about in the poem and the pace is excellent. A number of friends have said they "couldn't put it down."

There are also all the German, French, English, and Italian plays about C that intervened between Shakespeare's first and second coming.

Well, give us a buzz!

/ · /

Professor Rand: E. K. Rand, a famous Harvard classicist, author of *Roman Virgil*.
Bill's versions: William Shakespeare's.
Harry Stottle: Ezra Pound's name for Aristotle.

38. TLS-1   Thursday

DEAR JAY:

Thanks for sending me your essay, which has flattered me no end. I think it is an excellent piece of

work; there are a few errors of detail, which I have
noted in the margin, but the whole recitation of fresh
facts started my mind moving again, which was a
pleasant thing, since I have been stupid as a stone for
the past six weeks. One contrast you might have
done much more with, the contrast of Plutarch and
Shakespeare. This shows itself most, I think, in what
S. *omitted* from Plutarch, while taking so much, and
the whole comparison of the Elizabethan mind with
that of the classical one could serve to illustrate many
things.

The Paris *Coriolan* was a production of the play in
1934 in which the class-war was over-emphasized,
it seems, to please the 1934 audience. As you recognized, it was precisely that kind of crudeness I wished
to avoid. The reference to Coriolanus in *The Waste
Land* seems to show that Eliot takes C. as the type
of the isolated individual (you remember Plutarch
also has evidence for that view), for in the context,
the thunder has just advised the protagonist or ego
of the poem to sympathize, *Dayadhvam,* and the
protagonist replies that each one lives alone in the
prison of his own being and is actually in the same
isolation as was C. when he had cut himself away
from all other human beings. "Triumphal March"
and "The Difficulties of a Statesman" seem to indicate another view of C., however; he is the aristo-
cratic statesman and the noble captain trying to
preserve the values of an aristocracy, which he has
inherited from, or been educated in, by his mother:
This view is not only different from the one in *The
Waste Land,* but C.'s quality is erased in this view in
that he no longer hates the mob, but, as an aristo-
crat, feels a social responsibility for them.

After much effort, I still find it difficult to find
anything to admire in *The Family Reunion.* I would
send you a copy of the review I wrote for *The Nation,*

if I had one, because differences of judgement like this interest me very much. But I am now willing to agree with you about Englishmen after meeting MacNeice last week, along with Horton and his bride: Next to MacNeice, Horton seemed to be a giant intellect.

As ever,
DELMORE

/ · /

The Paris Coriolan: A staged version of T. S. Eliot's failed poetic sequence, which was to include four long poems, of which "Triumphal March" and "Difficulties of a Statesman" were the first two.

MacNeice: Louis MacNeice (1907–1963), Belfast-born poet and translator.

Horton and his bride: Philip Horton (1911–1989), first biographer of Hart Crane and curator of poetry at Harvard's Widener Library from 1937 to 1942. His wife was Tessa Gilbert, a painter.

39. TLS-2   Wednesday

DEAR JAY:

Sorry to intrude on your monumental labors, especially since I am now going to stage last year's act all over again, the well-known Schwartz delay. I mean to say that I think I had better postpone my book of essays until next year or the year after that. There are several reasons for this change of mind: One of them is the fact that I have not been able to write either the Williams essay or complete the long introductory essay to my satisfaction and another is that I want to have the time to write something about *Finnegans Wake* (Joyce's funeral). What has happened during the past two months is that I have tried to write criticism when I really wanted to write works of the imagination, the result being that I did not do anything satisfactory. The book of criticism can certainly wait until next year and be a better book with better essays as a result of the pause; then, if I do not have a new work of imagination finished (although I think I will), there will still be the book of criticism to keep me in the intellectual eye. If you want to insist, and you can you know, I could get finished by the first of October; but you and the bookstores have that autumn assignation, and as I say, it would be well to wait a year: Art is long . . .

If you want something to brighten your list, perhaps you'd like to print the translation I did several years ago of Rimbaud's *Une Saison en Enfer*. It would make a beautiful small book of about fifty pages, and if you wanted a greater length, I could write a short *Vie* and introduction: It is a great work. I'd prefer not to write the introduction, because I am so full of poetry, but you decide whatever there is to decide.

May the Lord God witness the fact that I hope I am completely wrong, but I think you are wrong in printing Patchen: His first book dropped dead immediately, his poems after that look like pure opportunism to me, and no one likes him. You could have done much better with almost anyone, Berryman, Mary Barnard, Elizabeth Bishop. But I have been wrong before and I hope devoutly that I am wrong again.

I am delighted to hear that *IDBR* is being bought and it makes me sure once more of at least this much, that I can be interesting to all kinds of readers, if nothing else, and when I get a book of fiction finished for you, perhaps we will really go to town.

We wanted to go to Bennington again, but we just can't muster up enough money to afford the necessary car as well as cottage. However, I can wait for the royalties until the proper time when you dish out each boy's cut. We also wanted to go to Yaddo, but they have made a fine rule that the creative husband must come without the non-creative wife (it is obscene, the desire to separate whom God hath joined), and since Gertrude has been planning to leave me since we were married, I think I had better stick around while she is still able to endure me. So we will be in NY most of the summer and when you come here you can stay with us and we will all sweat together. You ought to come to see the Fair and as a matter of fact we ought to see it ourselves.

I hope you do credit to old New Directions in the examinations. Let me know about the Rimbaud, but otherwise don't let me interfere with your studies.

Yours,
D ELMORE

/ · /

the Williams essay: Schwartz's review of *Collected Poems: 1906–1938.* See notes to Letter 35.

Finnegans Wake: James Joyce's novel, published in 1939.

translation I did several years ago: Schwartz had begun the Rimbaud translation in 1934. He was so full of the French poet, one saying of the times was "The trouble with Delmore is, he's always chasing Rimbauds."

Rimbaud: Arthur Rimbaud (1834–1891).

Patchen: Kenneth Patchen (1911–1972), American poet and painter.

Berryman: John Berryman (1914–1972), American poet.

Elizabeth Bishop: (1911–1979), American poet.

Yaddo: The writers' and artists' colony at Saratoga Springs, N.Y.

the Fair: New York World's Fair, 1939–40.

in the examinations: The "Divisionals" JL had to pass at Harvard that spring.

40. TLS-1   April 19, 1939

DEAR DELMORE:

I'm afraid we may not get so far with our plan to have you and Gertrude come to Norfolk.

I wrote to Aunt about it and she replies in the nixative. She fears, I think, for your influence on me. She read parts of the book and was a good deal shocked, I guess. She seems to think you are a mixture of sex-fiend and Communist from whom she will defend my innocence to the last breath.

That makes things rather difficult as I can't possibly afford to live anywhere else, or have the office anywhere else, than at Norfolk. Not for the moment anyway.

As you may have gathered, I have a good deal of trouble with my family about the books. Aunt liked the idea at first and gave me money for it, but when she found out what sort of thing I was doing she was horrified. Now she just tolerates the books in the hope that I'll reform.

It isn't an easy situation, but I have to put up with it for financial reasons. And also I am fond of her in spite of her prejudices.

I'm sorry. I'll work on her when she gets back and try to smooth it out somehow. These things have been done before. But it may take time. So you had better not count on that immediately. This is a blow, really, I was getting quite cheered up at the idea of having some intelligent people in Norfolk.

Please return the enclosed letter from Eliot.

Yrs through this vale of adversity!
J

/ · /

I wrote to Aunt: There had been talk of Schwartz working for New Directions in the Norfolk, Connecticut, office. But Laughlin's aunt, Mrs. Leila Carlisle—on whose estate the press was housed in a former stable—had objected to Schwartz on the basis of alleged obscenity in *In Dreams*. (The word "fuck" appears twice.) See Atlas, p. 146.

41. TLS-2   Tuesday

DEAR JAY:

I like your poem and will tell the *PR* boys to print it. There are, however, five of them to get past and they usually only believe me when I am jeering at some effort.

The news about your aunt and the job is quite a blow, especially since I have heard nothing from North Carolina for two months now, which must be their Southern way of getting me used to the Final No. It is a pity I did not get a chance to speak with your aunt last summer, so that she could see how far from a sex-fiend and Communist I am. However, it would have been difficult for me to stay at Norfolk all year, anyway. My impression was that we would be in Boston most of the year, or rather Cambridge, and as a matter of fact, I would have to be near a big library, if I was to write the critical articles I keep getting and which are my only financial consolation for being a poet. One idea occurred to me, that Gertrude and I might take a big apartment in Cambridge, half of which you could use as your office; but don't take the trouble to say anything about this, if it would not work. At any rate, I have begun to take desperate measures to avoid landing in the poorhouse with little Gertrude, the terror of 105th St.

Pound arrived last Thursday and immediately made a damned fool of himself by announcing that Mussolini was a great man. Naturally all the reporters were merciless after that announcement. But about blasting in general, and Pound's blasting in particular, I think you underestimate all the good he did when he was still in his right mind. He really made decent writing possible by yelling all the time: That was the way he managed to get Eliot printed. As far as the Bogan review goes, there are fourteen inaccuracies of fact, as I said, not to speak of the stupidity of judgement: Fourteen mistakes, you must admit, are quite a total, and even if Olympian calm is your program, that record deserves some notice. Thanks for getting after *The Nation.*

Horace *is* poetry and I fail to grasp your remarks about his character; so far as his character goes, he just did not like bastards, so far as I can see. Saroyan is at The Great Northern, N.Y.C., and said he would stay until the World's Fair was under way. I suppose he wants to see if he can beat it.

Fergusson's dramatization was postponed because some epidemic worked its way through the whole college. One more problem is going to make trouble for us, namely, the first short novel I give you either next year or the year after, which will certainly be obscene at least as the whole thing exists in my mind right now. I think you ought to do something about getting rid of the family censorship before then. I don't especially care to be known as an obscene writer, but the subject of this story and, anyway, of human relationships as they exist right now require, as I suppose I need not tell you, some free speech.

As ever,
DELMORE

P.S. Pound said that the only American poet he could read was Cummings, that damned fool: You would think that he had never heard of WCW, the greatest American poet since Emily Dickinson.

/ · /

nothing from North Carolina: Allen Tate had made an offer to recommend Schwartz for an opening in the Philosophy Department at the Women's College in Greensboro, N.C.

Mussolini: Benito Mussolini (1883–1945), Italian prime minister, called the Duce, and first of Europe's Fascist dictators, who ruled Italy for over twenty years.

Horace: Quintus Horatius Flaccus (65–8 B.C.), Roman lyric poet and satirist.

Fergusson's dramatization: Francis Fergusson's version of Sophocles' *Electra,* which ND took over from the original publishers, William R. Scott, in 1940.

Cummings: E. E. Cummings (1894–1962), American lyric poet.

Emily Dickinson: (1830–1886), American poet, known for her precision and delicacy when dealing with emotions and states of the mind.

42. TL-3   April 27, 1939

DEAR DELMORE:

I need hardly tell you that my relations with my family are one of life's chief problems. So I hope you will try to bear with the problem until I can get it straightened out. It is all a question of money. I would never put up with their ridiculous prejudices if I weren't dependent on them. I think Pound wrote a poem about that situation once—the dead hand, I think he called it. Well, there is a dead hand over New Directions all the time. They would love to stamp it out; on the other hand, they have the natural affection for their young. I am just sitting tight, trying to compromise—to keep New Directions going and still not alienate them altogether. They cannot disinherit me, because my father left money in trust for me, but the hell of it is, I don't get it until my mother dies and she is healthy as a horse. Fortunately I have a little of my own—enough to keep going for six–seven years at the present rate. My hope is that by that time they will have woken up to the fact that what I am doing is not a disgrace to the family but a credit to it, and will kick through again. As I told you, both Father and Aunt were very generous when I started the thing, because they thought it was going to be harmless and polite. I guess, Aunt froze right up as soon as she smelt sex. Often I have been about ready to tell them to go to hell. But if I did, I would just be condemning myself to inutility. There is no beating the game that I can see. It takes money to run a press like New Directions, and although the books might conceivably come to pay their way, you cannot count on that. The minute I began to count on making money, I would drift into printing crap. The only thing I can see to do is to focus on the quality of the stuff and take the gain or loss as it comes—keeping the two kinds of value rigidly separated.

There is just a chance that things may solve themselves a little sooner. My brother and I are now waging a legal battle against a bank in Pittsburgh which is trustee for the estate of one of my uncles. We are convinced that the bank has done us out of something we were meant to get. We won the first round in the lowest court and the opposition has now appealed to the next court. If we are reversed there we will push it up to the State Supreme Court. But that all takes time and I am not at all optimistic about it. We have what seems to us a clear case, but as you know right and wrong haven't much relation to law.

If that comes through everything will be OK as

the amount in question, although not large, would be quite sufficient for the needs of the press. We'll know about that within a year.

In the meantime all I can do is try to sit tight and hold everything. It isn't much fun, but on the other hand, you can't expect to have everything dumped into your lap.

I tell you all this because I consider you a partner in the enterprise, and want you to know just how things stand and understand why I do what I do. I'm not being ornery.

Don't worry too much about the censorship problem. We wouldn't be doing that novel before 1940, would we, and a lot can happen before that. I expect divine intercession from day to day, having led a blameless Christian life from the day of Baptism. Maybe.

Your idea of a big loft in Cambridge which would be combined living quarters and office is not so bad. I don't know what I'll be doing next fall, but I don't think I'll pass my Divisionals this year. I'm a fairly smart boy but I just haven't done enough work. I may have to take them again next year, in which case I would want to be handy to the library also. Of course it is much cheaper for me to live in Norfolk, but perhaps if I boarded with you we could get it down to a low figure.

I can envisage a kind of poetical rabbit & publishing warren in Cambridge that would not be half bad.

Well, let the thing ride along and maybe something will work out. As I say, I expect an angel to come down in his car any moment. Its car, I guess. Maybe you'll get the job in Carolina after all.

Thanks for the kind words about the Hitler poem. I have sent a copy to the *PR* gentry and hope they will do it. I would like very much to have that poem appear in that place. My connection with Pound always lays me open to attacks of being a Fascist and that is not very pleasant. The poem might help to clarify my personal position. I don't make political statements in *New Directions* because I want that to be strictly non-political.

I have given up trying to explain the facts of life to Ezra. If he wants to dig his own grave, all I can do now is try to keep some memory of what he once was alive. He is in Washington now. He wants me to come down there but I can't do that. Too busy with my Divisionals. And don't want to be his errand boy either. I'm all for his monetary principles but when he became a Franco & Hitler man, I found the going thick. I am willing to believe that the Duce has enlightened conceptions of finance, but that is as far as I'll go. If he does have understanding of social credit there is no need for him to bag *useless* colonies. That's what I think. It looks to me like wishful thinking on Ezra's part. Because BM is his pal he wants to make Christ out of him willy nilly.

What I object to in Horace is his bourgeois attitude which ruins practically all the odes for me. Things like that little duet with the wolf who went away because he could see H. was such a good man. Etc. He is much better in the epodes and quite good in the satires. And of course a marvelous technican at all times.

Pound probably didn't mention Williams because Bill has been telling Ezra to go to hell until he gets his nose wiped. Ezra was concluding his letters to Bill with "arriba España" and that was a bit more than Bill could keep down.

What do you think of this new mag in London edited by the Ceylonese gent? *Poetry* it's called. Have you seen? Drop into the GBM and take a look at it. They ought to print you and I guess they have some dough.

I'm enclosing a copy of our store release on the Joyce thing. How do you like the heading? I've just gotten it done and am planning to ship out these releases every so often to the stores and the papers to keep them wise to our doings. Think I'll do two on you fairly soon—one to the stores and one to individuals. Tell them what a nice chap you are, etc.

Don't you think it's a good idea?

Well, let's all keep our courage up, and here's to the lit'ry beehive. I think it could be damned good.

ETC.

/ · /

the Hitler poem: "A Letter to Hitler," *Selected Poems, 1935–1985* (1986), p. 35.

Hitler: Adolf Hitler (1889–1945), German chancellor and leader of the Third Reich from 1933 to 1945.

BM: Benito Mussolini.

duet with the wolf: Horace, *Odes* I, 22 ("Fuscu, an honest man . . .").

the Ceylonese gent: Editor from Ceylon who signed himself simply "Tambimuttu."

the GBM: Gotham Book Mart, now located at 41 West 47th Street, run by Frances Steloff (1887–1989).

the Joyce thing: In 1939, JL produced an American bind-up edition of *Our Exagmination Round His Factification for Incamination of Work in Progress,* with contributions by Samuel Beckett (1906–1989), William Carlos Williams, and others. Originally it was published in 1929 by Sylvia Beach at Shakespeare & Company in Paris.

43. TL-2

DEAR DELMORE:

I surely would like the book of essays this year, but one of the main planks of the ND platform is not to turn the writers into employees. So let your genius be your guide, remembering always that somebody or other who probably only had one ball defined genius as the capacity for hard work. With which morality—I have been preparing Seneca—I desist.

No, by all means do the imaginative writing. That is what is important. What are you working on? Something new?

I would like to look at the Rimbaud: He is one of my favorites, and I have had it in mind to do something of his for a good while. I was seeing Auden the other night and he highly recommended the translation of *Illuminations* by somebody named Rootham. Do you know anything about this?

Auden I just don't like, but please keep that to yourself. . . . [words deleted]. He greatly admires your book and thinks you are going to be hot stuff. I didn't try to get a statement out of him, as I don't like to ask favors of him. I have decided he is the Ovid of the day. . . .

/ · /

Seneca: Seneca the Younger, Lucius Annaeus Seneca (4 B.C.?–A.D. 65), Latin poet and satirist.

Rootham: Helen Rootham, governess and friend of Dame Edith Sitwell. She published *Prose Poems from "Les Illuminations" of Arthur Rimbaud* with Faber & Faber in 1932, with an introduction by Dame Edith.

Ovid: Publius Ovidius Naso (43 B.C.–A.D. 17), Latin poet.

44. TLS-2   Wednesday

DEAR JAY:

As you say, the Rimbaud is a great project and the sort of thing which might fertilize the imagination of a whole generation of poets—certainly some of this generation could stand some fertilizing and less fertilizer. I am perfectly willing to do the work complete and with your commentary—the commentary being absolutely necessary for some of the most important parts, because the Franco-Prussian War and the Paris Commune evidently is the background of some of the best writing, while the hatred of the bourgeois and the interest in Catholicism has much to do with *A Season in Hell*.

But there is this question to consider: My edition of Rimbaud is almost four hundred pages in length. If you are going to print a complete translation with original, your emendation, and perhaps an essay by Tate, if you want him, then that means an enormous volume of about nine hundred pages, much too expensive, to say the least, for most of the readers I know, not to speak of what it would cost you. Moreover, it would take about six months for me to translate the poems, about half of which are merely schoolboy exercises deriving from Baudelaire, Hugo and Verlaine.

There is this alternative, however. My edition of Rimbaud divides in half at p. 162. From 162 to 309 is mainly prose poesy—the prose poems of *Les Illuminations* and the *Season in Hell* with the interpolation of six poems in the latter work. The prose poems are evidently what Rootham translated and Faber published separately. I could get all of this done by the 1st of August at the very latest and you would have a volume of over 300 pages to publish this fall or winter, while you could announce the second volume for next year or after. The division in two volumes is made even more sensible by the fact that Rimbaud stopped writing in regular forms and began writing prose poetry exclusively at a certain point in his career. Furthermore, the prose poetry will create an interest in the strict verse, because in the former the leading obsessions are announced with great explicitness, while the strict verse, great as some of it is, does not yet show what Rimbaud was coming to, except implicitly—he was of course coming to the point where he felt it necessary to reject the whole of Western civilization, and become a gunrunner in Africa.

What do you say? The complete Rimbaud in one volume seems a virtual impossibility if we are going to be real scholars and print the original on one side, while the first volume I am suggesting has a real unity of its own and can be completed later. Another reason for printing one volume this year is that I will almost certainly have a book of my own for you next year. However, I am anxious to translate much of the verse also. I hope you can see this first volume for this fall—now is just about the time for the sticks of dynamite which the later Rimbaud was throwing at the disorder and conflict and disease of Western civilization, while by next year another war may be so brutal that verbal brutality will seem without relevance.

I would like to see your copy of Rootham very much and also the Wheelwright review of *IDBR,* and any other news about it. I could come up to Norfolk for a day to discuss the whole business with you, if there are still doubtful points troubling you.

As ever,
DELMORE

P.S. A second alternative: I could translate *everything* by August 1st, by turning the verse into prose, and adding a short *To the Reader,* in which I would point to the metrical-diction tension to be found on the other side of the page. This would be very good except for the fact that, as I say, there would be an absolutely enormous volume. The main thing that concerns me right now is getting at least one volume published between now and December. Prose translations are often the best: cf. the Herter Norton prose of Rilke with the equivalent Leishman translation. By the way, how are you set for your part of the work? I could send you a bibliography of what the N.Y. Public Library has on hand; there's quite an intensive commentary in French.

/ · /

the Paris Commune: More correctly, the Commune of Paris, an insurrection of Paris against the French government which took place between March 18 and May 28, 1871. It was the first organized Parisian uprising of the proletariat against capitalism.

Franco-Prussian War: More correctly, the Franco-German War (July 19, 1870–May 10, 1871), which marked the cessation of French hegemony in continental Europe and the foundation of the Prussian-dominated German Empire.

my edition of Rimbaud: Schwartz used the Mercure de France edition of the French text, except for pp. 251–53.

Baudelaire: Charles-Pierre Baudelaire (1821–1867), French poet.

Hugo: Victor-Marie Hugo (1802–1885), French poet, playwright, and novelist.

Verlaine: Paul Verlaine (1844–1896), French poet.

by August 1st: Schwartz was highly optimistic. He possessed what he himself admitted was a "high school" proficiency in French. (See Atlas, p. 148.)

at least one volume published: JL brought out Schwartz's five-year-old translation of *A Season in Hell* in 1939. It received a fine review in *The New York Times* and quickly sold out all 750 copies of the first edition. The trouble came later when more careful critics began to find all sorts of errors in the translation. ND brought out a corrected edition in 1941.

the Herter Norton prose: M. D. Herter Norton, wife of the publisher W. W. Norton, was a leading Rilke translator; she published seven titles in all, including *Sonnets to Orpheus* and *Stories of God.*

Leishman: J. B. Leishman (1902–1963), an Oxford don who translated Rilke's *Duino Elegies* in collaboration with Stephen Spender, published by W. W. Norton in 1939. New Directions published *Possibility of Being,* a selection of Rilke poems translated by Leishman, in 1957.

45. ALS-1

8 W. 105 St.
New York City
June 3, 1939

DEAR JAY:

I've been thinking about the translation of Rimbaud since sending it to you. Our new idea is that of printing the French text on the left-hand page, as Eliot did with his translation of *Anabasis:* It looks very elegant, as you probably know. Another thing is that it might very well help me to get a novel to translate from some N.Y. publisher—this is the sort of thing Gertrude and I can do quickly and it pays fairly well. Philip Rahv suggested this possibility the other night (G. just did a translation for *Partisan Review* and the result is that my eagerness to have you print *A Season in Hell* is much intensified). I also hope you decided to use Auden.

Yours,
DELMORE

/ · /

translation of Anabasis: A poem by St.-J. Perse (pseudonym of Alexis St.-Léger Léger, French poet born in 1887), translated by T. S. Eliot (London: Faber & Faber, 1930).

Rahv, Philip: (1908–1973), American critic, best known as co-founder and editor of *Partisan Review*. His writings on Russian and European literature were among his most influential.

to use Auden: Auden had sent Schwartz a letter praising his first book; Schwartz was urging JL to quote from it in advertisements.

46. TLS-1   July 30, 1939

DEAR JAY:

Enclosed is a copy of the copy I made of Auden's letter, and another version of the letter I enclosed for you to send to him. His problem of not knowing what to say could be solved immediately by his saying what he says in the letter: "I admire his work; he is very promising." That will do us no end of good, for Auden is here to stay, the unofficial laureate as authoritative as Lawn Tennyson. I will also try to construct an advertisement for ND and your catalogue which may suit you after we hear from him.

The translation of Rimbaud has just been surveyed intensively by an expert in the French language with some fine minor revisions suggested. Otherwise I have been too busy with two long articles to get much more done, but the main task which is left is the Introduction, nothing else.

A boy named Robert Hivnor, aged 24, resident in Akron, Ohio, came to show me some parts of a novel, and some of the writing is very remarkable, to say the very least, although he seems not to know enough yet about the basic problem of a complete narrative structure. He left some of the novel with me and I am going to show it to Dwight Macdonald and then tell him to send it to you. I'm sure that you'll agree that he has something really new in the way of prose style and sensibility and I hope that you will find it possible to write him a long letter of welcome and encouragement.

As ever,
DELMORE

/ · /

as *Lawn Tennyson:* Schwartz's pun on Alfred, Lord Tennyson.

a boy named Robert Hivnor: American playwright and fiction writer (b. 1915). ND gave him a small advance for a novel, *The Invader,* but according to JL, he was never able to finish it satisfactorily. However, his play *The Ticklish Acrobat* appeared in the ND *Playbook 1956;* another play, *The Assault Against Charles Sumner,* was published in *Plays for a New Theatre* in 1966.

47. TLS-1

DEAR JAY:

The limited edition would be fine, and the dollar royalty even finer; there must certainly be thirty people who would come across with the five dollars, so you ought to go ahead. I'll try to get the revised introduction to you as soon as I can; I think I maybe ought to mention the new War in passing; maybe not, I'll see.

Remember my mentioning Robert Hivnor, 1422 Hillcrest St., Akron, Ohio? He can't get printed anywhere else, but he is really extremely good; how good is not yet obvious. Would you take time out to send him a card declaring your interest? I've already told him to send you his parts of a novel, but he is slow and shy.

I await with much interest Carnevali, Nemerov, and Armageddon. One more thing: I wish you would enclose your dicta in envelopes; I come to breakfast and find that all the other seventeen writers at Yaddo have found out what you have to say to me; not that military secrets are involved, but it is none of their Goddamn business.

Yours,
DELMORE

/ · /

limited edition: In addition to a first trade edition of 780 copies of Schwartz's Rimbaud translation (which sold for $2.50), JL also produced 30 copies on Worthy Signature paper, bound in hand-blocked Carta di Firenze, and signed by the translator (for $5.00).

the new war: World War II began on September 1, 1939, when Germany—without a declaration—invaded Poland.

Carnevali: Emanuel Carnevali, an Italian dissident who was a protégé of William Carlos Williams. Carnevali died in 1942.

Nemerov: Howard Nemerov (1920–1991), American poet and fiction writer, a Harvard classmate of JL's. He had a poem in *ND* 10.

48. TLS-2   Monday

DEAR JAY:

Thanks very much for the check. It relieves a crisis which may not occur again if Morrison, Guggenheim, or Van Doren smile on me.

Sorry about the delay with the proofs; it won't occur again except if some of them come during the tail end of this week when we will be in N.Y., getting rid of our apartment and furniture. The desire for a home has become, in me, the desire for a place to rest my books. They have travelled thousands of miles in the last few years.

The Carnevali arrived the other day and I read most of it; I doubt what remains would do much to change my mind about it, which can be expressed as follows:

The book has many passages of fine writing, of the kind of freshness and clarity of observation which one gets from Williams (why don't you get him to write his "Vita"?). But I doubt very much that it makes a whole book, a genuine statement; what is lacking is some point of view which would make all the beautiful passages significant as examples of it.

The nearest to such a point of view is the implicit Bohemianism of 20 years ago—let us live, write poems, be free, sleep with Edna Millay and use her candle on both sides; that is what the advance guard all believed when Carnevali was a promising young poet. This book would have value *as a document* if Carnevali were sufficiently conscious that it is the attitude of a given period. However, the book is so frequently charming and moving that this might actually come through even to the majority of readers who, unlike myself, are not interested in the period.

What I would suggest is that, if you want to make peace with everyone concerned, you print a few chapters in your next year's anthology and see if the reviewers attend to it very much; then you can decide if it is worth printing in regard to whether anyone cares about Carnevali's life. And as long as I am making unrequested suggestions, I might as well add the idea that since Stevens seems to be writing poems at the rate of a mile-a-minute, you might be able to get a volume from him or print a collected poems— with Stevens and Williams in your stable, not to speak of your demon correspondent's next book, you would practically be in control of American poetry. It might also be a good idea to get Berryman, too; he gets better and better every day. However, be that as it may, I wish that hereafter when you send me a manuscript, and do so whenever you want, you keep my name out of it. Carnevali arrived via Ann Watkins, so that now if you don't print him, I suppose Kay Boyle will detest me as the frustrator of invalids or something.

Yours,
DELMORE

/ · /

Morrison: Theodore Morrison, instructor in Advanced Composition at Harvard.

The Carnevali arrived: Typescript of the poet Emanuel Carnevali's autobiography.

Edna Millay: Edna St. Vincent Millay (1892–1950), American poet.

the frustrator of invalids: Carnevali had been overtaken by a dreadful disease and returned to Italy, where he lived in torment for years, writing his American literary friends for financial support.

Kay Boyle: American novelist and story writer (b. 1903) who befriended Carnevali in Paris in the twenties and later compiled and edited his *Autobiography,* published by Horizon Press.

Ann Watkins: New York literary agent.

49. TLS-2

Yaddo,
Saratoga Springs, NY
Sept. 19, 1939

DEAR JAY:

Enclosed is the revised essay, and the paragraph for the jacket. You might, by the way, add to the other side of the jacket advertising *IDBR,* the words of MacNeice, especially, and any others that can be included—did Auden ever reply?—the longer the more likely to produce results. Will you see that I get the Rimbaud proofs all at once, not in separate parts; it is a waste of time when they come dribbling in, and interrupt a mind focused on other problems?

I read the Nemerov essay, or as much as I could stand, and I am sorry to report that it is just no good at all. Not only are there numerous errors of fact, and a good deal of misinterpretation and misunderstanding of sources, but when he does say something true, it is so obvious and commonplace that one wonders how anyone would take the trouble to write it out once more, except to please an instructor. The very first page contains one of the fanciest examples of the mixed metaphor I've ever seen—it might be called the delta mixture: "These two notions find common ground in a deeper current," and then, not satisfied, "of which they are perhaps only the symptoms." I'll send the manuscript back to you after the Carnevali, and with a piece, very poor, that Ronald Duncan has just sent me to pass on to you. Your essay on "Coriolanus" is back in our apartment.

We are probably going to stay here most of the winter, at least until the 1st of December, for the simple reason that we are incapable of paying the rent elsewhere and here we are rent-free. Such being the economic condition, I would like you to give me an advance on future royalties to the sum of $150; the Rimbaud book ought to take care of at least half of that amount, and you can make the whole thing out as a loan, which you will of course get back as soon, if ever, as I get a job or a Guggenheim. Certainly I am going to make that much money in royalties sooner or later. I dislike making this request, but I have already tapped every other possible and nearer source of funds and I have no choice but to ask you.

Yours,
DELMORE

/ · /

Ronald Duncan: (1914–1982), English poet and playwright, educated in Switzerland and at Cambridge. He edited the Songs and Satires of the Earl of Rochester and Pope's Letters. He was editor of the London literary magazine, Townsman, which became a vehicle in which Pound planted his disciples.

50. **TLS-1**   September 21, 1939

DEAR DELMORE:

I am enclosing a check for $150.00 as advance on
your future royalties. I'm confident that your books
will make this for you in due course and I hope it
will tide you over until better times. There is no need
to make out a note on this as long as we are agreed
that New Directions is to publish your books.

Thank you for reading the Nemerov. I agree with
you. It struck me as the most awful, pompous bilge.
But I just wanted to check on it with an authority.

I think I told you my position on the Carnevali. I
think it is a valid human document but a step backward as far as New Directions is concerned. I don't
want to do it. But Kay Boyle is hounding me about
it and, as I'm very fond of her, I would do it to
please her if I could be convinced that it would not
be bad for the press.

Duncan also sent me a pretty sad piece of a play.
He is all stirred up by the war. His letter hints that
they are going to jail him or something. I'm sorry
for him and admire his struggle to permeate the slime
of London, but I just don't like his work. I never
brought myself to use part of his other play in *ND
39,* though I would have, had there been room.

Auden has not answered my letter about the statement.

Look, Buffalo Bill, you didn't catch on about the
proofs. You've got to correct them in sections and
in a hurry, too. You see this is foundry type. It don't
come out of a machine. God made it. And He only
has so much of it. He has used all He has to set up
what you have proofs on now. He can't set anymore
till He has printed this lot. So hasten Jason with them

proofs. We're back in LA and hurrah for art and the handy crafts. Ah Beauty! Be not a Beast.

J

51. TLS-2   Yaddo
                            Saratoga Springs, N.Y.
                            Nov. 6, 1939

DEAR JAY:

I presume that you have now returned from your selling trip and can get rested up for the long Southern trip, which is now sewed-up. (I managed to get the subject switched—Wolfe was too appalling); you might do some salesmanship down there, by the way. I don't know why I am doing this—the benefits being so vague—and the four thousand miles round trip will have me sleepy and listless for weeks after; but I do like to make trips. We're both invited to stay with the Tates overnight (before starting) at Princeton, and you ought to invite Tate to come with us, if he decides to go to the MLA meeting. He can be amazingly interesting in many ways, and towards the end of the trip we would be able to look in on the cream of Southern intellect—Faulkner, Katherine Anne Porter, et al.

Your ND ad was beautiful, and the statement on top very dignified and impressive. This reminds me to say that on a certain subject concerning which I vowed to remain silent, and in which you seem to me to have made a ghastly mistake, I have heard various reports from several quarters. There is no sense in saying anything now, but I will send myself a dated letter or something predicting what is going to happen just to prove to you that the opinion I expressed last May or June was neither a matter of rivalry, lack of awareness, or anything but pure prediction. Forgive me this mystery, if it is one, and we shall see.

You'll certainly have a new book from me next fall, probably my book of criticism; I could get it ready by the spring if necessary, but since it is not necessary I won't, and hereafter, I am not going to get things done in a hurry by September, losing all the opportunities for revision and improvement and then have the printer linger over the thing for the next three months. I wish you would get your hired help to send me a batch of catalogs for distribution.

Yours,
Delmore

p.s. Please don't go and change your mind about the New Orleans trip—I just don't have the money to go there by train; and if I don't get there I'll be blacklisted academically.

/ · /

the long Southern trip: The Schwartzes and JL were to travel to the Modern Language Association (MLA) convention in New Orleans over the Christmas holiday.

Wolfe was too appalling: Schwartz had been asked to deliver an address on Thomas Wolfe. Instead, he substituted one on "The Isolation of Modern Poetry."

on a certain subject: Schwartz had insisted it was a mistake for JL to publish Kenneth Patchen, the poet and painter.

to go there by train: They traveled south in Laughlin's new car, and when Laughlin decided to remain longer, he subsidized their return trip north. See Atlas, p. 160.

52. TLS-2

Yaddo,
Nov. 17, 1939

DEAR JAY:

I wrote you yesterday at New Directions, but only God knows what happens to some of the mail, which is what I was saying yesterday: Eliot wrote me a fine letter and sent it care of New Directions; by the time it arrived here it must have been opened four times. As I said yesterday you can open all my mail, if you like, but I don't want him whose name I don't like to mention digging into my communications. The envelope was obviously opened and then re-sealed by an amateur hand.

I wish you had let me know about the job just one week sooner; our time was up and Mrs. Ames asked us to stay until Christmas and when she said she could not be certain for later, we delivered our ultimatum, just like Hitler moving into Czechoslovakia; April 1st, rent-free, or we go, and we started to pack (all this is in complete confidence, by the way), and this broke down the lady and she said in a broken voice, "April 1st."

The point is that after raising that scandal, we can't pick up and go until the 1st of March at the very earliest. But the essential point is this: *That you keep that job open for us until the 1st of March.* Forgive me the italics, but reassure me. You can get temporary help for the two months, and then we will come down there and show you how we really love New Directions. I suspect that your aunt will really like Gertrude; women always do. Now for God's sake, don't go and give someone else the job when your poorest author really needs it.

Gertrude thanks you for asking her to come; she

has not yet decided whether she wants to go or not. We ought to have a fine time.

I said yesterday that I was trying to get Miller's book for review. As for nameless sponsors, you know that Williams will praise anyone unless he writes blank verse and his name is Schwartz. He's a great writer, all right, but you know as well as I do that he can't tell a poet from a hole in the ground; to say that nameless is like Donne is insanity; the old doctor probably never has read Donne. Bishop praises everyone too; you ought to hear what Tate and Rahv say about nameless.

Wait until you hear what the old master mind of *The Waste Land* thinks about me, now that he has finally taken the trouble to read my book.

I don't know how you stand up under all that driving; I get worn out when I take the car and go the forty miles to Albany to get away from the silence and investigate the night life there.

Don't we take Tate along? He'll probably decide that he does not want to come, anyway, but it would be polite to ask him.

Now it is about time I returned to my deathless poem.

DELMORE

/ · /

him whose name I don't like to mention: Kenneth Patchen, who with his wife, Miriam, ran the ND office in Norfolk, Connecticut, for over a year.

Mrs. Ames: Elizabeth Ames, executive director of Yaddo.

keep that job open for us: JL proposed to move the New Directions office to Cambridge, where one or both of the Schwartzes could have a job with the press.

asking her to come: To accompany Schwartz and Laughlin on the motor trip to New Orleans.

Miller's book: Henry Miller's *Black Spring* was published that year in Paris by the Obelisk Press.

nameless: I.e., Kenneth Patchen.

Donne: John Donne (1572–1631), English poet and dean of St. Paul's.

Bishop: John Peale Bishop (1891–1944), American poet and novelist.

the old master mind: T. S. Eliot.

take Tate along: In the car to New Orleans.

my deathless poem: He was writing *Genesis, Book One.*

53. TLS-3   Yaddo
                                     Saratoga Springs, NY
                                     Dec. 6, 1939

DEAR MASTER MIND:

Cambridge is just the place so far as we are concerned. I have wanted to go back ever since I left (I
was there last week trying to promote my job) and
it is really the proper site for such a highly intellectual outfit as New Directions, especially the girls.
The old master mind could not have figured out
anything to please his future assistants any more.

One minor but important problem, however, arises
at this juncture. It is absolutely impossible for me to
make out just how serious you are about Francesca,
Paolo, and it is hard for me to see myself (assuming
that you are serious) standing in the same room with
my sister and anyone else but keeping a straight face.
We Schwartzes always giggle at the wrong time.
Furthermore, I know about a hundred people in the
old college town, some of whom are coming to see
me and most of whom know damned well that I
have no sister. For example, one of the first things I
would have to do in the old college town is ask my
old benefactor, David Prall, to dinner: Now he knows
everything about me, including when I first com-

mitted coitus, and he knows damned well I have no sister.

May I suggest, then, that it would be wiser if she were Gertrude's sister or my cousin? If old Jason Directions would just break down and uncover to his well-wishing future assistants the complicated motivations of his complex mind, then they would know just where they stand with regard to their future lying.

I can understand perfectly well why Francesca would have to be someone's relative in Norfolk in your aunt's shadow, but in Cambridge Francesca would have a perfect justification for being where she was, in the small house outside the city limits, just as one more office worker on New Directions along with Gertrude and myself. Conversely and inversely and perversely, anyone who is against coitus on your part is going to be against it whether or not anyone is a sister of mine or not, and anywhere and everywhere we go. This is merely a matter of detail, of course, but I may be spending the next ten years of my life in Cambridge (if I get that job) and I don't want to spend all that time answering polite inquiries as to where my beautiful sister is now, and how is she, and she was so charming. In fine: Just what is in your mind, and had not we better settle the fair lady as Gertrude's sister or my cousin? I know she looks like me, but then I don't look like my very brother.

To rise now to more urgent issues: When I last saw Tate he asked me if it would not be possible for him to come along with us if he decided to come; or perhaps it was my suggestion. The point is, if you don't want him for one reason or another, let me know immediately so that I can start making excuses; perhaps this means that we will not visit Tate, or perhaps we will, we'll see. But let me know. I can tell him that you have to go to Florida after New Orleans and can't come back right away. It would be pleasant having him, however, and without him we have no entry among the Southern intelligentsia except in the home of *The Southern Review,* also G. M. O'Donnell. However, there will probably be too much to see anyway. But what about Tate?

My driver's license ceased to exist thousands of miles ago and I have driven thousands of miles without one; but I'll get another one immediately just to please you.

We will meet in New York, I take it, at an address I will send you when we know where we can stay while there. But let me know immediately the precise day when you intend to start; we will want to have two or three days in NYC before we go.

I am delighted to hear you met Barrett and doubt very much that you shocked him. He is going to be a great man. But how did you get hold of him?

In Cambridge everyone was asking for you and talking about New Directions; anytime you want to change places with some of these boys, it ought to be easy to arrange—they would all like to be publishers.

If you have nothing else to concern yourself, let me ask you this: How about publishing my book of criticism in late spring or early summer, instead of the fall—assuming I could write it over again as I want to do, in time? We would get more and better reviews then than in the Christmas rush and you could still peddle the book across the counter as now in the fall tour.

I have never read a happier more hilarious letter than your last one. I guess that girl must have something. And with regard to your curious suppositions that my sister would want to commit incest, will state that I have not been so much flattered since a

dripping faggot told me I looked like Dietrich with
my eyes closed. The former is as likely as the latter
is true.

Signed and resigned,
Delmore

/ · /

just the place: JL had decided to open a ND office in Cambridge.

since I left: Schwartz had left Cambridge and Harvard, without taking
a graduate degree, in March 1937.

to promote my job: He was still hoping for a teaching job at Harvard.

about Francesca: It appears Laughlin intended to install a female friend
in the Cambridge house and pass her off as Schwartz's sister. Delmore's joke here is an allusion to the Paolo and Francesca story in Dante's
Inferno.

David Prall: Harvard faculty member to whom Schwartz dedicated the
poem "Sonnet: The Ghosts of James and Peirce in Harvard Yard."

G. M. O'Donnell: The poet George Marion O'Donnell, whom JL published in *Five Young American Poets of 1940*.

you met Barrett: William Barrett (1913–1992), an editor of *Partisan Review*
and future author of *The Truants: Adventures Among the Intellectuals*.

hilarious letter: It has not survived.

that girl: The aforementioned Francesca.

Dietrich: Marlene Dietrich (1904–1992), international film star.

54. TLS-2

Pigsburgh
Tuesday

Satanic Throne:

The business manager of Faber & Faber is interested in your Rimbaud. He's getting a copy, as also
the agent. Hopefully.

Now don't count your Cambridge until you're
there. That's just a hope. Maybe rents are too high.
And it would be outside in the country. I insist on

that. But you will have a station wagon to use. And we might not move up there before the summer. I dunno. It all depends on a complication of factors that would make old Jerksilly Ibsen blush.

Your idea of doing your essays in the Spring seems to me pretty impractical, but I'm not altogether opposed, if it would help your career. It's something to think about anyway.

All right, she's your little old Irish grandmother. I don't care what she is, but she's got to be something. She can't live in the same house with us unless she is some close relative of yours and I won't play if I can't have my delicious Polish bacon. So you work it out to suit yourself. I still say sister is fine. Prall is a good man. Well, you work it out.

I dare say you will be bored with your sister. C'est une vraie Vulpius. Which is what attracts me. Not beautiful. Not bright. But marvelously and sometimes pathetically human. A little girl from the styx who dreams of better things and uses big words she can't pronounce and wants to learn to play the piano. That's what breaks me down. She doesn't ask for clothes, but just can she have piano lessons. You will probably think I'm crazy. Maybe I'm all wrong about it. It hasn't anything to do with love. It's just a scheme to get one's bed warmed by somebody who will not make demands of time and has enough native style to merge with the furniture. The trouble with girls of "my own class" is that they use up so damn much time. In order to go to bed with them, you have to give them hours of attention every day. I have a terrible lot of work to do and I don't want any interruptions and when I get to bed I want to find a white mouse there. The fact that she can type, book-keep, etc. and has ambition is just so much gravy. And, as you know from my deathless poetry, I am fascinated with the object. This is an object if ever was.

Maybe I'm too cold-blooded about it. But hell, Europe has been run on this basis for years. This girl is not an American. I mean, not really. She has American ambition but also, I think, the European idea of what a woman is for. Well, you'll see. I hope it won't be a cause of grief to you. She'll have to be taught a lot. But, as I said, she likes Hemingway and Dos Passos to begin with and that's a good sign.

I don't think Tate can go with us. He is going to have his appendix out at Christmas. So we may not even be able to visit them. I may want to be here a little longer before Christmas than planned. There is a great intrigue going on in the family business and I seem to be in the thick of it. It looks like it will end in a proxy war. Those foxes the Jonses are trying to take the simple-minded Laughlins into camp, and the prospect of blood and fire all rather delight me.

So I think you had better try to stand ready to depart as soon as the 19th or 20th. I'm going down to Washington Thursday. My address there is care of Duncan Phillips, 2101 Foxhall Road, Washington. I'll be there Saturday and Sunday. I think I'll drive up to Norfolk and pour oil on the waters. Let me know where to pick you up.

Be sure to get that license. If they stopped you and you hadn't it and were driving my car, they would put you in the bagnio. And then no Orleanseo.

Invitation from the Erskines to visit Baton Rouge. I shall take my typewriter on the trip and dare say that it will do for both. Don't bring too much stuff. You can buy a pair of slacks and some polo shirts in Florida for five bucks and go native. I do not contemplate wearing a white tie in even the highest-class brothels.

Adieu, adieu, noel, noel,

J

/ · /

Ibsen: Henrik (Johan) Ibsen (1828–1906), creator of modern realistic drama, hence the reference to situations which would make even Ibsen blush.

vraie Vulpius: Reference to Christiane Vulpius, the rather stupid young girl who consoled Goethe in his old age.

the Jonses: Benjamin Franklin Jones (1824–1903) and his wife. Jones was a founder of the Jones & Laughlin Steel Corporation.

Duncan Phillips: Art historian and pioneer collector of modern art. The Phillips Collection in Washington is now open to the public. He was a first cousin of JL's father.

the Erskines: Albert Erskine, of the Louisiana State University Press and subsequently Random House, was then married to the novelist and short-story writer Katherine Anne Porter.

55. TC-1   [N.D.]

DEAR DELMORE:

Ok ok don't take on so, I just asked you a question. Either we'll have the office in Cambridge or I will provide you with such stipend as may be necessary to keep the wheels of literature rolling smoothly. I'll see you soon.

                                                    J

56. TLS-3   Friday

DEAR JAY:

In immediate reply to your inimitable communications, I would like to begin by clearing up one thing. The job is Gertrude's, not mine, if you give it to us and we take it; I will be her part-time assistant, since the thing obviously requires help, having downed two grown men. But my assisting would occur in the evening and late afternoon. Poetry is first, second, last and always in Schwartz's life. If I wanted to do anything other than write poetry I could get a great deal more than fifty cents an hour. I am now at work on a deathless poem which will obsess the nation, and in addition I am writing my book of criticism, for which the demand increases daily, and I also have to write articles now and then. However, I seldom if ever do anything in the evenings but reach out for the applejack and dream of fame and the grave, so that it will be a very simple matter for me to work from seven to eleven, five nights a week. Gertrude is available for the whole day, and though it may take her a month or two to get the whole thing straight, she is extremely efficient; and the both of us, out of pure nervousness, usually do whatever has to be done with great haste.

I think it's best to get these things understood before we do anything more; otherwise this might turn out to be the end of a beautiful friendship.

Secondly, you have got to eliminate the thirty dollars a month rent. Surely your aunt can be persuaded to let that go, or if not, you can do something else about it. We stay here at Yaddo for nothing a month, and that includes coal; and we can stay here for years (some people have) because Mrs. Ames loves Gertrude and reads my writing day and night. We would have to be damned fools to kick this away in order to go and work for the money to pay the rent and nothing else. So far as I can see, most of the year we would be working for twelve dollars a week (id est, four hours a day) which would leave us eighteen dollars a month surplus after the rent has been paid. Not to speak of what coal costs in the winter, and the fact that there would be little to save.

I don't know whether or not this means that you would have to pay us thirty dollars a month more than anybody else. But I think that we could make it worth the difference to you. To begin with, you would be getting two people for the price of one, or rather one and one-half, considering that poetry comes first. Then I could do some of your manuscript reading for you, if that is necessary. Then you would be helping one of your authors and the Lord knows that he needs your help and you will remember that you avowed a certain responsibility in that matter.

The business with Mrs. Ames can be arranged, but only at the cost of making it certain that we could not come back here again; for she is a fine woman but forgiveness is not one of her virtues.

Now don't let the rent stand between New Directions and the hard-working Schwartzes. It is just barely possible that I will get a Guggenheim (will you let me know if they write you?), or that I will get that miserable job at Harvard, but neither remote possibility would do away with arrangements: I could come from Cambridge to Norfolk for three days of the week and Gertrude could stay there all the time, I mean, stay in the office; the Guggenheim would not make any change at all. I can only do a certain amount of writing a day, Guggenheim or not, and I can do it at Norfolk as well as elsewhere.

I've painted the negative side of the matter out of pure honesty; the positive side ought to be this, an improvement over our predecessors if only in that two are usually better than one.

I have studied the last paragraph of your letter a number of times and still cannot say that I understand it well. My first impression was that you were proposing a new design for the covers of my book, a nymph or goddess in gold. I see now that the whole thing is not only licentious, but a great blow to the Schwartz escutcheon. Seriously, however, you can invent all the sisters you want for me, but if this is a scheme to delude your aunt, I can tell you from sad experience that a deception like that never works: never; it begins after a while to require more lies than one is capable of spouting with any fluency; you may be making a lot of trouble for yourself and getting us kicked out by your aunt. But as I say, call her my sister, aunt, or niece, if you want; remember, that Francesca is a name with ominous associations: Could we not call her, rather, Vienna Schwartz? I have wanted to call a girl Vienna. As for incest, when you know me better you will know that no one loves me and I have to buy love, and I do not have enough money to pay for Vienna. I would relish more details in regard to your plans for Vienna; why don't you take her along with us to New Orleans; she can keep Gertrude company when I go out to buy love and you are engaged in scholarship.

> Eternally yours,
> DELMORE

P.S. The business of opening letters is not important if Patchen is not going to be in the office to open letters. But for the pure sake of keeping the record straight, it is a hundred-to-one that Eliot's letter was not opened by mistake, but deliberately. The evidence is the envelope itself; when you open a letter normally, you cut or tear it on top; this letter was not cut on top, but steamed open—the marks of the heat have crinkled the flap; and then resealed. Not that it matters, but you don't have to be so trusting; and when Patchen says he hates Eliot, it is pure defense-mechanism unless he is even dumber than it appears either likely or possible.

/ · /

stay here for years: Schwartz was exaggerating. The usual invitation to
Yaddo is for a matter of months, at most a season.

to call a girl Vienna: Schwartz also named a bar "The Vienna Woods."
See his short story, "Tales from the Vienna Woods: An Inside Story,"
Partisan Review, 20 (May 1953), 267–81.

57. TLS-1   Yaddo
                                                      Jan. 8, 1940

DEAR JAY,

    We came back yesterday. The trip cost $56.20. You
gave me $25. and $5. was left of the previous sum,
so that I am out $36.20, some of which I had to bor-
row. Will you send me a check as soon as possible
so that I can pay my debtor?

    The 18 copies of *A Season in Hell* which are due
me have not arrived. Please tell the outgoing admin-
istration at Norfolk to send them here or all my
friends and benefactors will be mortally offended
because they did not get the compliment of a copy.

    The Mizeners stayed at the best hotels and restau-
rants and we divided the costs of gas and garage with
them, which was small enough recompense for being
cramped in the back seat, half the time, amid hat
boxes. There was also the $5.50 which had to be
paid to send three suitcases by express.

    Can you manage to fix it so that we can move to
Cambridge and start work even before the 1st of
February? I want to get settled in order to be able to
do some sustained work for a change.

    You will have to give up the idea of calling any-
one my sister. A simple matter of honor is involved,
not to speak of all the explanations I would have to
make to my family. Your family ought to be able to

reconcile themselves to your having a mistress who is not my sister. Or you might tell them that you are an unpierced virgin.

Let me hear from you very soon about the above burning questions.

Yours,
DELMORE

/ · /

The Mizeners: Rosemary and Arthur Mizener, who accompanied the Schwartzes back north after the New Orleans stay. Mizener (1907–1988) was Professor of English at Cornell. He was later to write *The Far Side of Paradise* (1951), the pioneer biography of F. Scott Fitzgerald.

58. TLS-1   Yaddo
                                                   Jan. 17, 1940

DEAR JAY:

We want the job and, as you know, we need it badly. I will spare your delicate sensibilities a picture of this our exile at Yaddo; the main thing is this business of living at the edge of being penniless all the time; *it interferes with the functioning of the creative artist.* Something has always turned up but one of these days something may not turn up and we'll be eating peanut butter sandwiches all day.

Your fear that I will get another job and go away is groundless; where are these jobs that I am going to get, where are they hiding? If by some chance I should get something which paid a young fortune, I promise you this and may the Lord God strike me down if we do not keep to it: *Gertrude will stay at the office for one full year more,* while I go wherever this fantasy of a job is located. That is a promise. We can

bear the separation for a time much more than we
can bear our present economic status. Moreover, you
don't know yet what a gem of efficiency Gertrude
can be; with a few Harvard boys at her beck and call,
she will amaze you.

The possibility of a Guggenheim does not alter
the problem. It lasts one year, and then we are right
back where we started, worry day and night. With
the job, I can be independent about any teaching job
I might get, quitting it if I find it thwarts the operations of my deathless mind.

Random House has called me and the LSU Press
also renewed their offer of last year. I am your serf,
I need hardly say, but I wonder whether you know
how much money in advances I have turned down
in the last two years? I wish I had Random House's
letter to send you right now, but I sent it to my
mother, to show her that I was not the complete
failure she insists on calling me because I don't make
five thousand dollars a year.

What about my MLA paper? Ransom seems to be
willing to print it even though you do also. All the
addresses of MLA members are in one of their publications which can be secured gratis at any library.

Yours,
DELMORE

/ · /

my MLA paper: "The Isolation of Modern Poetry" was published by
John Crowe Ransom in Kenyon Review, III (Spring 1941), 209–20.
Ransom (1888–1974) published his influential The New Criticism with
ND in 1941.

59. ALS-1   Monday

2 / 5 / 40

DEAR JAY:

We just took a fine apartment with one big room for the office. Our rent is $50, so the office will cost $15. The address is 41 Bowdoin St. And we'll be moving in tomorrow. Bring up everything as soon as you can and the wheels of industry will start turning as soon as you come.

The rooms are unfurnished, so you will need a couple of chairs and a table.

DELMORE

/ · /

41 Bowdoin St.: In Cambridge, Mass.

60. TLS-1   Sunday

2 / 11 / 1940

[No salutation]

I did not send Eliot a copy. Tell the business manager that a revised edition is being prepared. I gave you back all the copies I had not already given away. The corrections can't be made overnight. Copies have arrived from the bindery. If you have any extra furniture, you might have it sent here, since the ND room is stark and bare. If you want to use it for sleeping quarters when in Cambridge, bring a bed. It is expensive to rent furniture here, as we have been finding out painfully.

D

/ · /

a revised edition: Reviews of Schwartz's Rimbaud translation were coming in, and most were highly negative. Schwartz was preparing a revised
edition with the aid of William Barrett.

61. TLS-2   Sunday

DEAR JAY:

We've just come back from NY, toting my books
here (for the first time I realize that they are by now
part of my body), and here we stay until asked to
go, so that you can shoot the proofs to me whenever
you like and I'll get them right back to you.

The advertisement is very handsome and I certainly would like to have folders; they could be thrust
into my next book, the way some magazines enclose
a card for subscription.

While in NY, Philip Rahv asked me whether or
not you could be persuaded to let him write an
introduction to Kafka's *America.* I also discussed
Hivnor with him, since I've been trying to get *PR*
to print a part of his book. Macdonald wants to,
Dupee and Rahv are severely opposed. My own
feeling is probably like yours, I don't like that tendency in writing too much, but Hivnor is able to do
something with that style which is sometimes
remarkable. He came here to see me the week before
last and it turns out that what he wants is a guarantee
that his book will be published so that he can finish
it with some assurance. I think that he is bound to
produce something very much worth printing,
especially by one with your purposes, but I think it
would be a mistake to guarantee him anything for
the time being, except publication in your anthology. This book might turn out to be completely

immature—there is no sign so far of any real unity—
and there is all that tendency to being precious and
literary in the worst sense: It is one more step at times
to James Branch Cabell, and he seems wholly
unmoved when he is told that names like Juniper,
Nedina, and the like are the farthest from what they
ought to be, to use a surface example.

On the other hand, with proper handling, Hivnor
ought to produce a five-star final either in his first or
second attempt, so I think you ought to print him
extensively in your anthology and give every assurance, if you can, of the possibility of printing the
book when finished if it suits you then, or if not, his
second one: Practice makes perfect, and Hivnor needs
much practice, but is otherwise the real McCoy, and
if you think so too, you can help him a good deal by
telling him you do.

I'm delighted that you like the war manifesto. I
think Dwight collaborated with someone else on it.
That son of a bitch Roosevelt, if he gets the Embargo
Act repealed, will have us all in the trenches by
Spring, that is, just in time for the next Democratic
Convention to re-nominate him. As my grand-
mother would say, let him drop dead.

Have I ever pointed out to you the remarkable
passage in my story (written in 1935) and on page
18: "Again and again, the photographer comes out
from his hiding place with new directions," O my
prophetic soul, "The photographer only scurries
about apologetically, issuing new directions." Was
that you, Charley?

Well, all right then,
DELMORE

/ · /

the proofs: Of the revised edition of the Rimbaud translation. The first edition had sold out by March.

Kafka's America: The title of the novel, published in 1927 and translated into English in 1938, is usually spelled *Amerika*. It was published by New Directions in 1940.

F. W. Dupee: His *Henry James* appeared in The American Men of Letters Series.

James Branch Cabell: (1879–1958), American novelist whose works were highly individual.

the war manifesto: Probably a piece written by Macdonald when he broke with *Partisan Review* on the war issue.

in my story: "In Dreams Begin Responsibilities."

on p. 18: Of the first edition of Schwartz's first book.

62. TLS-2

41 Bowdoin St.
Cambridge, Mass.
April 2, 1940

DEAR JAY:

. . . I've been reading the new cantos with the greatest pleasure. The man may be the biggest jackass in the world and working hard at getting even bigger, but he has the best ear for versification since Milton, and maybe the best ear that anyone ever had who used the English language. Poets will be learning their metres from Pound for the next two hundred years, and it ought to be no small change to you that you are printing him. Your concern about attacks on the Jews can be dismissed. Outside of the first page, in which he quotes a passsage from Franklin, which is, I am told, a fabricated remark which Franklin never made, there is nothing at all about us poor bastards.

I'll get to work on the revised translation as soon

as your corrections arrive; you don't have to tell me
to work hard at it, I know perfectly well what I owe
you and myself in the matter. There is a review in
the new *Kenyon Review* which is the worst yet; not
that I don't deserve it.

I've not yet heard from the Guggenheim people
about holding down a part-time job for the latter six
months of my fellowship, and I'm beginning to get
scared. I really have to hold the Harvard job (which
would only be two hours a week, that is, one section) so that I won't be out in the cold the year after
next. The Guggenheim people gave me $1800 but
$500 of that would have to go immediately to pay-
ing debts which would make it impossible to save
anything.

In any case, I intend to take my stand in Cambridge, though maybe I'll leave Gertrude here one
month and go to Mexico for that time in order to
get rid of my staleness. Gertrude says she wants the
job, no matter what, if her work satisfies you sufficiently. She wants to be independent, and to have a
place in life, a function. Of course, if you want to
give someone else the job after September, when our
lease is concluded, that is your business. It is no longer
a case of need on our part, not financial need, anyway; though actually *psychological* need, on Gertrude's part. Well you let us know your feelings in
the matter: It is just barely possible that I won't get
both Guggenheim and Harvard jobs, but only one
or the other. I don't want to hog everything, but
I've had nothing for years and I don't want that time
to return.

Have you any suggestions about Mexico; I mean,
people worth seeing and talking to there? Probably
I won't go, but it is pleasant to consider the idea.
Vice, idleness, and procrastination are not, how-

ever, the perils of my immortal soul; though I suffer
from worse ones.

DELMORE

P.S.: Shall I send you my Pound (Farrar & Rinehart)
volumes, so that you can see for yourself?

I'll send you my revised Rimbaud sections for you
to check as I go. I intend to do nothing else until that
is done.

How about my offering, in the revised Rimbaud,
to give any owner of the 1st a copy of the revision if
he sends me the first one? This would show shame
and penitence, and though it would cost me money
(I assume you would sell me copies of the 2nd edition at the 50% author's discount), it would be worth
it.

/ · /

the new cantos: Pound's *Cantos LII–LXXI,* just published by Faber &
Faber.

Milton: John Milton (1606–1674), English poet.

a passage from Franklin: In *Canto LII,* Pound writes,

> Remarked Ben: better keep out the jews
> or yr / grand children will curse you . . .

the new Kenyon Review: Justin O'Brien, in his review of the Rimbaud,
called it "something like a sacrilege."

63. TLS-3

c / o Henry Carlisle
2511 Broadway
San Francisco
[N.D.]

DEAR DELMORE:

Do you think there is any book of Va. Woolf that we ought to try to wrangle into the NC? I'm not sure it could be done, but might try.

I am charmed with this little piece of Brecht that your enlightened student has translated. I take it one shd interpret it that the revolution will do things differently? If you like, you might have Albert approach him about it for *ND 41*. I think it would make an interesting contrast with *Mother Courage*. I think he should fix the line, "that the quick return home demanded." That's not clear. Otherwise it seems a nice translation.

Tell Albert to pubfile the youth. And I hope you have been religious in passing on to your unequaled spouse at all times names of suitable persons, by they freshmen, professors, or large broads, that you meet on your nights off. I believe that the broadest possible view should be taken of everything. I have lately found great spiritual solace in a young person of Greek origin whose life work it is to dive into a tank of water from a high ladder. This shows that absolutely everything is relative and, as you so often point out, full of choice and decision.

What Ransom says is true, but I hope you will not let these lonely old men turn your head. They, in their way, want love. Just as you want love. But you must get it in the grave. An artist's life is a sad one, says Mr. Herbert Read. That is sure true. Yes sir. I commit you to melancholy. . . .

. . . I will read the Gide book with all my soul, IN

SPITE OF David Diamond. My mind has not been fresh and strong for many years, in fact, not since the day when, at age 4, the ponycart ran over my toe. Nevertheless, I will TRY.

As to the Brecht novel in NC. That will depend on the cost. I'm not really sold on it altogether. It bogs down awfully in the middle. Hays says it is taken from the opera, and the opera is much better. Maybe we should look at that. Will you? Please reply.

Yes, I will also give my whole soul to Nabokov. *Onegin?* I could never stand all that stuff. Like *Werther*. Ugh.

Yes I will write stern god-prompted words to Hivnor. Henry Miller is here in town. I have not seen him yet. He goes around to the bookstores and asks if they know what a great writer he is. Ben Abramson is bringing out his new book, *The World of Sex*. Avukah.

Yes, you are right. Do not become a professional teacher. That would be a waste.

Pacoima is way out beyond Burbank. But it's on my way North. I will stop by for a moment if the hour is propitious.

Kerner I will write to again. He is like Horace. He wants to put it in the trunk for eight years.

I disagree about *Miss Lonelyhearts*. I don't think it is quite that good. However, if the plates would fit our size I would be willing to try it.

Life is ever curious. I was walking on the beach. Who do I meet, in a beautiful white bathing suit with her sumptuous golden hair trembling in the wind? The most beautiful of the Sun Valley mistresses. Ah shame, she has sold her lovely body and godgiven soul to a very rich young Parisian embusqué refugee who winters at Sun Valley. His home was on the Avenue de la Grande Armée. Her father is a Mormon farmer, a settler in the Snake River Valley. These

mixtures of culture are very beautiful. He gives her
a penny for her piggybank whenever she teaches him
a new English word. She disdains the French tongue,
the language of Proust and Ronsard and Madame
Grandeçon of the Place Pigale. Tomorrow they are
setting out for Acapulco in his elegant Cord. My
heart quivers. As you said that morning in the station square of New Haven, "Ah, Love, ah Love . . ."

J

/ · /

Va. Woolf: Virginia Woolf (1882–1941), experimental British novelist
and essayist.

NC: New Classic Series—inexpensive reprints of important modern
literary texts.

have Albert approach him: Albert Erskine had moved from Baton Rouge
to Cambridge to become managing editor of the ND office when it
appeared JL would be drafted.

contrast with Mother Courage: Only H. R. Hays's translation of the Brecht
play appeared in the issue.

lonely old men: John Crowe Ransom was fifty-two at the time!

the Gide book: Lafcadio's Adventures by André Gide (1869–1951).

David Diamond: (b. 1915), American composer.

the Brecht novel: Der Dreigroschenroman (1934) by Bertolt Brecht (1898–
1956), novel with songs translated by Desmond Vesey and Christopher Isherwood as *A Penny for the Poor* (1937), retitled *The Three Penny
Novel* (1956).

Onegin: A. S. Pushkin's verse novel, *Eugene Onegin.*

Werther: The Sorrows of Young Werther, Goethe's epistolary novel.

Ben Abramson: A fabled bookseller in Chicago. His shop was a meeting
place for writers.

Kerner: David Kerner, whom Schwartz described in one letter as "the
Joyce of Philadelphia," was in several early ND annuals.

Miss Lonelyhearts: Novel by the American writer Nathanael West (1903–
1940), parts of which appeared in *Contact* (1932), which West edited
with William Carlos Williams. The novel was published in 1933.

Cord: A sporty car produced in the late 1930s.

64. TLS-1   Memorial Day

DEAR JAY:

  To the Lighthouse is, I think, Virginia Woolf's best novel. *The Waves* has much good writing, too. I should think that you would be able to get either of these, if you wanted them.

  What do you think of a dialogue or exchange of *billets doux* between Levin and myself on the subject of the return from Naturalism? Nabokov and De Rougemont might do well, but nothing of theirs that I have seen suggests the literary theorist: I mean, the theorist of literary method. They're both theoretical enough in other ways. . . .

  I heard of some new authors in Chicago and took the liberty of suggesting they send mss. to ND. One of them, without hearing of Kafka, has written, I am told, a long story about a man who suddenly finds out that he has turned colored. . . .

  . . . I look forward to your comments on Gide. Brecht's opera is in verse and would be, I think, hard to translate at all well. As it is, I am told that much is lost in *A Penny for the Poor* because of the translation. The dog in the manger in me hears with a certain zest of all mistakes in translation. I was told that the King James Version of the Bible has thousands of errors.

  No tears come to my eyes when I hear of the setbacks of your libido. I read of it with great interest, as I would read of Asia.

  I heard the other day that Wallace Stevens had offered a new manuscript to Knopf's. This is your chance, if you want it. You might offer him many things Knopf never has given him and have in return not only the best poet in America, but one whose books will be asked for until the year 2000. Did you

ever inquire about *The Sacred Wood,* which was published by Knopf in 1920? What prestige for ND: Stevens and Eliot. . . .

I hoped to be finished with my poem by now and
have a genuine vacation for the first time in many
years. But it is clear now that I will have to work all
through the summer. As Yeats says,

> The intellect of man is forced to choose
> Perfection of the life, or of the work—

DELMORE

/ · /

Levin: Harry Levin (b. 1912), author of ten books and the first Irving
Babbitt Professor of Comparative Literature at Harvard. His ground-
breaking *James Joyce: A Critical Introduction* was published by ND in
1941 and revised in 1960.

Nabokov: Vladimir Nabokov (1899–1977), Russian-American novelist.
ND published his *The Real Life of Sebastian Knight* in 1941.

De Rougemont: Denis de Rougemont (1906–1985), Swiss writer and
critic, author of *Love in the Western World.*

new manuscript to Knopf's: Parts of a World (1942).

The Sacred Wood: Subtitled "Essays on Poetry & Criticism," this volume of Eliot's was first published by Methuen in November 1920, and
was reprinted by them eight times before going into other editions.

"The intellect of man . . .": Schwartz quotes the first two lines of Yeats's
"The Choice."

65. TLS-1   [N.D.]

DELMORE:

Will you look over these Marguerite Youngs and
grade them lightly in pencil in your indelible fashion???

I think of them for *ND 41* if you approve of them,
a group of perhaps ten pages.

She has had a book so cannot *FYAP,* and she's too obscure for *Mopo.* From now on no more obscureys in *Mopo.* Will kill it.

Yes, I will write to Clark Mills. I met this McGahey girl. She writes pretty stuff. Belongs to a little group who meet in a basement corner Page & O'Farrell Streets and pore over each other's mss. under the guidance of a sort of Sunday School seer named Lawrence Hart. They have a whole school of ideas and their own cult terminology, a separate term for about everything you can do with language in a poem. You otta see. Lot of bunk, I think, but their air of mystic holiness is wonderful. They all call each other "Mr." and "Miss" and sit up very straight and don't cross their legs and don't drop ashes on the floor. Oh boy. But the McGahey girl writes pretty stuff. She is the one that Stevens thinks well of. I'll be sending you a batch of her stuff probably to pass on.

I have been giving Albert hell recently because he won't condescend to answer the questions in my letters. I think we had better pass him on into a nice English instructorship at Haverford College. With his personality he can be Head of the Department at 48 and President at 56. However, this is all confidential. Strickly, Candidly, Problematically.

J

/ · /

FYAP: Office code for *Five Young American Poets,* the anthology which ND published in 1940.

Mopo: Poet of the Month series of poetry booklets, issued monthly by ND in uniform format.

Marguerite Young: American novelist who has managed to keep her birthdate out of reference books. Author of *Miss MacIntosh, My Darling* (1965). Schwartz took eight of her poems for *ND 41.*

Clark Mills: Appeared in *Five Young American Poets 1941.*

this McGahey girl: Jeanne McGahey (b. 1906), who also was published in *Five Young American Poets 1941.* Her *Homecoming with Reflections: Collected Poems* appeared in 1989.

Lawrence Hart: Source and mentor of the so-called Activist movement. He and McGahey were married in 1944.

66. TLS-2

San Francisco
Monday

DEAR DELMORE:

Your other letter didn't say anything about wiring. You imagine. I wrote at once.

Have you actually read Taupin's piece on Pound, or do you just say that from general principles?

I want very much to read the Gide book. You have only to have Albert put it in one of his express packages and I will devour it.

Think I will ask Harry if he wants to do the return to the myth article. I adore his style.

Rexroth's poetry may be mediocre but as a person he is delicious. Haven't been so diverted by anyone in years. He gives off.

You're right Albert is serious but so SLOW. As far as I can gather he is not getting ahead with things at all, rather falling behind, which is ridiculous when there are no new books except Ransom, no advertising, no selling, practically nothing for him to do. He has not undertaken any of the new promotions that I wanted done, has done nothing to bring in any new business, etc. etc. Just no zip to him. Too Southern. If I get drafted I will keep him on. Otherwise I will try somebody else. I mean to keep right on looking till I find one that runs like clockwork and at high speed. Such people do exist. I have seen them in other businesses. I will find one or bust.

As to the tone of my catalogue copy, how many times must I tell you the audience is dumb and must be talked down to? The highbrows who read the *PR* will buy the books from the author's names and from reviews. We must try to catch the fringe and you have got to talk their language. You really ought sometime to go out on the road and find out what the USA is like and just how lowbrow 98% of bookreaders are. This dry Ransomey stuff—tho it may be the truth—will not appeal to them. You have got to give them the old George Macy. That man has made a fortune with his bilge. The *mopo* prospectus is a parody of his style. It should work. Nobody in my family ever heard of Donne till we published him. Isn't that neglect? And of course it's a problem play, the problem is what to call the child, it has them all guessing.

You know really sometime for your education you should make a little tour of the back country and see what America really is. New York and Cambridge are not America. You just don't know till you see for yourself.

Re: Albert as litterateur. That's just what I don't need, as long as I have you to tell me what's what. What we need is a business man, with a real nose for promotion and sales pressure. The hell with literature in that job.

Send me that Maisel letter about de Rougement. I don't want to offend Gregory, but am inclined to agree with you that de Rougement would be better on Kafka than he would.

J

/ · /

Taupin's piece on Pound: René Taupin, French literary critic.
Harry: Harry Levin.

Rexroth's poetry: Kenneth Rexroth (1905–1982), American poet and critic, much published by ND.

George Macy: Publisher of The Limited Editions Club.

it's a problem play: Schwartz's *Shenandoah*.

Maisel: Edward M. Maisel, translator of Denis de Rougemont.

Gregory: Horace Gregory.

67. TLS-1   Tuesday, June 3

DEAR JAY:

In answer to your query, about my long poem, which I have almost decided to name *Genesis,* I must keep striving until September. I want to be sure that it is as good as I can make it, not be haunted with remorse at what I might have done and did not. Nothing is more ridiculous than an ambitious *fiasco.* Not only that, my impression endures, mistaken though it may turn out, that it might be popular as well as good. Though the popularity would depend on an accident, let us not forget how many good things are the result of accidents.

Received the other day your packet of manuscripts, plus the handsome copy of *Girl Beautiful.* Of the latter, I would like to say that I welcome and enjoy all discarded pornography, especially yours, but it only brings me more strongly than ever a sense of the gulf between warm-and-moist hand-feeling of actuality and the pale representation, which, as Plato says, is but a copy of a copy, while the real thing is in that Aeolian harp, the nervous system. Not only that, I want by explicit statement to make it clear that I am not deceived: I know very well that what you send to your friends *you have first procured for yourself—*

I have done no more than glanced at the Jeanne

McGahey and the Marguerite Young manuscripts; as an initial report, of the former especially, I think that you might be rushing her by putting her in *FYAP*. Though gifted, she seems to be one of those many—by whom you have more than once been deceived—who get a false poetic aura by the process of using words in disconnection from a definite meaning: The movement and choice of words is dictated by an effort to achieve a feeling of profundity which is not backed up by any genuine meaning. There is a false mysticism of precious syntax and unusual or unusually used words. This is not always true of la McGahey; in about ten poems she keeps clearly in mind a definite subject-matter which her words explore. But she ought to be urged to practice this all the time.

There has been a veritable flood of mss. lately and I have found more than one of exceptional promise; particularly one by a fellow who rejoices in the well-omened name of Georg Mann. I will mark them with comments and send them on to you soon. I also went through Goodman's novel before it went out to you; do you want me to report on that? I have also just read F. O. Matthiessen's new book, and he strikes me as a candidate for a book on Melville, who ought to be done in any case. I also saw the letters to be filed in which, despite my pleas, you make a special point of telling some people that I have been reading mss. for you, also a letter of mine in which I comment on Albert. I forgive you, but wish you would try more often to bear in mind my position, in condemning mss; and also how Albert might regard my discussion of him. Thus this message, too, ought to be committed to the flames.

Seriously,
DELMORE

P.S. Just by the by, just what was the point of telling Dwight Macdonald that I devour all the mss; is that some frustrated resentment at work? Where else would such a reader of mss. be found—let alone for ten dollars a month?

P.P.S.: More translated Brecht is coming in the next express.

/ · /

my long poem: Schwartz was to work on *Genesis* for twelve years.

Girl Beautiful: A cheesecake magazine.

Georg Mann: Georg Karl Frederick Mann (b. 1913), published in *ND* 6, 7, and 17.

Goodman's novel: Paul Goodman (1911–1972), New York poet, fiction writer, fabulist, and playwright. The work was presumably a section of his four-part novel, *The Empire City.*

Matthiessen's new book: American Renaissance (1941).

Melville: Herman Melville (1819–1891), American novelist and poet. A selection of his poems, edited by F. O. Matthiessen, was published in the Poets of the Year series by ND in 1944.

68. TLS-2

Tuesday

DEAR JAY:

I've decided it would be best to publish a volume of criticism this fall or winter. You can announce it in this way:

THE ISOLATION OF MODERN POETRY AND OTHER PROBLEMS IN LITERARY CRITICISM
(Critical essays on Ernest Hemingway, John Dos Passos, Ezra Pound, W. B. Yeats, W. H. Auden, T. S. Eliot, Wallace Stevens, Allen Tate, and Thomas Hardy)

("In making this collection of essays, reviews, and lectures written for *The Southern Review, Partisan*

Review, Poetry: A Magazine of Verse, The Modern Language Association, *The Nation,* and *The New Republic,* Mr. Schwartz has done a most unusual and illuminating thing: He has written a long introduction in which he describes the way in which the general nature of literary criticism presented itself to him on each occasion and with each new subject. And he has written a *retroduction* for each essay, in which he attempts to criticize his own specific act of criticism in the given case. The result is a book in which the nature of poetry and literary criticism in our time is defined freshly and concretely. Added to this, there is the intrinsic interest in the subjects of the essays, some of the best and most significant modern authors. Mr. Schwartz's gifts as a critic are implicit in the fact that most of these essays were written for the most distinguished literary reviews in America.")

This is by way of giving you something to work on for the catalogue; I'll try again and try to be less pompous and clumsy.

You can announce the poem simply as: A long narrative poem; I've not yet decided between two titles.

Seeing as how Blackmur is getting $400 and Ransom $250, I ought to get at least what Ransom gets, since I am ⅝ as good as Blackmur and better than Ransom. As a matter of fact, I think the advance will almost certainly come back to you. Blackmur says that Florence Codman sold 700 copies of *The Double Agent* and has just given him $300 for his second collection. I don't want to seem greedy or ungrateful to you for other favors. But the book is worth that advance, the laborer is worthy of his hire, this is my chance to get out of debt, and I ought to get the same pay as the rest. Under socialism, social credit, or in the next life, I will work for nothing, but meanwhile, capitalism seems to be here to stay.

Didn't you like M. Liben's stories? I thought both of them were very good, especially the Kafka-esque one. Have you read Blackmur's novel yet? It sticks in my mind with a great deal of vividness.

Yours,
DELMORE

/ · /

the poem: Genesis.

Florence Codman: Publisher of Arrow Editions.

Blackmur's novel: King Pandar, R. P. Blackmur's unpublished novel.

M. Liben: Meyer Liben, who published stories in *ND* 5, 6, 7, 8, and 12.

69. TCS-1 [N.D.]

DEAR DELMORE:

Trust your Bennington appearance was a blazing success. Sorry I couldn't get up for it, but too much going on here. . . . Josephine Miles had just sent in a batch of about fifty poems for one of the Mopo series. These ought to be cut down to 27. Would you like to look them over and do the weeding? I suppose I could do it, but would prefer your judgment, if you would be amused to. . . . Just had a jubilant letter from Ezra, re: Kunk's declaration on gold. Ez says Europe will soon be running on HIS economics. . . . If Gertrude has gone, would you send down a few of the pale blue invoice forms—about fifty. We haven't a one here and need them to get out the orders with. . . . I may go over to see Katherine Anne someday this week. She has some kind of a journal she wrote in Europe which might not be bad. Thanks for the blurbs. Will comment on these later. Haven't studied them yet. Will be useful.

JAY

/ · /

Josephine Miles: (1911–1985), American poet published by ND on several occasions. She was a professor of English at Berkeley.

Kunk's declaration on gold: Typographical error for "Kung's"; Kung is the Chinese name for Confucius.

to see Katherine Anne: Porter was a resident at Yaddo at this time.

70. TLS-1   Sept. 22, 1940

DEAR JAY:

I'd like you to postpone the publication of my book of criticism until May (which is the date for which you've already scheduled one book, the *Faust*).

The following reasons make me want more time. Working on the title essay has kept me from my poem for the last few weeks. I must get enough of it into presentable form by the 1st of January to get a renewal of my Guggenheim fellowship, and with my schoolwork, this is almost impossible unless I concentrate on the poem. From $900 to $1800 hang in the balance, for the Guggenheim committee will have to be shown something three-quarters finished before they give me a six-months' or year's addition.

Besides this, external financial reason, I'm anxious to give as much thought as I can to the central problems of the book and to go on revising the different chapters just as the revisions occur to me, not under pressure of a deadline. I can hardly afford to appear

at anything but my best, such as it is, after my inglorious translation.

I realize that this delay might make trouble for
you and for the salesmen (though I suppose the sales
of this book won't be a great matter in any case).
But you remember that you gave me a similar
extension of time on my first book and the four
months' additional work made the book much better. I doubt that anyone has ever injured his book by
doing more work on it and delaying its publication.
Many books of criticism, by the way, have appeared
in the middle of spring; Wilson's last book, one of
Eliot's, and Winters' *P&D,* and I suppose it's just
possible that that may be the best time, for in the
winter the spotlight is on the novels.

Hivnor came to see me yesterday and I tried to
explain my critical feelings about his book, but
without much success; I don't know whether this
was because I was not expressing myself well or what,
but no progress was made. I've looked some more
at the version of *Faust,* and I think you'd better get
an expert to pronounce judgment; my own impression is that the German text is necessary to make it
worth publishing.

Yours,
DELMORE

/ · /

the Faust: A new English translation by Carlyle F. MacIntyre and JL,
illustrated by Rockwell Kent. Bilingual, published in 1941 at $3.50.
(100 copies signed by Kent sold for $7.50.)

the title essay: "The Imitation of Life," never published.

my inglorious translation: Schwartz's Rimbaud.

Wilson's last book: The Triple Thinkers (1938) by Edmund Wilson (1895–
1972).

Winters' P&D: Yvor Winters's *Primitivism and Decadence* (1937).

71. TLS-1   Tuesday

DEAR JAY:

Struck to the quick, I can only say let us reduce
the rent from $16 to $10, beginning with October.
All right? Hate to seem consumed with avarice, and
so let me explain that my net income barring G's
earnings is $1600, minus $432 which I owe Harvard.
Next year it will be even less unless my Guggenheim is renewed. Not that this is a subject of intense
interest to you, but I want to be sure you have a
noble image of me.

If I were you, I would think four times before
sticking my neck out too far on Hivnor's book; as a
whole, it reminds me of the state of Gertrude's office
before her reformation; plenty of brilliant sentences,
but as old Gertrude Stein remarked, "Remarks are
not literature."

                                Yours,
                                THE BOWDOIN BARD

/ · /

Gertrude Stein: (1874–1946), American writer, often termed Cubist.

72. ALS-1   Friday

DEAR JAY:

I'll do Berryman's piece for him *unsigned,* but don't
tell him that; I suspect the whole show is staged just
to get something which will distinguish him from
the other boys. He'll be here in two weeks and then
I think I can drag the thing out of him in a kind of

interview sort of way and write out two or three pages after that. . . .

The Rimbaud is finished but needs checking. What I want to do is get Berryman, Barrett, and whomever we can drag in and read the whole thing through one night, someone watching the French, etc. What about waiting until the 1st of Oct. so I can do that?

In fact, what about not rushing me on anything? I enjoy doing all these things, but the rush is shortening my life and you're always in a rush. At present, I have to do the following: Write a piece on Trotsky for *P.R.*, a piece on Fergusson's show, two articles for the *S.R.*, a review for the *Kenyon Review*, work on my 40-page introduction, write a piece on Stevens for the *Advocate*, and also do my daily minimum on that immortal poem which will surely start a new school of writing if I ever get it done. All I ask is not to be rushed.

Your description of Berryman in bed was wonderful.

The Pound thing is almost done. By the way, I took it for granted that it was going to be unsigned, though I may use it in my book.

D

/ · /

show is staged: JL had visited John Berryman in Princeton and found him in bed, pretending to be dying. The performance was so convincing, JL sent for a doctor.

Berryman's piece: Berryman's poems in *Five Young American Poets 1940* were to be accompanied by a personal introduction. According to one of his biographers, "He felt disabled from writing an introduction; diffident and lacking conviction, he could not speak about his own beliefs and practices in poetry. He eventually drafted at least seven prefaces, and sent the last to Laughlin late in August"—John Haffenden, *The Life of John Berryman* (1982), pp. 127–28. Laughlin disliked the effort.

Eventually Berryman produced "A Note on Poetry," which was a paraphrase of his own poem, "On a London Train."

a piece on Trotsky: Unpublished.

a piece on Fergusson's show: The Sophocles *Electra.*

two articles for the S.R.: "Poetry and Belief in Thomas Hardy," *Southern Review,* VI, 1 (1940), 64–77; and "The Poetry of Allen Tate," *Southern Review,* V, 3 (1940), 419–38.

a review for the Kenyon Review: "Neither Historian Nor Critic," *Kenyon Review,* III (Winter 1941), 119–23, a review of Van Wyck Brooks's *New England: Indian Summer.*

my 40-page introduction: A shorter version appeared in *Kenyon Review,* III (Spring 1941), 209–20.

a piece on Stevens: This was never published.

that immortal poem: Genesis.

The Pound thing: Both Schwartz and JL had written critical notes to be used as a promotional pamphlet for Laughlin's edition of Pound's *Cantos LII–LXXI.* Schwartz's piece was signed "S.D." and JL's was signed "H.H."

in my book: The Imitation of Life.

73. TLS-1   Wednesday

DEAR JAY:

Ship me a check for $300 as an advance. You agreed to this a few weeks ago, and in any case, an advance is calculated on previous sales, by all publishers. Let us forego further discussion, for I am entitled to that much money.

As for your advice against it on the grounds that I will spend it, this is correct: What do you think I want the money for except to spend it? Please send it soon, because I need it.

The contract figures are impossible in several ways. For one thing, royalties go up to 1000 copies, not 2500. The business about splitting royalties from an English edition, which seems rather academic at the moment, and anthology fees, makes urgent the following question: Do we have a contract or not? Every time it suits your convenience you change the terms of the contract. Furthermore, I do not understand your attitude: Are we friends or business acquaintances? If the latter, then let us get out the old contract, have it properly certified, and fulfill all its terms, on both sides.

If we are friends, which is what I hope is the case, then you ought to stop breaking verbal promises of one kind or another when the mood takes you. For example I was to receive all anthology rights, not split them. The sum of money does not matter, it is a question of your attitude. If I am a friend of yours, I assume that you will not count copies sold in accordance with how much royalties you feel like paying.

Your escape from the war does not seem to have improved your character or disposition.

Reports on *Genesis, Book One* continue to be extremely favorable; I will send you some soon.

If you had read my letter with care, you would have found that I have no objection to your thwarting my enemies or getting friendly reviews; I was merely objecting to your quick follow-through. I have worked out a plan of campaign which should be very helpful and which will keep both of us from seeming like disingenuous scoundrels.

Don't say anything about the possibility of a new magazine being postponed indefinitely until the book is out. What is the very latest deadline for the *ND* essay?

Your devoted friend,
DELMORE

/ · /

as an advance: Against future publication of *Genesis.*

escape from the war: JL's draft board classified him as 4–F. He did perform some war work training paratroopers to ski in Utah.

Reports on Genesis: According to Atlas, Schwartz reported that "Berryman had said it was brilliant, that Matthiessen was preparing to lecture on it, and that Van Doren, Blackmur, Conrad Aiken and James Agee had praised it" (p. 215). Agee (1909–1955), the American novelist, film critic, poet, and journalist, was a friend of Schwartz's.

74. TLS-1   Nov. 1, 1940

DEAR DELMORE:

[. . . .] How essential to your economy and happiness is Gertrude's job? As you know, if you really need it, you can have it, but, if you don't need it, it would be most practical for Albert to locate in New York, close to the printers and the nerve-centers of the book business. I think too that he would like to have a trained book-keeper and stenographer.

On the other hand, I consider you, Delmore, quite apart from personal considerations, our most valuable asset, and I would not do anything to alienate your affections from the establishment which I expect you one day to glorify and enrich. So I leave the decision up to you. Take your time and think it over . . .

I imagine I'll be coming up Wednesday or Thursday.

JAY

75. TLS-1   Monday

DEAR JAY:

By this time you must have received translation and introduction. No sooner had I sent them to you than two things began to occur. 1) I began as usual to make revisions, and 2), your postcard came.

Please give the introduction to the printer last. I will send you the final version within the next two weeks: Judging by last year, it will take that long to get the rest of the book printed anyhow. Secondly, do not use pp. 251, 252, 253 of the Mercure de France edition of the French text. This is a deliberate falsification of the text by the editor for the sake of proving Rimbaud was a good, simple Catholic instead of the particularly modern one that he was, and has been attacked as such by many French critics, including Catholics. If you have Daniel-Rops' *Rimbaud,* you can find one attack on p. 23. What the editor did was to add one of the *Illuminations* to the head of *A Season in Hell,* just like that; his earlier editions of Rimbaud have those pages as a separate prose poem among the *Illuminations* and the edition which Rimbaud gave to and took from the printer is the one I have translated. Let me know how you feel about the translation.

I saw Morrison today and so far as I can make out, I was no great success. A job for this year is improbable and although there seems, from what he says, to be a fairly good chance for next year, I have no idea of how I am going to get along until then. He said that you had sent him a copy of my book, but nothing about the book. Was that after or before I told you about the prospect of a job? Thanks for doing so, although, considering what his poetry is probably like, it may have done nothing but harm.

I have five different items being published in England and America during the fall, and the whole thing will net me about $225—I'll be rich in no time.

As ever,
DELMORE

/ · /

translation and introduction: Schwartz's Rimbaud.
Daniel-Rops' Rimbaud: Published in 1926.
a copy of my book: In Dreams Begin Responsibilities.

76. TLS-2

Laguna Beach
May 9, 1941

MELANCHOLY, FATE-DESTINED BARD:

Your reprisals rec'd and duly digested. Very well. Jack Donne is the bedside companion of every high school girl in Wichita. O my Amerika. Have it your way. You can lead the hub of the universe to water but you can't make it forget the *Maine*. Or something like that.

I enclose check for $30 down on *Shenandoah* and ten months' stud fees. I dare say *S* will earn more than that. Has Albert fixed you up with a satisfactory contract on that? I trust so.

What do you think of my plan for a great contest for the soldiers and sailors and an anthology of their resulting writings? What I am looking for is good documentary stuff recording the minutiae of this grisly farce. We'll doubtless have to conceal our intentions to get the cooperation of the powers, but we could simply toss out the roseychrome junk and use the straight stuff. What do you think of this idea?

I am also thinking of rushing Wordsworth into the *mopo*. England's hour, or something like that. Such a good chance for easy publicity. I am also terrified at the number of toughies I have gotten into the first year. They'll strangle it. Thank God yours makes ready sense. Wheels and Miles are real tough ones. You're right. She writes notes for poems. That's just what I was trying to tell her. Much of her ambiguity is in the remove of her titles. She never labels with a title. It is always a figure abstracted from the subject and hard for the reader to catch. I'm going to try to persuade her to supply little geographical notes in the margin like glosses. Ok?

I am in the middle of the Brecht book and just love it. Quel hexprit. If it's all so good we'll surely have to do it. Don't you think?

I agree with you that Williams' *GAN* shd be in the NC [New Classics] at some time but I don't think right away because it wd look funny to have 2 Wms before we had much of anything else. I save that for about 1943.

What are your plans in life? I hope you will keep me posted. I ask because if my draft board confirms the 4-F I will suggest to Albert in a nice way that he go on to greater things. That will mean that we will want to move the office back with you when his lease is up. That will mean that you will want to move into a somewhat larger place. No? This is all based on your staying at Cambridge and your wanting the job for Gertrude to continue. I am glad for her to have it as long as you want her to have it and will keep the office in Cambridge for her benefit. Should she want to give it up, I think I would move it back to Norfolk. Why don't you take a house or half a house? Something on the order of the Hortons'. I will help you with the rent as before, only more so if we need two rooms instead of one. When is your lease up? I have not said anything to Albert except that I am having Emily S. come on the job in June and for him to fill her full of wisdom as I want him to go on the road. When I hear finally from the army I will put it to him. Of course he can stay on until he finds a better place. I am not really angry with him and don't want to make trouble for him. I just don't feel that he is doing enough for the money he is getting. I will only have to pay Emily about half as much and I think she will do about 25% more per hour, because she works quicker. I will return from the land of the buffalo and put my shoulder to the wheel. I think Stewart will be a good salesman. We will keep Carmack out here and Jervis in the South. I will make a few trips here and there and try to locate somebody to cover middle western libraries. You can continue to set the high literary tone. Don't say anything to Albert as yet, but just keep me posted of your reactions and plans. Also, what about G's going to nightschool and learning short-hand and touch typing? I feel this would be good for her just on general principles. What do you think?

I await the Gide with interest. I take it you approve of the Flaubert *3 contes* if I can pry that loose from Knopf?

Oh, this Rilke situation re *mopo*. I went into it pretty thoroughly with MacIntyre, who wants to get his oar in, and I don't much want him. But he does know the stuff backward and forwards. It seems the only chunk of stuff left that has not been translated is the *Marienleben* and the *Stundenbuch*. The *Marienleben* is all juicy religious stuff. The *Stundenbuch* is the book of hours of a Russian monk and pretty dewey. What do you think we had better do? Will you discuss the *Stundenbuch* with Phil and see what he says? Or have a look at it yourself. It would be good in the sense it is simple and pretty and will counterbalance people like Wheels and Miles. Shed the light of your etc. upon this knot.

I imagine Prof. Burnham takes a simplified view. I doubt if you can so easily reduce it to a pattern. I also wonder what are his views on money? You would never guess from Cowley, C being age 6 in such matters. As far as I am concerned, the guys who run a country are still the guys who control the flow of credit. Interesting, however.

We'll wait on the Taupin. I think I have the book at Norfolk.

That bird Allen was working on a book on the little mags. At Purdue. He had done a lot of research. It wasn't bad. I will try to stir him up.

I too am melancholy. It is a strange and perplexing life. The consolations appear to be few.

UNCLE REMUS

/ · /

my plan for . . . an anthology: Never published.

rushing Wordsworth into the mopo: Never published.

Wheels: Nickname for John Brooks Wheelwright, whose *Selected Poems* chosen by R. P. Blackmur was published in the Poets of the Year series in 1941.

Miles: ND published Josephine Miles's second book, *Poems on Several Occasions,* in 1941.

Williams' GAN: William Carlos Williams's *Great American Novel,* reissued by ND in 1956.

Emily S.: Emily Sweetser.

Stewart: George W. Stewart, sales manager for ND. JL rented space in his office on 44th Street in Manhattan when he moved the office from Cambridge.

Carmack: Jesse Carmack, book salesman who sold on commission.

Jervis: Ed Jervis, also a bookstore traveler.

Flaubert 3 contes: Flaubert's *Three Tales,* translated by Arthur Mac-Dowell, with an introduction by Harry Levin, published as No. 7 of the New Classics Series in 1944.

Rilke situation: ND brought out Rilke's *Book of Hours,* translated by Babette Deutsch, in 1941.

MacIntyre: C. F. MacIntyre, translator.

Phil: Philip Horton.

Burnham: Philip Burnham.

Cowley: Malcolm Cowley (1898–1989). ND published his poems, *The Dry Season,* in 1945. As critic, poet, editor, teacher, and literary historian, he helped shape twentieth-century American literature.

Taupin: René Taupin, French critic.

That bird Allen: Unidentified.

Uncle Remus: Pound's nickname for Eliot was "Old Possum," and Eliot called Pound "Brer Rabbit." Laughlin here enters the pantheon.

77. TLS-2   [N.D.]

DELMORE:

*please give me a report on the relation of *Sacred Wood* to that volume of *Selected Essays* that Harcourt brought out. If the bulk of *Sacred Wood* is still in print, is there much point in doing it again?

*please write me who publishes Virginia Woolf. Harcourt? I mean *Lighthouse* and *Waves.* What of Virginia Woolf is in the Mod. Libr? Just *Mrs. Dalloway?*

*I have asked Berryman to be a Poet of the Month in 1942. Do you approve? As he is doubtless too weak to lift a pencil to paper, I hope you will follow this up and let me know what he thinks.

*do you think we ought to ask Jarrell for 1942 too? is that ms. of his still there? If so you better send it on in an exp. pack for me to look at.

*I don't mean to make a policy of looking after our FYAPs forever, but I do think those 2 are fairly good and worth keeping on with.

*Rexroth says Jarrell is a barbarian.

*what happened to Tate that he soured so on his protégés in *PR?* Is that just that he is angry with me, or is he angry with all his past life? I don't care, really, but I think it's hard on those kids who had reason to believe that he was back of them.

*what do you think of the poetry of H. R. Hays? he has entered some in the *FYAP* scramble. Want to see it?

*do you think Marguerite Young suitable for *ND 41?*

J

/ · /

Mod. Libr.: The Modern Library, inexpensive Random House editions.

Selected Essays: Selected Essays of T. S. Eliot (1932; reissued 1935).

too weak to lift a pencil: Ironic reference to Berryman's feigned illness. See notes to Letter 72.

Jarrell: Randall Jarrell (1914–1955), American poet, critic, novelist.

H. R. Hays: Translator of Spanish American poetry.

---

78. TLS-1   June 8, 1941

DEAR JAY:

Quick as a flash, with the speed of Apollo, Thrower of Arts when Zeus commanded, I hasten to answer your queries.

The Sacred Wood has five essays not included in *Selected Essays,* also very interesting preface to 2nd edition. Has interest as a classic document and would, I think, be bought much.

Harcourt published all of V. Woolf, only *Mrs. Dalloway* is in Mod. Libr.

Best poems of Berryman and Jarrell are all in *FYAP 1940*. Berryman is ten times better than Jarrell, who just echoes Auden three years back. Jarrell mss. goes out to you, we do not see Berryman ever since Baby Buckman went berserk and threw him out for fainting before I was able to say "James Laughlin." By next year B. should have more good poems, maybe, but Jarrell bores me stiff and seems nothing but a wise guy. Many much better poets deserve *POM*.

Tate is angry with you, with me, and with Life because he has not been able to write a poem for six years. He is a despicable son-of-bitch for kicking boys who adore him that way because he knows they will continue to adore him.

I like what I have seen of the poems of H. R. Hays. I like a few poems by Marguerite Young, but not very many.

I will be delighted to write an introduction to that so great work of Gide's, though many others would write one well. There is no sequel. You may have thought so because there were two titles used at different times.

The Golffing outline strikes me half and half. He concentrates on technique, while the fact is that the Symbolists were what they were because they hated bourgeois life (so became Bohemians), and sought in poetry the satisfactions no longer available in religion or the community. Golffing seems to have no idea that poetry springs from the life that is lived by the poet in relation to his community and the great beliefs of the whole culture. He echoes the stale false commonplace that poetry was trying to become music in the S's and makes what I regard as being other errors in detail. He derives too much from Winters in a mechanical way. On the other hand, close attention to a technical evolution is of course valuable, his translations seem fairly good, and would increase the value of the book, and there is probably no one else who is prepared right now to write a book on this so important subject.

Hivnor arrives Friday night and we are going to have a long conference on his book, in which Hivnor will agree with everything I say, and then go away and do nothing. My idea was for him to span temporal developments with long chapter heads describing events: In this way, the plot would not seem to be jumping about like a grasshopper.

You might tell Rexroth, since you have already told him too much, that he was better off when he wrote the most obscure poems ever written. Since he has become clear, even barbarians can see what commonplace thoughts were concealed in his obscurity.

When *Main Currents of American Culture* (in the 20th Jahrhunderts) is written, and the chapter called "Orson Welles, James Laughlin, and others born between 1910–20" appears . . . I will continue with the prophetic utterance in my next—

Seriously, Consummately, Candidly,
DELMORE

/ · /

Jarrell mss.: DS uses the plural form, mss., when he means ms.

Baby Buckman: Gertrude Buckman.

POM: Poet of the Month.

two titles: Les Caves du Vatican (1914) was translated as *The Vatican Swindle* (1925).

The Golffing outline: Proposal for a book by Francis Golffing, a disciple of Yvor Winters, to be called *The French Symbolist Poets.*

in the S's: In the Symbolists.

the most obscure poems: Schwartz refers to early poems which Rexroth called his "Cubist period." See "Phronesis" and "Easy Lessons in Geography" from his *Collected Shorter Poems* (New York: New Directions, 1967).

79. TL-1   Monday, June 16, 1941

DEAR JAY:

As I said before, I think my old play revised would look well in *ND 41*. It is rather long, remember, and is not likely to get shorter in revision, so keep room, not like last year.

Emily arrived today, looking as if she had managed to lose her virginity since last seen: Less nervous tension, and as lively and likeable as ever.

Hivnor was here Friday, Saturday, and Sunday on his way to Yaddo. On arrival, as on all his previous visits, he expressed great tiredness and asked to be allowed to sleep for several hours, which he did. He is a pure romantic and regards all his fautes as decrees of eternity, karma, and nemesis, that is, never to be changed forever. Seems to have used the last few months writing a long play which sounds like *Bulldog Drummond*. But he promises to be pure work for the next six weeks until his novel is finished. . . .

I hear that Knopf will not let the Gide book go. What a son of a bitch: It is out-of-print and he probably will never do anything with it.

I am glad to hear you took on Golffing, although I doubt that he will transcend the technical. But it should be a valuable book anyway. If you see him again, ask him how come he thinks Laforgue is a better technician than Corbière? It is an original opinion to say the least. Also that Laforgue must have read a great many more German metaphysicians, besides Schopenhauer (the one he notes), after he finished reading to the German Empress; and also that it might be worth saying something about Laforgue's prose, *Six Moral Tales*.

I will soon send back the Modern Library list; it

has a number of items which will add infinite prestige to ND.

I compared the 2nd ed. of *The Sacred Wood* with what is in *Selected Essays* and was just about to write you that, on latest thought, it was not worth doing. Are you going to do a Pound *Collected Essays*? With a grand preface by someone like Marianne Moore (I bet she would be glad to write one)?

Blackmur was here last week and he said Stevens told him he made $60,000 a year and always took a whole floor at the Waldorf: Will I ever receive that salary even if *Genesis* is a masterpiece? No, I will not.

See in the newspaper's objective mind how F.D.R. had had diarrhea and sore throat for the last few weeks, well-known signs according to St. Freud of a man afraid of a choice he is about to make. He will burn in hell for this War: I have the page reference in Dante.

Did you see the prospectus for *The Viking Book of Living Verse: From Beowulf to Schwartz*?

Trash is trash,

P.S. If you want to read a really good book, read *Darkness at Noon* by Arthur Koestler, Macmillan.

/ · /

old play revised: *Paris and Helen,* which appeared in *ND 41.*

Bulldog Drummond: British inspector in Paramount films of the 1930s and a popular WOR radio series in the 1940s, revived in 1953.

Laforgue: Jules Laforgue (1860–1887), French Symbolist poet who influenced Eliot. ND published his *Moral Tales,* translated by William Jay Smith, in 1985.

Corbière: Tristan Corbière (1845–1875), another French Symbolist poet.

Schopenhauer: Arthur Schopenhauer (1788–1860), German philosopher.

Marianne Moore: Moore (1887–1972) did not write such a preface. (She did, however, praise Pound's music and defended his obscurity in her review of *A Draft of XXX Cantos,* which appeared earlier in *Poetry,* XXXIX [October 1931], 37–56.) ND published *The Literary Essays of Ezra Pound* with an introduction by T. S. Eliot in 1954.

Blackmur: Blackmur was a high priest of the New Criticism.

$60,000 a year: Stevens did not make this from his poetry; he was an insurance company executive.

Arthur Koestler: (1905–1983), British novelist, journalist, and critic-philosopher.

80. ALS-1 Friday

DEAR JAY:

1) Mudge is an intelligent poet but boring, like Empson. No ear. He'd do, but I think Prince would be better. Or Durrell's poems, since he's bound to go far as a novelist.

2) Bertolt Brecht is *wunderbar.* I tried four or five times to get you to read his novel last winter, but you were too busy with your four or five lives. He's a good poet, good novelist, and good dramatist. Like Silone but better. Like Jonathan Swift, like *Gulliver's Travels,* really wonderful. Shall I get it from the Widener for you?

Letter to me from Hivnor, asking for your address, and saying he plans to finish book on 31st of March (date of the beginning of Easter vacation), and needs money like breath. I wrote him, quoting myself:

> How many lives the Pleasure-Principle
> Rules like a sick King,
> Rules like a Leader . . .

Letter to me from Fergusson, certifying *Shen.,* but suggesting an important change. This summer he's going to put on one play of mine—has not decided which one.

Letter to me from D. Macdonald, wants to print abridged version of *Shen.* I take it you have no objections to my getting the extra $75 and audience? The pamphlet version will have things in it not in *P.R.* preface and Fergusson's suggested expansion. This may or may not mean 1-month delay on pamphlet.

Have founded a new school of writing, the peripatetic-dart-throwing school. I write, then walk, then throw darts, to free the caged sedentary animal. Next month I may go further *and write standing up*!

DELMORE

/ · /

Mudge: Evelyn Leigh Mudge (1879–1962), English poet.

Empson: William Empson (1906–1984), British poet and critic. ND published his *Seven Types of Ambiguity* in 1949 and *Some Versions of Pastoral* in 1974.

Prince: F. T. Prince (b. 1912). *Poems* published by ND in 1941.

Durrell's poems: Lawrence Durrell (1912–1990), British novelist and poet.

Silone: Ignazio Silone (b. 1900), Italian novelist and journalist whose real name was Secundo Tranquilli.

Jonathan Swift: (1667–1745), British novelist and satirist.

Bertolt Brecht . . . his novel: Brecht (1898–1956), German playwright and poet. The novel here is *Der Dreigroschenroman* (1934).

Shen.: Shenandoah, the verse play.

D. Macdonald: Dwight Macdonald was acting on behalf of *Partisan Review.*

standing up: Probable allusion to publicized writing habits of Thomas Wolfe and Ernest Hemingway.

81. TLS-1   Alta, Utah
                                               [N.D.]

DEAR DELMORE:

Your salty communications much enjoyed. Tell
Gertrude to send along her pay sheet for the last
month and I will remit. I enclose yr February ck. I
would rather that parts of *Shenandoah* did not appear
in the *PR* because I would like it to be a virgin first.
So that you don't lose money, I wd. be glad to fix
yr. advance on this at $100. Will that be all right? I
don't think we have a contract for *Shen.* Ask Albert
to draw one up—he has the sample forms there—
and send it to me to sign. I will forward the ck. at
once. While the pamphlet will hardly earn that much,
I feel that the dough will be well spent in advertising
the series. I haven't received the ms. yet. Imagine it
is at Sun Valley, where I will soon go.

Yes, you certainly handled Untermeyer well.
That's fine, I think I deserve some credit, tho. After
all I kept eating away at his underpinnings, a slow
but constant termite.

I agree with you about Schubert and Shapiro for
FYAP. The others, I dunno. Think it wd be good
to get Goodman in there too. Need a woman also.
Stevens writes well of McGahey in Cal. Will look
her up. Young is out, as she had a book with Macmillan. Think I'll let Warren cool a while. Austin,
that is. I think he is losing his mind. He is in love
with a priest in a monkastery and they write each
other back and forth witty sacrilegious letters, which
he reads aloud to E. Sweetser so she will bully him,
which gratifies him. Oh this life. He became ill at
my lecture and had to leave. But the others swallowed it down.

The Laughlin elegies are around the office somewhere, I think. Ask yr wife, chief of filing dept. Ok let's make it Prince for the English poet. I'll have Albert write him. Yes do send me anything you have of or on Brecht. Send to Sun Valley. H. R. Hays is also sending me translations of his plays or something. Sounds good.

I won't give Hivnor any more money unless he has really done some work on the ms. I wrote him to send it out to me. His mother wrote to me, a sad little note. I don't think they will let him starve. I've asked him if he wants me to try to get him in at Iowa City this spring. Might be done, perhaps. But I think what he needs is to go back to Akron and sweat and bleed, just like Churchill. He don't coddle good, that egg.

My muse is roaring along at a great rate in the best *Collier's* and *Liberty* vein. You will not speak to me, I have no doubt, when you see it. Better so. Nobody will confuse me with Parker Tyler.

Twelve feet of snow here. I have a pocket edition of Jane Austen and read it going up in the chair lift. This amazes the inhabitants and keeps them in their places. Well, continue to breed immortal lines.

J

/ · /

Untermeyer: Louis Untermeyer (1885–1977), American poet and anthologist, known for his collections of American and British poetry which are widely used in schools.

Austin Warren: (1897–1986), American poet and critic.

Schubert: David Schubert (1913–1946), American poet, published in ND's *Five Young American Poets 1941.*

Shapiro: Karl Jay Shapiro (b. 1913), American poet and critic, also published in *Five American Poets 1941.*

Goodman: Paul Goodman was also included in *Five Young American Poets 1941.*

Iowa City: The Iowa Writers' Workshop, founded by Paul Engle.

Collier's and Liberty: Popular middle-brow magazines of the day.
Parker Tyler: (1907–1974), American author, poet, and film critic.
Jane Austen: (1775–1817), English novelist known for her satirical por-
traits of the gentry.

82. TLS-2   Thursday

DEAR JAY:

Your pleasure in my *jeu d'esprit* (jew d'esprit)
pleases me very much. I intend to take both of your
suggestions: "Foreskin" is more exact than "penis,"
and the crotch line was pure decoration.

After much thought, I've decided to withdraw the
play from *PR*. I wish you would hereafter let me
know how long in advance you want me to keep my
efforts from periodical publication. In this case, it
makes no difference to me, obviously, whether I get
$100 from you or $25 from you and $75 from Mac-
donald. (Actually I would have gotten more, because
they pay verse one dollar a page more, but I won't
haggle.) *And I would have enjoyed the additional audience.* However, such is my love for you and my
Rimbaud guilt and my debtedness for G's job that,
in this showy way, I will make the sacrifice. We must
all make sacrifices, said Roosevelt the other night.

As you may have heard by now, I won another
Guggenheim, this time for six months and nine
hundred dollars. My monstrous face was in the papers
and I have just finished giving a *Transcript* reporter—
who insisted on calling you Henry Laughlin—an
interview, advertising The Poets of the Year in particular. The important thing about this news is that
my long poem has passed its first test with flying
colors. I don't know who the boobs were who read

it, but should judge that their mentalities resemble those of The Book of the Month Club. They had a hundred pages to read, which was fair enough for a trial.

Castellon and David Diamond also scored, and while I am speaking of others, Philip Rahv married Nathalie Swan and went off to live in Chicago with her, which implies parental anger.

Tired of regarding maneuvers passively, I invited Theodore Spencer and Albert to dinner last week. This puzzled him, but the old boy came right back by giving Albert an album of Shubert's C major *Quintet*. At dinner he became intoxicated and said many things which I am just barely well-bred enough never to repeat, but will say that the English Department seems like a snake-pit to me now. I have never seen so many friends hate each other with such intensity.

I agree that putting Goodman in *FYAP* next year would be a good way of getting him to the kind of readers who would take to his writing. But I hope you know that he is not really a poet at all; some of the virtues of his prose get into his poems once in a while, but he has no metrical sense, no feeling for versification's methods, and tends to get coy and childish. For example, that Trotsky poem is full of figures like the one calling Trotsky "our hero" and "the chief of excitement." One would think that the Russian Revolution was a kind of amusement park. This deliberate infantilism mars his prose, too, but not as much. There is room for a fourth poet even with Goodman; I wish you would at least ask Clark Mills to let you see what he has. Blackmur thinks he's very good.

I hear you landed in Class-1, and though unasked to express my attitude, I hope you have no qualms about doing everything you can to stay out. I do not think God cares very much for either party in this war.

Berryman took the Brecht book from the library and refuses to give it up, on the grounds that he is smarter than you. When he gets through with it, I will send it to you. If I ever say anything in favor of that incredible fool again, I wish you would throw something at me. There's an article on Brecht in the current *P.R.*, not very good but gives an idea. Can you read German well enough to read one of his plays which are full of slang?

I think it would be a very good idea to publish that old play, revised, in *ND 1941*. I wish you would also consider seriously re-publishing my essay, "The Isolation of Modern Poetry," there too; it is in the current issue of *The Kenyon Review* but it is a theoretical statement of the reason for modern poetry (and for New Directions), and also a preview of my book of criticism; it is quite short, would not take much room. What do you say?

Packard just called about the Victrola record business. When you read my long poem, you may be able to see why I refuse to be joined even in an album with the Whiz Bang exhibitionist and the girl whose poems are like a bathrobe. I want to be alone.

What did you tell Hivnor about the future? Getting his mother to write you does not sound like cricket to me. But then again, who is playing cricket?

Elinor came one day to say you were getting married to a Grecian princess.

I enclose a letter which was written for popular consumption, because I think it is about time to begin to lay bare some aspects of my irrefragible ineluctable immortal work.

Yours as always,
DELMORE

P.S. What about the book, *Aurelia,* Clara Cohen has? You might add that to the check for *Shenandoah,* and write her that you are willing to take it out in trade. P.P.S. I note your loud silence on promoting me to associate editor and my feelings are hurt; you'll be sorry, you'll be sorry.

/ · /

Transcript: Boston Evening Transcript.

Henry Laughlin: JL's cousin, president of Houghton Mifflin, the Boston publishers.

Castellon: Federico Castellon, artist who did drawings for the ND edition of *Shenandoah*.

Theodore Spencer: ND published his poems, *The Paradox in the Circle,* in 1941 in the Poets of the Year series.

that Trotsky poem: "The Death of Leon Trotsky, 1940," by Paul Goodman.

Clark Mills: (b. 1913), Poet who did the English version of *Fata Morgana* for *ND 41*.

class 1: Draft Board classification; JL was actually classed 4-F.

old play: Paris and Helen.

"The Isolation of Modern Poetry": The essay was reprinted in *ND 41,* pp. 687–98.

Packard: Frederick Clifton Packard, Professor of Declamation at Harvard, who launched the Harvard Vocarium, a series of recordings of poets reading their work.

Elinor: Elinor Blanchard, a Radcliffe student with whom JL kept company. She was the niece of Cleanth Brooks.

Clara Cohen: French translator who worked as an editorial assistant on the Surrealist anthology in *ND 40*. She translated Gérard de Nerval's novel, *Aurélia,* which was not published by New Directions.

83. TLS-1   San Francisco
                                              Wednesday

DEAR DELMORE:

Since you think so much of it, I see no objection to your running the play in the magazine, though it

detracts from the excitement of the pamphlet. However, perhaps you can write a special introduction
for the pamphlet, explaining how the stage is just
wonderful and Emmy Sweetser is just wonderful and
Francis Fergusson is the most wonderful of all. Consult with Albert on length, etc. And you might also
get Albert to draw up this luminous contract that
you speak of, which I will file away with my shares
of the Pittsburgh Mercantile Company and other
illegal enterprises that make one rich. Oh yes, please
also tell whoever publishes it to give us a free page
advt. for the *mopos,* as my cut for letting them have
it. Make that a condition and don't let them take it
out of your check. In fact, I wd. make them bid
against each other for this literary jewel. Like a
tobacco auction.

Hivnor writes that you impressed at your NY
reading but that you read "as if contemptuous of life."
That sounds very nice. Kindling love with proud
disdain. H. says nothing of having done any work
on the novel. What a man.

Hays seems to think we can have the Brecht stuff.
That's to the good.

I really think Rexroth is one of the most superior
humans alive. He reminds me extensively of Wheelwright—a Wheelwright without the psychic kinks.
R. seems to enjoy life. A vast store of anecdotes
delivered in an intermountain drawl. We spent Easter
rock climbing down in the mountains and you have
no idea how near you were to coming into your small
fortune. We did a small, very vertical chimney and
on the way down my extremities became completely dissociated from the petrine substance. Fortunately the sovietic bard was belaying me with his
rope from above and by intellectual ruggedness
maintained me in the air, for all the world as Virgil,
to whom my poetry has so often been compared,

would say, like the wily spider dangling from his self-begotten silky cord, until I retrenched myself in the rock. R. is doing some translations of Martial that are very good. Will do for a *mopo*, I think.

Etc.

J

/ · /

the play: Paris and Helen.

the pamphlet: Shenandoah, which ND also was publishing in 1941.

the Brecht stuff: Hays's translations of *Mother Courage,* which appeared in *ND 41,* and *The Death of Lucullus,* which was the March number of the Poets of the Year series in 1942.

Wheelwright: John Brooks Wheelwright.

small fortune: JL had made Schwartz beneficiary of his life insurance.

Virgil: Publius Vergilius Maro (70–19 B.C.), greatest poet of ancient Rome.

Martial: Marcus Valerius Martialis (fl. first century A.D.), Latin writer of witty and ribald epigrams.

84. ALS-2   July 1st, 1941

DEAR JAY:

The Modern Library list goes back to you today, marked up. I doubt that you can get the best books on it.

Delay and silence caused by my masterpiece. Either it is a masterpiece or I am demented, perhaps both. But my fingers may be finished before the book is, from excess typing which is why this is not typed.

I think you are making a mistake by not printing Pound's *Collected Essays* as soon as possible. Might be a gold mine, like Eliot's *Selected Essays,* and is full of great essays which made the Age.

For *FYAP,* I would suggest Snider and Karl Shapiro, both are much better than McGahey or Goodman, who is not a poet at all but a short story writer, as you can verify by consulting other authorities. What did you think of Snider? I liked the others a good deal, Mills, Schubert, Brinnin.

Delighted that you like G. Mann and that you are going to print Nabokov. I hope you know that you are doing it for love, he will not be much bought. Though he's just had a story in the *Atlantic Monthly* (circ. 110,000) which shd. help.

You can call Nabokov's book a profound comedy of identity, about those who are *lost* (expatriated) in the modern world—

Who is Harry Bull? . . .

This is not a fashionable neighborhood, but anyway there's a price-fix in Cambridge, all the landlords keep prices up and keep a housing shortage. However, we will manage: G. is looking about for quarters. Philip pays same as we do here.

You might try more discretion. Emily says you told Eudora Welty how you felt about Schubert who told K. A. Porter who led you to Schubert. Gratuitous unnecessary hell is raised.

Shenandoah in *Kenyon Review* is being hailed. What do you think of enclosed addition, which will make your version practically a new come-on? Let me know quickly if it goes to printer soon. Wouldn't it be best to publish it in September?—better month than August?

DELMORE

/ · /

best books on it: For JL's New Classics Series of reprints.
my masterpiece: Genesis.

Snider: Poems by Charles Snider were included in *ND* 6 and *ND* 13.

Mills: Clark Mills.

Schubert: David Schubert.

Brinnin: John Malcolm Brinnin (b. 1916), whose *The Lincoln Lyrics* was published in the 1942 Poets of the Year series.

Nabokov's book: The Real Life of Sebastian Knight, published by ND in 1941.

Harry Bull: Editor of *Town & Country,* for whom JL wrote articles on skiing.

Philip: Philip Horton.

Eudora Welty: (b. 1909), Mississippi novelist.

in Kenyon Review: The shorter version was published before the ND pamphlet (*KR*, III, Summer 1941), 271–92.

85. TLS-1
July 26

DEAR JAY:

The enclosed may be a bit laborious, but you can fix it. I would willingly without charge collaborate on future jacket prose. I thought the remarks about C. Mills' poems were very good criticism.

I suspect that the books outlined in Nabokov's novel—supposedly plots of Knight's books—are really stories or novels already written by Nabokov; it would be just like him, and if so, they are better than this book, at least in synopsis. Did you ever do anything about the Pasternak trans.?

The choice of expression in the enclosed illustrates the leit-motive of my academic career: Every expression is surrounded by alternative expressions, some of which may be better.

It occurs to me that if you like my *ND 41* play enough when you read it, perhaps it would be worth printing as a pamphlet like *Blood Wedding,* since the cost of composing it is already taken care of, and so forth—

Hivnor has passed his physical examination and says he thinks he will be inducted soon. Could not something be done, such as saying he needs to be deferred to finish his novel? The Army will annihilate that wandering boy, so full of unrest and opposed to discipline, and besides, it looks like once you're in, you stay in. You might be able to find out if you could help in Akron on your way back.

Harry was here the other night, not yet finished with JJ and so forth—

DELMORE

/ · /

The enclosed: Copy for the inside flap of *Shenandoah*.

Pasternak: Boris Leonidovich Pasternak (1880–1960), Russian poet and novelist. ND published his *Selected Writing,* by various translators, in 1949.

Knight's books: Written by Nabokov's fictional character, Sebastian Knight.

ND 41 play: Paris and Helen. Unlike Lorca's *Blood Wedding,* which appeared in the Neiman translation in *ND 39* and also was reprinted separately, Schwartz's play received no separate publication.

to finish his novel: The fact that Schwartz suggests the Selective Service System might give a man a deferment, during wartime, to finish a work of fiction is both charming and indicative of his lack of touch with reality.

Akron: In 1992 JL does not believe he ever was in Akron, Ohio.

JJ: Harry Levin's book on James Joyce, which was to be the first volume in JL's Makers of Modern Literature Series, critical Baedekers to the moderns, priced at just one dollar.

86. TLS-2   August 14, 1941

DEAR JAY:

Gertrude has changed her mind and I have gone ahead and taken the house on Immemorial Drive.

She has promised not to abandon me for at least a year; but if she does, I will of course bear whatever cost the upset occasions you. This arrangement will be less expensive to you, as you know, than if you had to help out my $884 from Harvard with advances.

The Prince poems are chosen. A sequence at the end had to be left out. It is fairly good, however, and I suggest that you use it in the poetry pages of *ND 41*. Also for *ND 41*, I think, is a wonderful poem of about ten pages by Dylan Thomas in the latest or a recent issue of *Horizon*.

What did you think of the Chicago boys? Have you written to Auden? Harry and I are evolving what is, I think, an interesting scheme.

Under different cover, Goodman's prose, all that he sent but the poems (save the mark!), go to you. I suggest that you make him write an entirely new foreword for *FYAP*. What he has written abounds in stupidity. Note the nonsense, which will cause ridicule among reviewers, about how he pronounces his verse, making one syllable two syllables, et al.; this is just an effort to deny the fact that he does not know how to wrench metres. His references to crime, hints at homosexuality, and other poses, plus his mention of unpublished works as examples, although everyone has not read them, are also likely to make unnecessary trouble. His pose as the great rebel is the most ridiculous thing of all; everything he does springs from an aesthete-homosexual point of view of his work which he has adopted only since being published by *Partisan Review*. Then there is the statement that all his characters are equally learned: Now what author in his right mind would think it a virtue that all his characters were equally learned? The poem on Trotsky ought to be omitted; Dwight said it had been universally damned. I will make my choice and send all to you.

I freely confess that the harshness of these remarks may be in part not as objective as possible, since Goodman's personal slanders of years' standing to our common friends in New York seem to continue with new and fresh invention. But if you don't trust me in this matter, I pray you, consult with a good poet somewhere on such a matter as how to pronounce "child" and "appears." Ask Y. Winters! Or Blackmur.

The enclosed clipping was found by my wandering girl who takes an intense interest in pictures of your friends.

Tiredness made me unable to respond properly during our Social Credit argument. I do not know if you care very much about the whole thing, but 1) the people will not have faith in invented money when it is clearly invention, nothing else; the notion of faith in this sense reminds one of Christian Science; 2) as for the rich patronizing art, you must know that you are phenomenal in this regard and that literature has been backed by the lower middle class for over a hundred years while the rich when aware of the arts at all, buy Old Masters and mausoleum-museums; 3) the acquisitive instinct is annihilated by capitalism after one generation; 4) do you think the rich young men of your class are not brutish oafs, by and large, who do nothing with their resources? 5) Are not all or most of the people whose work you respect tormented all life long by economic need in this economic system, while the idle oafs swoon in creature comforts? (I grant freely that they are victims, rather than agents and prime movers of their own decay: But that's just my great rhetorical point, that the rich as well as the poor are exploited and victimized by capitalism.)

I don't want to bore you through the mail but I

cannot bear not having the last word in an argument.

In New York, I encountered further examples of the fact that my work is going to have more and more popular appeal. On my return, I read some more of *Genesis,* and now fear that it is so good that no one will believe that I, mere I, am author, but rather a team of inspired poets.

I sent Beilenson the play, re-typed, and the essay. The essay will have an appendix, quite brief, very novel, in which is described various audiences' questions when I read the essay and how their questions prove the isolation of modern poetry. This is brand-new and justifies even more using the essay in *ND 41.* I am disheartened at my inability to inject the epigram about the human crotch anywhere in the play. I have removed the penis erect at your suggestion. I think the play is better (ie., more than just "entertainment") than you do, but perhaps I am wrong.

> Yours always,
> TELLMORE SHORTS

/ · /

changed her mind: According to Schwartz, Gertrude had threatened to leave him. But Atlas (p. 192) calls this "a sardonic intimation." As it happened, they moved to a new apartment on September 10, taking the ND office with them.

Immemorial Drive: The actual address was 908 Memorial Drive.

$884 from Harvard: Schwartz owed the university previous fees.

The Prince poems: Work by F. T. Prince, to be a part of "A Little Anthology of Contemporary Poet" in *ND 41.* Thomas (1914–1933) was the leading Welsh poet. These were not reprinted in *ND 41.*

our common friends: Schwartz portrays Goodman and his circle in the story "The World Is a Wedding" (1948).

Social Credit: The economic theories for credit reform propounded by the English engineer C. H. Douglas. His plan called for a national dividend and the just price mechanism for controlling inflation. Douglas's work may have influenced Ezra Pound's theories. At this time JL was a member of the Boston branch of the Social Credit Party.

Beilenson: Peter Beilenson, of the Walpole Printing Office in Mt. Vernon, N.Y., a fine designer and printer who produced many of the very beautiful early books for ND. He eventually became publisher of Peter Pauper Press.

the play: Paris and Helen.

an appendix, very brief: The essay did not have an appendix when it appeared in *ND 41.*

87. TLS-1   August 22, 1941

DEAR JAY:

I've read the Eustis story and think it excellent, except for the prelude, which, though well-written, is not sufficiently relevant to the whole, and could be left out. I take it that it is a fantasy—a little too dependent on Kafka but it does not matter—of how Fascism can take hold in America; an especially brilliant touch is that a Jewish girl is involved in bringing about the Fascist regime; Fascism with Democratic ties. I can't understand why you think the Fisher story trash. The *Criterion* volume is out at the moment. I will get it soon; I remember the Roughton story with pleasure; do you want Dorothy to type it out? If so, send a special order, since Albert resents every move I make as part of your denunciation of him. What a mess that is—

I can't send you my immortal work because the only carbon copy I have is of an unrevised version and I am not going to trust all that breathless matchless writing in the mails across the continent. Or if you want, I will send you a synopsis of the plot and suggestions for catalogue. One of the things achieved in it is a theology of modern life—the real deities of the present are shown in action, moving private lives; the result is that the story is told in what is, I think, an absolutely new way. Another note is that I am now, I think, the poet of the Atlantic; of the Atlantic migration, which made America. I have been carefully reading the whole, waiting for revulsion and disillusion to begin, but find, so far, that I was never so sure before.

For the catalogue blurbs, I insist that you use Aiken, Ransom, Stevens, Tate, Van Doren, MacNeice. Let's not argue about this, no matter how you feel about some of them; no one is likely to say anything better about me than they have—until *Genesis* appears. I hear that you have bought paper for it, but only for 418 pages; that's certainly not enough.

I will see to it that Harry comes through and will write to him from Cummington the opening letter. I go to Cummington Sunday for a week and will surely propagandize and take addresses as instructed. Blackmur said that there was an 18-year-old girl there who was very good at verses.

When are you coming back East? Read the giant work then, and see how with the right handling it will bring in kudos and O above all dollars!—When you read the Chicago boys, let me know what you think of them?

DELMORE

P.S. My address until the 1st of September will be: The Cummington School, Cummington, Mass.

/ · /

the Eustis story: "The Factory" by Helen Eustis, which appeared in *ND 41*. She was the wife of Alfred Young Fisher.

the Fisher story: Rejected story by Alfred Young Fisher.

the Roughton story: "The Sand Under the Door," by Roger Roughton, published in *ND 41.* The story was first published by T. S. Eliot in *The Criterion.* JL was unable to communicate with Roughton; there was a rumor he was killed fighting in the Spanish Civil War. JL felt that the remarkable story should be shared by American readers.

Dorothy: Employee in ND Cambridge office whose surname has been forgotten by JL.

a mess that is: Albert Erskine was leaving Cambridge for New York City. Eventually he became an editor at Random House.

418 pages: Genesis, Book One, had a total pagination of 208 pp.

Cummington School: Schwartz was invited to spend a week in residence at The Cummington School of the Arts, in Cummington, Mass.

88. TL-2   September 4, 1941

DEAR JAY:

I am engaged in trying to pack for moving, trying to finish my Yeats essay for a *S.R.* deadline, trying to fight off a cold, and trying hard. Hence it may be a week before you get the 300 words for the catalogue. Inspired words which will please both you and myself will only come from trying hard; at the moment, they seem like squaring the circle, but be at peace, before a week is over, I will send you what is my idea of what should be said.

My stay at Cummington was one of the great weeks of my life.I saw the new generation, recognized that I was no longer young, enjoyed the sight of young ladies paying $40 a week to be there and also waiting on tables, drying dishes, and making beds. As to this new generation, they appear to regard sex as a form of violent exercise a little less serious than tennis. The co-operative activity inspired me to the idea of a long story entitled "Grandeur and Misery of Socialism."

I met Fisher who struck me at once as the supreme apple-polisher of our time, better even than Arthur

Mizener. He forced a sixty-three page manuscript on me which I want you to return to him; it is a long essay on aesthetics too full of abstractions in the grand manner. One girl student there is so good that you must without question publish her; I will send you a group of her poems soon; they are probably better than Marguerite Young and Elizabeth Bishop put together, and would look well in *ND 41*.

I am delighted that you decided to help Hivnor. I note that it was useless for me to ask you, you had to hear from two soldiers who never had my education, not to speak of my prose style and social insights. I should say too that I, for my part, as a result of Hivnor's last message, refuse henceforth to have any truck with so great a crybaby. He would like a convocation of the League of Nations every time he suffers a hang nail.

Your so-called fatal longing for Jewish flesh interests me profoundly; when I have time I will copy out for you the very interesting words of Maimonides, the Aristotle and Aquinas of his people, on a similar phenomenon in the sexual taste of the Moors in the eleventh and twelfth centuries. Are you a Moor? Amid your climaxes I trust that you forget the presence of the daughters of Israel and remember that their forefathers were scholars, poets, and metaphysicians when yours were grubbing about fen peat or is it turf on the Scotch heaths or the Irish moors?

I have taken care of Golffing, Eustis, and Brinnin. Fisher is sending in the last two books, never published, of his long poem. They might be good. He wanted to know whether he could put you and me down as sponsors for his Guggenheim application. I told him I would be happy and thought you would be happy too.

Thanks for the first month's rent. I take it that this means that I am no longer to receive $10 a month for my advice, but since you fell into this out of kindness and since I am sure that it is only your feeling that my services as a reader are inestimable and can not be measured in dollars or cents, let us reduce this to the lordly sum of $1 every month just so that I will feel that I am not being too much of a sucker. One dollar every month as a symbol of my being a dollar-a-month man and I think it would be appropriate if I received it separately.

Harry has still not finished his Joyce book and God only knows when he will; plays with the child all day. Maybe you had better get Auden to write the first letter; faced with the prospect of being left out, Harry might make a move.

As to the line-up of the poets of the year, I am destroyed by my own vow to keep eternal silence on the subject of one of the world's most painful vulgar banal and incredible human beings; you can guess his name. However, I have made no vow on the subject of Charles Henri Ford and think you are misled by your . . . I started to write ruthlessness-with-weakening-at-the-end, but I do not see how you could make a greater mistake than in letting that . . . [words deleted] translate Baudelaire. He can't write English verse, he knows nothing of the spiritual conflicts behind Baudelaire's poetry, and probably takes him for a decayed surrealist . . . like himself. I bet Winters and Golffing would know someone who could do a really good translation of Baudelaire; Winters himself would be wonderful at it, since he suffers from the same malaise as Baudelaire.

You do not know what a gem this Dorothy is; asked as to her religious beliefs and whether she was an atheist, she replied, "No," she said, "I am an antagonist!" This is the best yet since David Diamond explained to me at Yaddo that I would love

Paris and not mind the rainy weather, because in Paris "it was a dry rain." When I explained that this was a contradiction, he said, "O Delmore, you're always so bookish!"

AN ANTAGONIST

/ · /

my Yeats essay: "An Unwritten Book," *Southern Review*, VII, 3 (1942), 471–91.

Fisher: Alfred Young Fisher was teaching at Smith College in Northampton.

one girl student: Jean Garrigue (1913–1972). ND did publish her in *Five Young American Poets,* Third Series (1944), and later brought out her book, *The Ego and the Centaur* (1947).

Maimonides: Rabbi Moses ben Maimon (1135–1204), Jewish philosopher who attempted to reconcile Rabbinic Judaism with Aristotelianism in Arabic form.

Aristotle: (384–322 B.C.), Greek philosopher.

Aquinas: St. Thomas Aquinas (ca. 1225–1274), Italian scholastic philosopher.

Charles Henri Ford: (b. 1913), American poet, brother of the actress Ruth Ford.

guess his name: Kenneth Patchen's *The Teeth of the Lion* was one of sixteen books from which the 1942 MOPO series was to be chosen.

89. TL-1   908 Memorial Drive
                                               Wednesday, Sept. 10

DEAR JAY:

I hope you use the enclosed, whatever its faults, just as it stands. If you do not, I want to see what you do to it before it goes to the printer; don't be high-handed about the whole thing, let collaboration, conciliation, consolation and consultation rule between us.

Gertrude and I moved on Saturday, the office

moved yesterday, and there certainly has not been so much disorder since the Jews left Egypt. You ought to get back to Cambridge as soon as you can.

I am told that *Shenandoah* has occasioned an article entitled "Schwartz the Dramatist," which will appear in *The New Republic* as soon as the pamphlet is published, which will probably never happen; why do these things happen always only to me?

I hear that Williams wants to go elsewhere and hope that you bend every effort to keep him, since he is a great author and you have only one other one.

I think that it would be a very good thing to announce, in one or two sentences, the publication of *The Imitation of Life,* for late spring or summer. It will be finished by then, and I want to publish another creative work next year, a work consisting of a story, a long poem, a group of lyrics, and a play in verse, all of them written but the lyrics. The long poem is "God in 1920," outlined, if you remember, in my Guggenheim project; it was supposed to be an interlude of sixty pages in *Genesis,* but I saw that one cannot have sixty-page interludes.

The enclosed check was wet by the water from a fallen glass full of flowers, presented me by a sleek sex-machine who lives next door and who will undoubtedly attract your "attention."

Yours sincerely,
*

/ · /

the enclosed: Document unidentified, perhaps reworked copy for the inside flap of *Shenandoah.*

Williams: William Carlos Williams.

only one other one: Schwartz most likely refers to himself, not Ezra Pound.

90. TLS-1 Sunday, Sept. 14, 1941

DEAR JAY:

In the process of moving, I mislaid or lost or did something I can't remember with the check for royalties: See enclosed statement and send me another one. I am appalled by the state of being which could permit me to mislay such an amount. In one of my economic status, it smacks of intellectual and moral chaos.

Furthermore, I must have my dollar a month, which you can add to the check for the rent if writing the check separately will tire you so much. It is a symbol and I am a symbolist, among other things. The schizophrenic separation of mind from self which I often celebrate in my immortal verse makes my mind say to you: Is it not unwise to refuse such minor demands, precious only to the soul of the poet?

Furthermore, our telephone bill has been $3.25 until now, every month. It will probably go over that and I want you to add the difference between $3.25 and whatever it is to Gertrude's check. E.S. will be using the phone a good deal for business purposes. If you cannot part with that sum, tell E.S. not to make the calls.

I would gladly compose the sestina you want except that it is as impossible as an immaculate conception; you have listed seven rhyme words.

I told Golffing his note would be improved by elaboration, but we would use it, in any case, if he did not want to elaborate it. I took several of Brinnin's poems, enough for a group, and gave the rest to Albert to send back. I made Eustis consent to leave out the unnecessary part of her story; sent it back yesterday, revised as suggested and it will go tomor-

row to Beilenson, who has received the corrected
proofs of my play and will soon get the corrected
proofs of my essay. I agree with you about Goodman's story and have given it to Albert to send back
with request for more mss., although they all look
alike to me. I took a few of Hays' poems and will
give the rest to Albert to send back. All this is done,
as you suggest, for love; love minus $1.00 per month.
On your way to the private parts of some poor
female, spend $1.00 a month less on flowers and
gems: This will make it come out even in the budget
and you will get just as wet.

This reminds me that I do not mind your vulgar
question as you call it about the girl poet, who is
really very good as you will soon see in *Poetry*. But
are you quite willing thus to betray to me by such
questions your own tastes and inclinations? Taste is
good.

To continue with my Cummington memoirs, as
you so well entitled them, I told the new generation
to write every day, imitate great authors, imitate style
and not subject-matter and thus arrive at a style new
because transformed by their own subject-matter, but
above all to eat well, since a poet needed a great deal
of energy . . . This last maxim pleased them so much
that I followed it with a suggestion that chastity was
good for the poet since coitus was such a drain on
the spirit as well as the body . . . This shocked them;
many felt then that they knew now why they had
written little since coming to Cummington, so to
speak.

Shenandoah still remains just a dream of Hornby's;
you might if you felt like drumming up business,
send Fadiman a note pointing out that he might be
specially interested in it for regional reasons; and
besides, is not his name Clifton?

Send me, not Albert, the catalogue page I sent you with comments; what makes you think I have any influence over Albert?

If you would but return my letters to me, I would abandon my unnatural reticence . . .

DELMORE

/ · /

E.S. will be using the phone: Emily Sweetser.

seven rhyme words: A sestina usually is unrhymed, using instead of rhymes the six end-words of the lines in the first stanza as end-words in the remaining stanzas, and doing so in a particular order.

Hays' poems: Six of H. R. Hays's poems were published in *ND 42*.

the girl poet: Jean Garrigue.

a dream of Hornby's: George Hornby, whose Domesday Press in Manhattan was printing the play for ND. At this time he was nearly two months late in delivering the printed book. It was part of the charm of ND's Poets of the Year series that each was printed by a different press.

his name Clifton?: Pun on place name of Clifton, New Jersey, and given name of Clifton Fadiman.

91. ALS-1   Thursday, Oct. 9, 1941

DEAR JAY,

I acceed to your imperative and have chosen the poems as best I can, which is not very good. I wanted not to be judge at all, because of my present state of "nervous depression," if that is what it is, in which I see all things as equally gray and boring. Don't blame me if you'll be dissatisfied with my uninspired choices.

The enclosed poems by one of the Cummington students seemed excellent to me weeks ago, and cer-

tainly ought to go into *ND 41*. If you don't want
them, you write to H. Duncan.

I hope to see you soon.

D

/ · /

one of the Cummington students: Probably Jean Garrigue.
H. Duncan: Harry Duncan, one of the partners of the Cummington
Press.

92. TLS-2   Friday, December 16, 1941

DEAR JAY:

I am sending you the first two hundred pages of
Genesis today in a copy which is a mixture of carbons, revisions, and older versions, but as close as I
could get to the final version without parting with
what I need here. These 200 pages are substantially
the basis on which I was given a Guggenheim
renewal.

I want you to publish it separately. It can be called
Genesis or *Genesis Part I* or *Made in America* or *Made
in New York* or *An Atlantic Boy* or *A New York Childhood.* Many other titles might be considered to take
care of the fact that it is just the first part—*The
Beginning,* or *Book One.*

This publication of the first two-fifths of the poem
seems by far the wisest policy to me for a number of
reasons, intrinsic and extrinsic. The intrinsic reasons
are bound up with the difficulty of getting a proper
conclusion right now. If I try to force one, I may
wake up in six months and be sorry. But these 200
pages I am certain of, I have tried them out on myself
in the worst despondency and lack of energy and I

am sure they mean what I want them to mean and what they ought to mean. And if they don't, there will still be time to make changes whenever the whole poem is published. Long poems have been published in parts from *The Divine Comedy* to *The Cantos,* and no comparison in quality is needed here: The form is the same, the long narrative poem can be published in its natural divisions. But more than that, it is too much of a risk right now, with everyone thinking of war, to print 500 pages and expect it to get attention between one crisis in the Far East and another in Iceland and a third in Libya and a fourth in Southern Russia.

The fact that the Philistines of the Guggenheim committee were pleased with this two-fifths should serve as a good external gauge. Some of the internal gauges worth mentioning are as follows: It may seem for a while that the alternation of Biblical prose and blank verse is too predictable, but it will, I think, be felt as an acceptable *formal* device, like the refrain in a ballad or like rhyme or like a tragic chorus. If the dead as a chorus seem bizarre, remember that Dante wrote the best poem ever written *by using the dead as voices*. If the fusion of narrative and commentary seems strange, remember that, as I intend to point out in a short preface, this story-succeeded-by-commentary is one of the profoundest most deeply-rooted and most accepted experiences in modern life: The newspaper story-editorial, the play-and-review-of-the-play, the travel film with voice as commentator and newsreel with commentator are all primordial examples of what is going to be an inevitable literary form (inevitable because the life we live forces it upon us). In any case, as I just said, the chorus is one of the best and most popular devices invented in any time. Louise Bogan made a fool of herself again by denying this in reviewing *Shenandoah* (she says that the poet always disappears from the scene when Dante walks half the way through Hell and Purgatory with a poet next to him and stops to discuss versification with other poets on the way).

If you don't want to get in back of this separate publication in the way that you would back up the whole poem, that suits me perfectly. I feel that this is more than good enough to make its way to the point where, when the reviews are in, you will feel no further need for caution about my staying powers as a poet. You can regard it as a trial balloon, which will cost you no more than the new Miller book.

The Christmas vacation comes in two weeks and by the end of the month, at the latest, I will be able to type final copy of the two hundred pages I want you to print, with a bridge passage at the end intended to make the reader look forward to more. Then I can *wait* (as all good poets should and as fruit-trees wait for the proper season) until the right conclusion comes; I can wait through the summer when I do not have to mark eighty abuses of the English language a week. Perhaps I can write a first version of a first novel, or at least enough of one to make you think I am worth my leisure time.

I have a good deal more to say about this 200-page section in itself (especially about the roadhouse scene as the proper end to this separate publication), but it is pointless to do so until you have the mss. [sic] at hand and have read some of it.

I also want to answer your letter in detail as soon as I have time. One point worth mentioning in advance is that the question of matching another publisher's advance is beside the point. Whether I am worth what I am told by some publishers I am worth I may never know; they say they would spend from five to ten thousand dollars advertising a novel

of mine. Not only would you not do this, but the
organization of ND gets worse all the time and you
have just put it all in the hands of one who, though
a fine person in many ways, has just been running it
into the ground because of ignorance, hysteria, and
neuroses unequalled on the Eastern Seaboard. The
only reason you put it in her hands is that you are
busy with the ski hotel: What reason has anyone to
believe that you will not always be busy with something else besides ND? It strikes me that the whole
thing would be much better moved completely to
Hollywood, since you obviously intend to be in Utah
most of the time. In fact, that seems to me the only
possibly reasonable arrangement, moving everything including E.S. (who would do well enough
with a superior nearby) near you. ND needs you as
a bow needs an arrow. However, be this as it may,
it is nothing I intend to do anything about until I
give you a novel.

Another thing I ought to answer right now, since
it may shine on the mss. I am sending is that, lucky
or not (and I was not very lucky with Rimbaud, for
if I had not been at Yaddo because of poverty I would
have shown it to someone at Columbia), and intrinsic merit apart, it should be clear to you by now that
what I write attracts a great deal of attention (did
you, for example, see the spread for *Shenandoah* in
Sunday's *Times?*). Perhaps it is a streak of vulgarity
or something else, but almost everything I have
published has rung the gong for four years; the
instance of the translation shows that it is not my
beautiful eyes or winning personality or Aryan
background which is responsible; it is the work itself,
whether for the wrong reasons or not I do not know.

Please read the mss. as soon as possible and with
the best attention. Printing this first part will solve
many problems at one stroke. I will try to get a final

version to you quickly; don't let rough spots here
and there throw you off.

Yours,
DELMORE

/ · /

the new Miller book: The Wisdom of the Heart, a collection of essays and
stories by Henry Miller, published by ND in 1941.

the roadhouse scene: The book concludes with an end to childhood innocence when Hershey Green and his mother confront his father dining
with a whore in a roadhouse.

ski hotel: JL was running the ski lodge in Alta, Utah, in Big Cotton-
wood Canyon above Salt Lake City.

93. TLS-1   December 27, 1941

DEAR JAY:

I sent you at Alta a rough approximate copy of
the first part of *Genesis* the same day that I wrote you
about publishing it as a part. It should have arrived
at least two weeks ago and perhaps it did, among
other packages you have put aside or not looked at.
It has a ND label on it, and looks like most of the
ms. packages you get. The idea of its being lost scares
me because there is a stretch of thirty pages of which
I have no copy other than three revisions back. We
have just started an air mail tracer. Will you look for
it right off and read it as soon as you can and write
me immediately? I have to type out the whole two
hundred pages for the printer and the new conclusion to this part, and I want to write a short introduction explaining the method of the poem and the
dual use of blank verse and Biblical parallelism. The

numbers, by the way, are out, since they look pretentious and the paragraphing will serve the same purpose of a formal distance and rhythm.

I am certain that you did not pay for the Viking anthology. You can check by looking at your checkbook for the time when you paid Thomas and Williams, for you received one check for the three of us and probably wrote them checks: Of course, you may not have paid any of us. If you like, we can go back to the principle of splitting such fees as a symbol of the fact that with luck and leisure I will be a rewarding investment. Your remarks about deciding about backing a novel strike me as fair enough. But it is not just advertising or just the organization of ND, but both and a number of other factors. However, I will produce the novel, the desirable nature of which you describe well, and that will be the test: I will have to show you, but you also have to show me.

I look forward to seeing what you said against the war. It was a noble gesture, anyway, but I am sure you are right in taking it out now when it would merely be resented. When the war is over, everyone will decide that it was wrong to go to war.

In the script of the first part of G. which I hope you have, some of it may seem, at first reading anyway, episodic in character. This was necessary to the structure of the whole thing. The conclusion I have just written generalizes the whole part, however, and apart from this, the episodes have a temporal order which carries them and which, at the very least, is not different from Thomas' *Portrait of the Artist,* with the additional strength that it is not straight fiction and is like Dante and Virgil passing from episode to episode also. (This comparison is descriptive and not evaluative and not my head swelling, as of your recent letter), that poem having been published in parts also and although I must admit conditions have changed somewhat, it is still being read mostly in parts.

DELMORE

/ · /

you did not pay: Permission fees to reprint some Schwartz poems.
the first part of G.: Genesis, Book One.
Thomas' Portrait of the Artist: Dylan Thomas's *Portrait of the Artist as a Young Dog,* which ND published in 1940.

94. TLS-2
Thursday, 11 A.M.
Jan. 7, 1942

DEAR MR. LAUGHLIN:

Henceforth I will communicate with you in the cold objective style. This may or may not prevent you from remarking from Norfolk to romantic Alta that I am a drunkard. Your new method of getting at me and insulting me appears to be imputation. First, I play the part of Judas and write the *Advocate* review; then I write when drunk. I drink only to get to sleep when I have been writing all day; to drink at any other time would be a waste because I would then have to drink so much more to sleep.

Send me back my two Monday letters, so that I can make out what it is, except an epistolary style modelled or rather inspired by yours, that made you think I was drinking. Also send me back my poem. I want both these things and I want them very much, so let us not argue about it.

Answer me about Kazin: Did you tell him I was going to review his book? I take it you are not interested in the story; this suits me, since I can get paid for it now. Also I demand a retraction again; what makes you think you can call me a traitor and schemer in that way without offense?

Why won't you be persuaded that jacket quotes are dangerous in this case? First, you may not even be able to get them because even those who much admire me think I have already been praised too much for a young man. Second, the reviewers will spend their time fighting the jacket quotes. Third, I can't postpone reviews and poems beyond March, and if I don't do them, the editors will be displeased with me. Fourth, the reviews I've already persuaded some of my friends to write on the ground of your putative campaign against me won't be written because of the delay and also because the jacket quotes will make it clear that there never was a campaign, only resentment, expressed loudly to you because it is thought that I have influence with you.

Never was there anyone so influenced by momentary fashions as you. Just because quotes work with Villa, you think it will do good in quite a different case, a long poem in which such a one as Louise Bogan will think this is her last chance of stopping me this side of immortality. If you visit the right editors, then we will get honest and sympathetic reviews, and this book can get along on its own speed.

The decision, perforce, is yours, but you'll be sorry if this book is not an immediate success because you won't want to meet the offers I've gotten and can get from other more well-to-do publishers when my novel is finished, as it probably will be by fall. I can get three thousand dollars instead of three hundred for a novel and in addition not be insulted as a drunkard, nor terrified by imaginary campaigns against me; nor would I have to fight to get the proper amount of advertising for a novel, namely, an amount which exceeds what you spend on all your books.

I have all the fame I want for the time being; now I want power to protect it or money and probably both. If this seems a drunken statement to you, come to Cambridge and I will make it in person after walking a straight line.

As for Arthur, I like him, but never admired him because he has nothing but his capacity to flatter. In that *Kenyon* review, he praised all who might do him good and damned those who could not harm him, such as poor Berryman.

For example, in sneering at those who praised Villa, he carefully omits to mention Van Doren, whose boots he has already licked earlier in the review. He kicks Berryman in the face, but is careful to put in a soothing word to me. Next time you see him, ask him how the shoe polish tastes which the Tates use. You can get a certain distance by bootlicking, *if* you have talent. Arthur has nothing but glibness; I suppose I ought to be sorry for him, because they scared him at Yale and it must be hard to be a Mizener and Moore in a time of raging anti-semitism. But I am sorrier for Berryman who does have talent. Another instance of your fickleness: Last year, on reading his poems, you told me you thought he was really first-rate. Now Arthur says no, dishonestly, and you change your mind. Why are you so unsure of your own taste? Who scared you?

We must get another picture, or the old one may be used and I am sick of being kidded about that and also disappointing the Radcliffe girls. I am nervous and sensitive, and don't want to be kidded.

Furthermore, I am going to get a five-year contract from Harvard in May. One possibility which may interest you is that the Army may put all instructors into uniform and make them officers (since most of the students will be in uniform and it has been difficult to maintain discipline at training schools with civilian instructors). The classes will march into school in platoons and the first time this happens I will doubtless turn and run into the blackboard, thinking, Jay was right after all, there *was* an organized campaign against me, there are Patchen, Prokosch, and Barker coming to shoot me down.

As for Williams and his light o'love, this is an example of how your wish to have everything is impossible of realization. You say you want only good poems and an anthology with staying power. In the same paragraph, you say you want Patchen, Brown, and God knows what other bad poets included, all in 128 pages. How can this be? Will you explain? A good anthology full of bad poets? It might be done if we had four hundred pages. But 128 pages? It is you that must be drinking, James.

Which preface do you want me to write, the ghost book or the artist book? I would prefer the ghost one, since I already have thought about it a good deal, and have a lot to say.

Gertrude does not know which store ordered 50 copies. You have an exaggerated view of her interest in how many copies my books sell. She thinks, probably, San Francisco.

Now I have wasted all this energy on you, which would otherwise have gone into a new chapter. Enough of these insults and imputations. Please send me back poem and letters and please answer all the questions I've asked.

Yours truly,
M R .   D E L M O R E   S C H W A R T Z

P.S. If you must have quotes, why won't old quotes do? Maybe it is the extreme excitement of writing better than ever before that seems like drunkenness to you, when I relax into letter-writing?

/ · /

the Advocate review: "The Ultimate Plato with Picasso's Guitar," *Harvard Advocate,* CXXVII (December 1940), 11–16. Not listed in Zucker bibliography.

Kazin . . . his book: On Native Grounds (1942), by Alfred Kazin (b. 1915), which Schwartz did not review.

Villa: The poet José Garcia Villa (b. 1918) later worked in the ND office in New York. ND published his *Volume Two* in 1949.

As for Arthur: Arthur Mizener.

the Tates: Allen Tate and his novelist wife, Caroline Gordon.

that Kenyon review: Mizener's piece.

Prokosch: Frederick Prokosch (1908–1989), American novelist and poet. ND published his translation of Hölderlin in 1946 and another of the *Love Poems of Louise Labé* in 1947.

Barker: George Barker (b. 1913), British poet. ND published his *Sacred and Secular Elegies* in 1948.

which preface: Schwartz was to introduce a ND volume of Henry James stories. Instead, ND issued *Stories of Writers and Artists,* edited by F. O. Matthiessen (1944).

95. TLS-1   [N.D.]

DEAR JAY:

I will try to make a list of suggestions for the Penguin volume after I see the new volume of *ND*.

Harry reported, in many paragraphs, that Hivnor's novel was "frightfully bad." As you know, Harry tends to be inordinately harsh, but there was a striking correspondence between his specific remarks about how adolescent some of it seemed and what Rahv has to say. I myself lacked the strength of attention to read right now, and it still seems to me that, despite the disorder of narrative form and gaps, there is a remarkable sensibility there, and something ought to be done about it. I suggest that you try it out on a few more people of good taste before you make up your mind. Something certainly ought to be done to keep Hivnor going and even the risk of certain and costly failure might be better as an experience for him than just getting the mss [sic.] back and told to rewrite it.

There is still no word about the mss [sic.] Please make one more effort to find out if it is not mislaid somewhere in the ski-jump. If I hear nothing by the end of next week, I will have to re-write the passage of which I have no up-to-date version. I trust that you have not forgotten your promise about getting someone capable, at least within reason, of running the business, since you have obviously decided to spend your life skiing and falling off roofs, or whatever it is you find so engaging in romantic Alta.

DELMORE

P.S. You might ask H.L. for his impressions of Hivnor. They are worth hearing.

/ · /

Penguin volume: A proposed anthology of selections from *ND*.

Harry reported: Harry Levin.

Rahv: ND published Philip Rahv's essays, *Image and Idea*, in 1949.

Hivnor's novel: The Invader, which was announced for publication in an advertisement in *ND 41*, scheduled for release in the spring of 1942. It was never published.

about the mss.: Schwartz had sent his only typescript of *Genesis* to Laughlin in Utah, where it got lost. After a four-month search, it was found under the floorboards of the Alta, Utah, mail truck. See Atlas, pp. 213–14.

H.L.: Harry Levin.

96. TLS-1   Friday, Jan. 17, 1942

DEAR JAY:

I said nothing to Spencer. You ought to know me better than that, or you ought at least to know that he fills me with too much pure discomfort for me to discuss anything like that with him. He did say to me that he had written you, but I listened and made no comment. He was just troubled about his pamphlet and feeling self-important. Would you like me to get him to confirm my silence?

I wish you would stop throwing the word, *neurosis,* about, at least with regard to my behavior. I don't want to get pedantic about it, but it is a technical term and means a state of mind which actually prevents normal behavior. My behavior is nothing if not normal; I teach, correct papers, and try to write every day. I resent the way teaching takes up time which might be spent in writing, but this resentment is perfectly conscious and non-pathological. I suggest that you just call me ill-tempered.

The express office has begun to stall about whether they have received word on their two tracers, so I suppose the whole business is hopeless and I will have to begin re-writing the pages of which I have no copy and also feeling for the corrections which were not made on the carbon. I confess that I do not look forward to this task: Is this too a neurosis?

In the light of your devotion to the daughters of the ancient people, and in proof of my ceaseless devotion to your interest, the enclosed letter is enclosed [sic], so that when you come East you can engage in further anti-insemination. I have not answered it, nor several others of different origin in race: How do you feel about the Free French? You can have some letters from them too.

Slocum and Pierce strike me as good tests, but you ought to get a third party of a more intellectual cast, since some intellectuals do read ND books.

I have not yet looked through the anthologies for suggestions for selections, but my story, in *IDBR,* and "Shenandoah," thirty pages all told, are the only selections I intend to insist upon. It occurs to me that the first five chapters of *White Mule* and the poems, "The Yachts" and "Elegy for D. H. Lawrence" and the chapter on Poe in *The American Grain,* and Fisher's story last year, and Goodman's "The Ceremonial" and Berryman's "Winter Landscape," "The Disciple," "The Statues," "On a London Train," both Kerner stories, and Harry's article in *ND 39,* and Fitts' poem about necking on a country road, and five of Mary Barnard and of Jarrell ought to be included. I leave you to make your own selections from your own verse, but I would suggest the one about Rockefeller City and the one about Pittsburgh at least. Also Howard Baker and Winters ought to be included as poets. From Patchen I would include nothing—but you will certainly include something.

Yours sincerely,
DELMORE

/ · /

Spencer: Theodore Spencer.

the enclosed letter: Unidentified.

Slocum and Pierce: John J. Slocum and Charles A. ("Cap") Pearce. Slocum was JL's classmate at Harvard and Pearce was a member of the publishing firm of Duell, Sloan & Pearce.

White Mule . . . The American Grain: All titles by William Carlos Williams. The title *In the American Grain* (1925) is paraphrased by Schwartz.

Kerner stories: David Kerner had stories in *ND* 5 and 13.

one about Rockefeller City: JL's poem "Above The City."

one about Pittsburgh: "Easter in Pittsburgh."

97. TLS-2   Jan. 31, 1942

DEAR WOMBAT:

I suggest that you stop yelling at me and stop being rude. My devotion to you is great, but not endless. I have not been in the office or spoken more than Hello to Emily at all since early in December. . . .

Enough of these discussions, however; you will have to find out for yourself. Enough also of writing to me as if I were Albert; struggling as I am to finish a work which, in spite of the Railway Express, the laws of chance, the Harvard freshmen, and other factors, including the World War, will last as long as the Pyramids, I expect to be addressed with a certain amount of respect.

Don't just drop Hivnor. In spite of the faults and the general immaturity, there really is something there and there may be more later on. The very least that can be done is to print about half in next year's *ND;* this would be 125 pages (since Hivnor's pages are very short) no longer than the G. Mann, and it would teach him a lesson through the reviews. It might make the *ND* volume a bit lopsided, but it is worth doing nevertheless, and it would have the advantage of not doing what you seem to fear, scaring the book-stores. Of course, it may be possible to do more than that with the book: You might wait and see what Pierce and someone like Georg Mann says about it.

Please put "Shenandoah" into the Penguin volume. If you want to substitute "Coriolanus" for the story, all right, although that will take a lot of room, but "S" will be good in such a collection for the English as a regional study, which is what the English always want from America, local color. This reminds me that you ought to put in the pencil poem and "The River." What a fine writer you could be, if you did not feel so devoted to your pleasures, such as running second-rate hotels. Did you include some poems by E. Bishop and W. R. Moses?

A good possibility for the poets-of-the-year would be a selection of the poems of that very great writer, Herman Melville (his poems are like Hart Crane, in diction). The selection could be done by Matthiessen (whose big book is quite a success) or by many another pundit.

Did you read the Roberts report on Pearl Harbor? If you look closely, you will find that on the 26th of November an ultimatum was sent to Japan which was meant to force a war. Of course, Friendly Frank expected an attack in Malaya and the Philippines, not in Hawaii, but the point is that he embarked on a step in foreign policy which neither Congress (which is supposed to have equal voice in deciding foreign policy) nor the people (who, in theory, ought to have their wishes carried into action in this democracy) would have sanctioned. In fact, since the arming of ships passed Congress by just one vote, it is clear that no one wanted him to do what he did. Now we will have a war until every Chinaman has to buy Gillette blades or lose his self-respect. I don't know why I make a point of speaking of this, except that it is depressing to think of five years perhaps of war, when it is not necessary. Needless to say, my feelings ought not to be broadcast, should the occasion arise.

Do you want the Quennell book on the Symbolists?

DELMORE

/ · /

the pencil poem: JL's "What the Pencil Writes."
"The River": An early story by JL about his life in Paris.

Moses: He was included in *Five Young American Poets, 1940.*

big book: F. O. Matthiessen's *American Renaissance* (1941).

Friendly Frank: One of Schwartz's nicknames for President Franklin D. Roosevelt.

the Quennell book: Baudelaire and the Symbolists (1929) by Peter Courtney Quennell (b. 1905), British poet, critic, and biographer.

98. TLS-1   June 12, 1942

[No salutation]

I owe James Laughlin the sum of one hundred and fifty dollars, payable on or before the 1st of October 1942.

DELMORE SCHWARTZ

99. TLS-1   June 23rd

DEAR JAY:

Please return enclosed with a permission which I can send to Kreymborg. His anthology won't appear until November and would anyway help *Genesis,* that liber mirabilis, almost finished now. The appearance of *Shen.* started sales going fast on *I.D.B.R.*

I am touched by your remembering the plot of my novel-to-be. I hope to start it this fall in order to keep myself from paranoia and megalomania when the reviews of *Genesis* begin. How much water has flowed under the bridge since you saw that synopsis, how many nations have fallen, how many women have been fornicated, how much was unforeseen!

I looked at the Nabokov again and think maybe with the proper luck in reviews, it might do well.

The enclosed piece by Jarrell is superficial in many

ways, I think—he does not understand that commercial publishers are the way they are and reviewers are whores *because the great public wants them to be that way*—but nevertheless worth your scrutiny. This is cut from my own copy of the *N.R.*, not yours.

I have read the Rougemont and think you ought to print the piece on Kafka in *ND 41*. Not only is it the best thing about K. I've ever read, but in principle it would be handsome to show that ND is aware and receptive to that kind of writing.

DELMORE

P.S. My new play in verse is all versed and needs only to be typed and is much better than the old one—especially for *ND 41*. So all that remains is the letters between Harry and me on "The Return from Naturalism in World Lit."

/ · /

Kreymborg: Alfred Kreymborg (1883–1966), poet and critic, who included *Shenandoah* in his big anthology, *Poetic Drama: From the Ancient Greek to the Modern American* (1942).

my novel-to-be: A *Child's Universal History*, never published.

the Nabokov: The Real Life of Sebastian Knight.

Rougemont: Denis de Rougemont's fictional piece, "Stages on Death's Way," appeared in *ND 41*, in a translation by Edward M. Maisel.

My new play: Paris and Helen.

the old one: Venus in the Back Room.

100. TLS-1   July 27, 1942

DEAR JAY:

The Fitzgerald project seems to me pointless on the face of it. If the book had any commercial possibilities, Wilson would not give it to you. The journal might be good, but that remains to be seen. Fitzgerald is the laureate of the Twenties in one great book, but the Twenties are twenty years passed. If you could persuade Wilson to write a Maker's book on Fitzgerald, you would be much better off. He would be worth the price he asked for.

Poor old Williams, how great an author he might have been, did he not have so immense suspicion of the intelligentsia. He is a great author, anyway, but he might have been much more; not that Jarrell represents the intelligentsia, or anything but an illustration of how easy it is to substitute wise cracks for perceptions; perceptions are hard and require thought. I look forward to ten years of Jarrell and Harry Brown trying to see who can make the most wise cracks.

Enclosed are some very beautiful poems by this year's star at Cummington. I have about fifty more, some of them very good, but in need of revision. She certainly deserves a group in this year's *ND* and ought to be in the next *FYAP;* or perhaps even a pamphlet. She has been printed in *KR* and *PR,* which should further exhibit her appeal. In any case, let me know what you think and write to her soon. I trust you will not make the same imputations as you did last year, for this is one of the wrong sisters, and seemingly tortured by it.

I saw the Fishers also, and the stately Alfred wants to know about the Penguin anthology, when it is coming out, and if he is included; Helen gave me two stories which I have not read yet, but will send you soon. I did not ask for it, she just gave it to me, after plying me with highballs. Such is the way of the world, but where else can one live?

I heard more of the antagonism I have evoked and its source appears to be my criticism, since I so seldom name anyone a Shakespeare, not even an

Edmund Wilson. But forbear to this business of keeping me posted; anger makes me able to go forward to eternity, posterity, and the praise of *The New York Times*.

DELMORE

/ · /

The Fitzgerald project: The Crack-up, a collection of uncollected pieces, notebook entries, and unpublished letters by F. Scott Fitzgerald, who had died in 1940 at age forty-four. The collection was assembled by his literary executor, Edmund Wilson. Many large publishers turned the book down before JL eventually published it in 1945. It became a bestseller.

a Maker's book: A book in JL's The Makers of Modern Literature Series.

the most wise cracks: Jarrell won. It was he who said of Oscar Williams's poems that they "gave the impression of having been written on a typewriter by a typewriter." See Jarrell's *Kipling, Auden & Co. Essays and Reviews, 1935–1964* (New York: Farrar, Straus & Giroux, 1980), p. 137.

this year's star at Cummington: June Cannan. Twelve of her poems were published in *ND* 8.

the same imputations: JL had accused Schwartz of having relations with Jean Garrigue the year before.

Helen: Helen Eustis Fisher.

101. TLS-1

20 Ellery St.
Cambridge, Mass.
Sept. 20, 1942

DEAR JAY:

Genesis is all dressed up in Sunday clothes, ready for the printer, posterity, and my hated enemies.

Let me know immediately whether to send it to you or straight to Beilenson, and don't forget the format you promised me, that of Thomas' *PAYD,* but with a blue cover.

It might be rushed and made ready before Christmas, I don't care whether it is or not, but you may— but I am in a hurry to get sheets to show Moe of the Guggenheim Board, for I seem to have a good chance of another Guggenheim, on the basis of *Genesis* as a half-finished work in print. Let me know how soon this can be done.

This is no doubt the worst time of all to publish such a work, the War being what it is. But I must get free of it and move on to the novel which my head is heavy with. I hope you are ready to do what must be done to give the book any chance of success, and at the very least preserving the prestige of a valuable property. I can see how you may well be skiing when the time comes.

When copies are ready, I will send you a long list of suggestions, such as, visit Irita Van Doren, and tell her what Mark Van Doren said of the book, write to Ransom and move him to tears as you moved me, by telling him of the cabal, visit J. Donald Adams and persuade him to read the poem, and explain to him what a cabal of enemies is ready, visit Margaret Marshall and point out that every one of my works has been attacked in *The Nation.* The main principle is to get these editors *to read the book.* The experience of sending it to many different hearts and minds this summer [sic] makes it overwhelmingly patent that it awakens the intensest interest and at any other time there would be a chance at popular success.

I want a three hundred dollar advance on the novel, and this is not meant as the beginning of bargaining. I can get three times as much anywhere else, you gave Hivnor and Nabokov that much, the ever-rising cost of living, the end of Gertrude's job, the necessity of not writing critical essays while I teach and try to concentrate on the novel—make me need that sum very much. Moreover, such an advance was part of your promise last Christmas. If you feel like gambling, I will go to the trouble of getting definite offers from other publishers, and then you can give me *half* of what they are willing to give me, which will be more than I am now asking you for.

Yours,
Delmore

/ · /

20 Ellery St.: The Schwartzes had moved in August to the house where Philip Horton and his wife had lived. The rent was $27 a month less.

Thomas' PAYD: Dylan Thomas's autobiographical sequence of short stories, *Portrait of the Artist as a Young Dog,* which ND published in 1940.

Moe: Henry Allen Moe, for many years director of the Guggenheim Foundation.

Irita Van Doren: Editor of *New York Herald Tribune Books.*

J. Donald Adams: An editor of *The New York Times Book Review.*

Margaret Marshall: Literary Editor of *The Nation.*

102. TLS-1

Friday,
Sept. 25, 1942

DEAR JAY:

I think Electra would be fine, but the Electra of Stevens' *The Man with the Blue Guitar,* which Wolff did, and not the kind used for McAlmon or Miller.

You decide about the size, but please don't use the decadent fin-de-siècle yellow paper of *IDBR,* and don't put the title between my two names, and use a blue cloth cover.

You can announce the book of essays for some time in the summer to come. One month's work is all that is necessary; but it is necessary. And I want to write a first version of my novel before I do anything else and before it stops brimming over in my head.

I need the three hundred dollars in order to be able to write it under reasonably good conditions. The difficulty you speak of does not exist for such an author as myself, whom you know to be industrious. I really have to have the money, and I don't want to write critical essays to get it. I have written some twenty-five during the past few years and that is enough for a time.

This reminds me that I must give you back the money you gave me for Berryman. Enclosed is the check.

I have read enough of Goodman's high-toned trash to last me some time. But he is going to be one of the characters in my prose fiction; if you think this new work will illuminate his character further, I would like to look at it.

This reminds me to say I told you so, mean though it is, about last year's *FYAP*. I chose the Shapiro group. Shapiro wrote commending the selection as being the best possible, and I told you not to include Goodman, who received a merciless beating. Hence, I hope you will let me have a hand in the next volume.

Scarfe's book is a curious mixture of perception and naivete, not to say stupidity. But, such are the rewards of journalism, it might very well be worth printing as the kind of survey which is much reviewed and helps the poets to get read. The Celtic anthology hardly seems worth more than good enough to be put into a number of *ND*. The best poems in it are ones by Thomas already printed in his volume. It is a shame that such a good idea was not better embodied.

Don't be mean about the advance, for is it not true that I am to be given what I would get elsewhere and certainly authors are given money to write books. Also, why have I not received a royalty statement? I am, although trapped by economic determinism,

> Yours always,
> DELMORE

P.S. If you destroy the check for Berryman and send me $150, each of us will gain a sum of $105, net.

/ · /

Electra: The typeface.

Wolff: H. Wolff, New York book production house.

McAlmon: Robert McAlmon (1896–1956), expatriate American poet and fiction writer. He directed Contact Publishing Company.

one of the characters: Schwartz wrote an entire 400-page novel about Goodman and his circle before abandoning it. The story, "The World Is a Wedding," from the collection by that title, is ten short chapters from the novel.

last year's FYAP: The 1941 *Five Young American Poets* were Jeanne McGahey, Clark Mills, David Schubert, Karl Shapiro, and Schwartz's bête noire, Paul Goodman.

Scarfe's book: British poet and critic Francis Scarfe's *Auden and After* (1942).

The Celtic anthology: A submission. ND published no Celtic anthology.

103. TLS-1   October 26, 1942

DEAR JAY:

What would you say to a *New Directions Anthology of Poetry of the Past,* to be edited by you and myself, comprised of all the out-of-the-way, little known, or experimental, or modern-like, poems—English and American—from the Elizabethan to Hopkins, with an introduction attacking the anthologists who so often choose the same poems or poems easy to discuss in classrooms?

There would be no permissions to pay for, or almost none if we put in some Emily Dickinson, and the only expense would be to pay for the rental of a typewriter for Gertrude and not even that if you have an extra one in Norfolk. The book could be any length you think feasible, and it would be a joy forever. Anthologies must be a gold mine, there are so many coming out, and in addition, this would obviously be a fine characteristic action for the firm.

An enormous amount of material has been accumulating ever since the revolution in taste which Pound and Eliot began (one of the things worth doing would be simply to follow the suggestions in Eliot's criticism of the Elizabethan dramatists and the Metaphysicals). Consider for example this beautiful thing which just one or two anthologists have had the sense to use:

> The maidens came
> When I was in my mother's bower;
> I had all that I would.
> > The bailey beareth the bell away;
> > The lily, the rose, the rose I lay.
> The silver is white, red is the gold;
> The robes they lay in fold.
> > The bailey beareth the bell away;
> > The lily, the rose, the rose I lay.
> And through the glass window shines the sun.
> How should I love, and I so young?
> > The bailey beareth the bell away;
> > The lily, the lily, the rose I lay.

I think maybe we might have to inquire as to whether you pay for permission when you take the text from some modern editor. This might be circumvented by using Widener and going back to older texts, although this would involve a good deal of

work in the Treasure Room. For my part of the work,
I'd expect the usual percentage of royalty, minus
whatever permissions have to be paid for. What do
you think?

Yours,
DELMORE

/ · /

New Directions Anthology of Poetry of the Past: It was never published.

The maidens came: Schwartz quotes a poem from the fifteenth or six-
teenth century which is given the title "Bridal Morning" in *The Oxford
Book of English Verse, AD 1250–1918,* edited by Sir Arthur Quiller-
Couch (Oxford University Press, 1900).

using *Widener:* The main library at Harvard University.

104. TL-1   [N.D.]

DELMORE:

Ever your slave, I enclose some other possible
sketches. Please return with comment. #3 might be
very sales-provocative if a really juicy page of the
ms. were selected for the underscrub.

Please return. In 32 the letters would appear like
blocks of wood, seen from looking down on them.

J

/ · /

possible sketches: For the dust jacket of *Genesis.*

page of the ms. were selected: The design was to feature an actual typewritten page with a red shape imposed upon it and the title GENESIS in
reverse.

105. TL-1   [N.D.]

[No salutation]

Your inspiration seems to have deserted you. Is it
fatherhood? Once you designed jackets so beautiful.
#2 impresses me as the least of the three evils. Why
not something like *White Mule,* in green, with black
letters? Or this: [Schwartz drew a jacket design, which
is very close to what Laughlin in fact used]. Enormous letters, blue on a green ground or green on a
blue ground. Green = Generation, growth. Big letters = Generation is important.

Biddy Fisher writes asking for her stories, which
I sent you in August. Let me know what happened.

You had better get someone to go over these proofs
with care. I can't see anything after hundreds of
readings of the poem.

Gertrude says my bill is $3.81. Can't you deduct
it from my royalties?

Your lack of enthusiasm about the anthology is
depressing; I have been a stalagmite for years.

If you are going away to ski or something, please
postpone publication of *Genesis* until you return or
are able to engage in promotion.

Sweeney in the Poetry Room of Widener wants
to put on an exhibit of my mss. when the book
appears. Have you the ms. of *IDBR?*

Can you get me, and when, a set of proofs to send
to Moe?

How efficient ND is! Neither Pindar nor Berryman can be found, as yet, in the Coop, and don't
forget this is a culture center.

Harry will now turn on the British Empire.

/ · /

fatherhood: JL's son by his first wife, Margaret, was born in October 1942, the year of this letter.

Biddy Fisher: Helen Eustis Fisher.

Sweeney: John L. Sweeney, Curator of the Poetry Room at Harvard. He edited *Selected Writings of Dylan Thomas* for ND in 1946.

Pindar: Some Odes of Pindar, translated by Richmond Lattimore in the Poets of the Year series.

Berryman: After Laughlin included Berryman's work in *Five Young American Poets* in 1941, he issued a separate collection, *Poems,* in the Poets of the Year series (1942).

Coop: The Harvard Cooperative Society in Harvard Square, which had a large stock, mostly textbooks.

106. TLS-1 [N.D.]

[No salutation]

I like the one on the other side very much, also that hairy paper.

Enclosed is the check.

I don't deny G's inefficiency, but you ought to remember that there was no system, only your improvisations and the accumulation of other inept clerks, all of whom you excoriated for the same reason.

Your cheery resignation to the fact that the Coop does not stock ND verse is really something. Any salesman who can't convince the Coop man on the basis of past records that verse is bought in Cambridge is no good, and you know it. If copies of *Genesis* are not bought in the city where I teach, where will they be bought? Can't you get them to take any on consignment? They do have a shelf full of books of poetry, you know. How am I ever going to get to earn a living, or even earn my advances, if you let things slide like that? *Genesis* ought to get a display in the Coop, and it is better to give Kerney the books, whether he pays or not, than not to get them circulating in one of the four or five culture centers of our great nation.

You say that ND is now a model of efficiency; what kind of efficiency is that? Bookkeeping is a fine thing, but getting books on display seems to be more important. This will indeed drive me to Hollywood, where I will play the regimental barracks in *The Golem*, or the Hudson River in *Shenandoah on the Albany Night Boat*.

Disturbed,
D

And furthermore, G. says the Coop had a standing order for the poetry! Did they cancel that as soon as you moved to N.Y.? What kind of madness is this? You said last month that the Coop had promised a display for ND? Was that a myth?

/ · /

G's inefficiency: Gertrude Buckman Schwartz's performance in the ND Cambridge office.

Kerney: Schwartz's misspelling of the last name of Gordon Cairnie, owner of the Grolier Bookshop on Plimpton Street, Cambridge, a center where poets met. In a letter to Cairnie, Schwartz declared, "the Grolier Bookshop always was a second home to me and to a lot of others. . . . And it was not the books but the proprietor who made us feel that way" (Phillips, ed., *Letters of Delmore Schwartz*, p. 350).

The Golem: Reference to a film version of Gustav Meyrink's (1868–1932) supernatural novel about the artificial anthropoid of Prague. The Golem of Meyrink's novel represents the human soul undisciplined by spiritual knowledge.

107. TCS-1   New Directions
                                      Norfolk, Conn.
                                      [N.D.]

DEAR DELMORE:

Well it's ok for Thursday. Will you look up the
trains and let me know what time you arrive at
Hartford station? I will meet you and stand on your
right hand. Trains run by way of Springfield. Be
sure to make it on time. I will pay you back for your
ticket. I'm telling them you will be ready to say a
few words about poetry, especially in reference to
Hartford's pride, and also to read from your work.
Be sure to read nothing "off-color." See if Elinor
wants to come with you???

                                      J

                          / · /

for Thursday: Schwartz was to give a reading at Trinity College.
Hartford's pride: Wallace Stevens.
Elinor: Elinor Blanchard.

108. TLS-1   [N.D.]

JAY:

I have gone over this twice, but, being over-
whelmed by its beauty, truth, solidity, lucidity, and
scope, I doubt that I have not missed some errors.
There is a serious mix-up in galleys 16 & 17, copy
pp. 52, 53, 54. Also the verse has not been lined up
properly with the prose many times. The beginning
of the prose paragraph should be even with the verse
line. Other lines of the prose should be to the left.

Please advise when I must send in copy for the foreword. It is already written, but I keep revising it, and it will help.

In days to come—mark you!—this poetic style will be seen as the beginning of Post-Symbolism, as Cézanne was the beginning of Post-Impressionism. As he gave to Impressionism the solidity of the museums, so I will give to the Symbolism that has reigned from Baudelaire to Eliot the solidity and the lucidity of the classics and the narrative ground of the epic.

The page opposite the title page should have a list of my books, so:

By Delmore Schwartz
In Dreams Begin Responsibilities
Shenandoah
Genesis
The Imitation of Life, and Other Problems in Literary Criticism *(in preparation)*

D

P.S. I want the mss. back for Harvard exhibit, and I want a set of page proofs.

/ · /

gone over this: Proofs of *Genesis, Book One.*
Cézanne: Paul Cézanne (1839–1906), one of the greatest Post-Impressionist painters. His works were influential in the aesthetic development of Cubism.

109. TLS-1   New Directions
                                               Norfolk, Connecticut
                                               Tuesday

DEAR DELMORE:

You won't have any charges for changing indentation, because there aren't going to be any changes. The book was laid out according to principles beyond your worldly comprehension and is going to stay that way. You will prefer the way it comes out to the many broken lines that would follow from your suggestions. You are almost totally innocent of any understanding of the technical problems of printing.

No, what will mount up will be the endless comma changes and little things like that. You don't seem to realize that each change like that costs about 25 cents, because heedless intellectuals following the false illusion of liberalism have voted for demagogues like Roosevelt, who have allowed the unions to raise wages to a point where anything like poetry cannot be commercially manufactured.

THERE is something to write a poem about—how the artist has destroyed himself by forgetting under what conditions his art can flourish . . . ah well . . .

My wife is eating up Kazin like ice cream, so now I KNOW he is no good. However, I have arranged to have him write something for the series. In fact I had a long time ago, or as soon as he took over the *NR*. He hasn't decided yet which one he wants to do.

I think the negative tone of your preface is a mistake, but I suppose you know what you're doing. It doesn't seem to me that you need to appear to apologize like that.

I'll work on the blurbs after I've read it again in page proofs, using the catalogue version for basis.

                                                      J

/ · /

eating up Kazin: Alfred Kazin's *On Native Grounds. A Study of American Prose Literature from 1890 to the Present,* was published in 1942.

negative tone of your preface: "I would like to try to remove some of the preconceptions and 'habitual expectations' which would condemn the formal character of the whole work," Schwartz had begun in his note "To the Reader." The piece got more apologetic as it continued.

110. TLS-1   Friday morning

[No salutation]

I am just about to send off the preface, dedication, and quotations to Reichl.

Last year's catalogue description would be fine on the jacket. In case you feel moved to add anything, I enclose the preface, which please return. At any rate, be certain to add an announcement of the book of critical essays, and sentences about my being a Briggs-Copland Instructor in English at Harvard (this pleases Morrison), and that this was written on two Guggenheim Fellowships (to please Moe); perhaps this will evoke the interest of librarians.

I hope you are keeping to your idea of circulating copies of the book for two or three weeks before the review copies go out. This may make much difference on who gets the book to review. . . .

DELMORE

/ · /

Reichl: Ernst Reichl, book designer.

the preface: Not reprinted here. See "To the Reader," *Genesis* (1943), pp. vii–ix.

111. TL-1   [N.D.]

[No salutation]

Genesis is the story of the making of an American, told in prose and poetry by a young poet whose interpretation of the meaning of modern life is original and illuminating. The American in question is Hershey Green, a New York child whose parents came from old Europe in the great Atlantic migrations at the turn of the century. In this boy, as he grows, we watch the complex struggle of forces that determine the nature and pattern of a typical American city life, and the "genesis" of a human being.

The way in which Hershey Green's story is told is in itself an important new direction in writing. The actual narrative of scenes and events is given in prose—the young man, lying sleepless at night, recalls his own life as a child and what he has heard about those of his parents—then in the darkness, in a state of hallucination, he hears a chorus of strange voices which comment, in poetry, on the things he remembers. These are the souls of the dead, interpreting his experiences from their vantage point of superior knowledge and trying to explain to him. These observers can trace and understand the remote causes of action which are hidden from the young man himself And these causes—historical, social, cultural, and psychological—are the "divinities" of our day, acting upon our free will as fatefully as ever did the gods of the ancient world. In their interplay the poet finds material for "poetic action" which is quite as dramatic as that in the scenes of real life.

Critics often point out that the best literature offers several levels of appreciation. This is true of *Genesis,* for here is a book which gives the reader of stories an engrossing tale to follow, which sets the thinker out on many new paths of fruitful speculation, and which will delight the partisan of poetry with countless fine lines and subtle poetic insights.

And critics have also pointed out that in the case of a new and experimental work, the reader ought to defer judgement until he is sure that he has responded to the work as a whole, and sure that he has not been prejudiced by the very newness of style and technique which makes the work important.

(Re-write this last paragraph, but be sure to put it in.)

/ · /

Hershey Green: Protagonist clearly modeled on Schwartz's childhood.

112. TL-1   December 16, 1942

DEAR JAY:

The proofs, as you learned by wire, have gone to Reichl. I had to make a considerable number of changes because of linguistic usages, and punctuation. Don't touch any of them, they are almost without exception necessary: For example, I did not know that *cantabile* had to be used only of instruments, never of the human voice.

About Williams' anthology: You would be insane to have anything to do with it. Williams promised contributors payment on a royalty-divided basis both times and has never sent anything, using the money himself and blaming it on the publisher. This is what you take for his ability to get poems for nothing. Did he tell you that? Please let me know. You arouse a sufficient amount of antagonism by your own financial methods without taking upon yourself

Williams' indebtedness. Authors who did not get paid by Williams would get after you. For this valuable piece of information, send me a copy of the MOPO Pindar.

Furthermore and wholly apart from Williams, I want to edit whatever anthology of modern verse you put out. Last year, I was on the verge of running everything but the adding machine; this year, I can't even get a free copy of Berryman's poems, because you don't send me one and he won't give me one on the ground that he does not like the edition. Yes! the idea grows handsome in my mind as I think of it, an anthology edited by Jarrell and myself, of the same kind as Williams, but much better. You ought to know by now that in my own way, I am just as good a promoter as Williams.

A further note on new ND efficiency came through last night when Wanning and Schorer were here. They said they had been getting two and three copies of some of the MOPOS. They get two and three copies and I get none! If you're intent on throwing copies away, why not throw them the way of one of your forever moneyless authors, who now teaches the Freshmen so that he can be published by New Directions.

Rahv would certainly write a good book on Dostoyevsky (whom you ought to get into The New Classics, for a new vogue seems to have begun), for Russian is his native tongue and he wrote a first-rate essay on D. some years ago. *Notes from the Underground* would be a good and easy-to-get book; also *Journal of an Author,* which is a miscellany of journal, essays, and stories.

Auden and Isherwood love Forster, to whom *Journey to a War* was dedicated, with a sonnet addressed to him. Years ago Arnold Bennett wrote an essay in which, I think, he said Forster was the best living novelist. There was an essay on F. by Belgion in *The Criterion,* but it was distinctly unfavorable, maintaining that Forster was an instrument of the Devil. There must be some more, but I can't think of them right now, my mind is tired.

Keep out of any reply to Williams, for he may very well be one of the reviewers of *Genesis;* although I would prefer reviewers with more sense, he would certainly not be a venomous enemy.

/ · /

Williams anthology: Proposed book to be edited by Oscar Williams.

Wanning: Andrews Wanning. While an undergraduate at Yale, he was one of the editors of *The Harkness Hoot,* for which JL was Harvard correspondent. In later years Wanning was Professor of English at Bard College, Anandale-on-Hudson, N.Y.

Isherwood: Christopher Isherwood (1904–1986), British novelist. ND reprinted four of his books, beginning with *Berlin Stories* in 1945.

Forster: Edward Morgan Forster (1879–1970), British novelist. ND reissued his *The Longest Journey* and *A Room with a View* in the New Classics Series in 1943.

Journey to a War: Collaboration by Auden and Isherwood (1939).

Arnold Bennett wrote an essay: "Books and Persons," *Evening Standard,* no. 32, 888 (January 9, 1930), 5. Bennett (1867–1931) was the author of over thirty books of fiction.

Belgion in The Criterion: Montgomery Belgion, British critic, "The Diabolism of E. M. Forster," *The Criterion,* October 1934.

113. TLS-2   Sunday

DEAR JAY:

What is this about losing the page proofs? At present I am so benumbed by what appears to be inspiration that I am incapable of anger, but do you not think that a little less frigidity might be expressed about this second loss, or are you kidding?, or do you think it would be a joke to undergo the ordeal of reading proofs again? Please advise. And please do something about it, not like the last time when four months passed before the mss. appeared. . . .

Yes, I would very much like to write the James preface. Blackmur did not mention all the good ghost stories so far as I remember, either the stories or his essay. I will send you a list one of these days; there must be more that could go in one volume. When do you want to put it out? It might be well to time it with the *Kenyon Review* James number next autumn.

I also want to go through with the anthology idea, but I am not sure, on second thought, that Jarrell is right as co-editor; too many people hate him, I don't know if he would do his share of the work, and he might make difficulties, for he thinks—for example—that Stevens is not a good poet. What about Berryman? His wife would type the letters, and he would be amenable to suggestion, and he would do his share of the work. Moreover, it would be a Christian thing to do, for he takes a dreadful beating while inferior poets like Jarrell, Villa, and other Filipinos get printed in big books because the Japs attacked the Philippines or Jarrell attacked Prokosch. The latest is Dunstan Thompson being printed by Harcourt, Brace. Why? Because he has attacked Jarrell, Prokosch, and Marianne Moore. One of these days I will attack everyone and win the Pulitzer Prize and the presidency of Harcourt, Brace.

(By the way, one incentive to your recovering the proofs is as follows: I have 1 chance in 1000 of winning the Pulitzer Prize, but the name of that chance is Mark Van Doren, who may be on the committee.)

If you don't want Berryman, which would be a shame, then I am willing to go and have Williams on the following terms: A written statement from you that royalties will be paid in advance. I have, as the others must, letters from Williams promising royalties and blaming all on the publishers. $250. is enough, but you have to pay something; of course, if the volume sold more, as it might, further royalties would also be divided. Williams will, I should guess, be pleased to have me as a fellow-editor, for he proposed something like that last year. I will bet you your Buick against my 1929 ownership license that I can get a poem from Eliot, which Oscar has not yet achieved.

Please advise. I have a legitimate right to my desire to be an editor, for I have the predisposition, the habit, the talent, and I do it all the time. Moreover, I will look like a big fool if I don't edit something after last year's hub-bub, created by you for your own convenience.

The way Williams gets the poets is through their fear of being left out. With me, there might be, in some quarters, an additional feeling of being pleased that I asked them.

Of late, I have made much progress with my novel, and made enough to think that maybe I can be done before next fall. If so, we will meet like Hitler and Mussolini at the Brenner Pass at Poughkeepsie, and you can be Hitler, I will be the Duce, since his mistress is 16, but if the new contract is not enough for me to lead a double life on, then I may turn out to be Darlan, who is fast becoming the Abe Lincoln of France.

Before you say anything to Williams, if you decide to be mean and turn down Berryman, please advise, for I have a few conditions to make, such as that I see carbons of letters from Williams to authors, so that he does not promise them the Woolworth Building.

Also, please stop writing me on post-cards. The postman, I see from my study window, pauses to read your prose style and God only knows what he thinks of such felicities as murderous Xmuss, maybe he knows French and studies *Finnegans Wake* at the dinner table.

Some Christmas,
NOAH GOLD

/ · /

the page proofs: Of *Genesis, Book One.*

the James preface: To the proposed edition of Henry James's tales of the supernatural.

Kenyon Review James number: Blackmur published one of his James essays, "In the Country of the Blue," in this issue (V, 1943), 328–52. Later JL would publish all of R. P. Blackmur's James essays as *Studies in Henry James,* edited and with an introduction by Veronica A. Makowsky (New York, 1983).

Dunstan Thompson: American poet and critic, co-editor with Harry Brown of the magazine *Vice-Versa.*

have Williams: Oscar Williams.

hub-bub: Over the dollar-a-month salary.

to be Darlan: Jean François Darlan (1881–1942), French admiral and high commissioner, who had just been assassinated in December 1942, hence the Lincoln allusion.

xmuss: An early JL pun on Christmas.

Noah Gold: Another of Schwartz's jokes playing on his Jewish surname.

114. TLS-1   New Directions
Norfolk, Connecticut
[N.D.]

DEAR DELMORE:

Had lunch with Rahv today. Never met him before. My GAWWWWD what a tank!

Do you think he is suitable to write on Dostoievsky for the Makers? Wants no money down but wants a contract. Let me know what you think before I commit myself. He says he reads Russian easily and will digest all the books on D in Russian. Please advise.

He spoke of changes at *Partisan* and wanted to know if I wanted to get into it. Certainly not. He said Dwight was going to have his own political monthly.

Also met Villa today. Marvelous little guy. Like an affectionate squirrel. He wants to be in P of Y. OK by me. Give the public what they like. He worships Cummings, which puts him in good with me.

I have your instructions about additions to preface. Can be done all right. Trust you have sent your version of corrected page proofs to Norfolk where I'll be tomorrow. If by some mistake you sent them direct to Reichl, you better telephone him to stop things. I want to go over it carefully myself.

That is nifty about Mallarmé and Old Possum. Aren't you the smart one.

I will write the blubbers when I have read the work again and shoot it up to you before I have it set up.

Unless my figures are wrong, ND is showing a profit of a few dollars this year. Receipts will run close to $15,000. Of course this is illusory because much of this is money that Buckman woman should have collected in past years and should have been applied to the deficits in these years. It also looks like we will grow rich at Alta. Booked solid for months ahead. In view of this, I am issuing a general order to cut all author's royalties 10%. ND cannot be tainted with any commercial practices.

Best,

J

/ · /

Villa: José Garcia Villa.
Mallarmé: Stéphane Mallarme (1842–1898), French Symbolist poet.
Old Possum: T. S. Eliot.

115. TLS-1   January 12, 1943

DEAR FRIEND:

Your last two letters, with Plan A and Plan B, are such clear evidences that you have been drinking that I do not intend to answer them until you sober up.

If you can detect the liquor on my breath all the way from Norfolk, Conn., how is it you cannot comprehend the basic loyalty of my character? If I wanted vast sums of money, I would have had nothing to do with you in the first place.

Unlike you, I intend to keep all my promises. Now, instead of all these plans, why don't you keep your promise of getting the book out *before* you take a vacation? After all, I have no vacations at all, now that we have to teach during the summer, and, granted that you are more important than I am, still you ought to do something, make some sacrifice, for a book which has taken five years and destroyed my youth.

When the page proofs did not come back from New York, why did you not go to New York and get them instead of spending your time staring at your son in the Men's Room? Or why did you not tell me to go get them? I would have been glad to.

As to the poem beginning to be good at p. 70, you may be right; but it is also possible that you just began to *tune in* on what I was doing at that point. The first time you read the book, you said that the first part was good, and then proceeded to fall asleep over the second part before my very eyes. By 1963 I expect a fair reading from you.

Still something could be said on the jacket about being patient. Also, you had better put in Jarrell's sentence; one quote will help.

Thanks for the volume of *ND* which has just come. Do you want me to express myself on Nardi?

A further note on what troubles me in you: First, you write me that Villa's poetry bores you stiff and then two weeks later you meet him in New York and sign him up for MOPO on the basis of his charm. Is personal charm your new criterion? Is it not rather that your chief standard is success, regardless of your own opinion? Is this the way you keep ND from becoming a clique, by publishing poets you don't like? Personally, I think Villa is pretty good, but the point is that I am made distraught by your fickleness.

Now stop drinking and stop figuring out new ways to insult me. The important thing is to get the book out in the right way. This is important for you as well as for me.

Soberly,
DELMORE

/ · /

at p. 70: On pp. 69–70 of *Genesis,* Schwartz begins to account for the naming of the child, Hershey Green. This is material he had well rehearsed in *Shenandoah.*

Nardi: Marcia Nardi, poet and protégé of William Carlos Williams. At William's behest, a large group of her poems appeared *ND* 7.

Jarrell's sentence: Jarrell had pronounced Schwartz "the most promising extensive poet of the time" in his review of *ND 41* (*Partisan Review,* 9, July–August 1942).

116. TLS-1   January 19, 1943

DEAR JAY:

I accept Plan B, if only to halt the flow of insane and drunken letters. However, in the interests of truth and my own intelligence and self-respect, may I point out that these fantasies of your not publishing *Genesis* and of selling my past and future works to another publisher—do not impress me. If you will inspect the contract you will see that if you do not publish the work by the 1st of February (time being of the essence of the agreement), you lose possession of the work. Not only that, but you are not one to let another publisher get all the credit that this work will gain.

Most of the facts you cite about how you have lost money in publishing my other works are of an inaccuracy which must have been inspired by an extreme and may I say unchristian desire for your ten percent.

You can have your ten per cent up to five thousand dollars on these conditions, neither of which seem very difficult to me, though God only knows what is going on in you these days:

1) You do not go away until the book is published;

2) You actually act as agent for my novels whenever it seems best that you do so. . . .

Make up the new contract and I will sign it when the book has been published. This letter will have to be your guarantee until then. I have no aversion to accepting the money of other publishers, now that you want me to do it.

I also want a contract right now for writing the preface to the James stories. I have begun going over them in order to make a list.

Among other inaccuracies, you say that you printed only 800 copies of *IDBR*. Look in the back and see; thus you prove that you have lost money on that book.

If you can get the book out within the next months, you will have a real success. The latest proofs have come and I will get them back tomorrow or the next day.

I am letting you have your way not because you deserve ten per cent of my putative earnings, nor because I fear that you will not publish my book, nor because I am impatient. O no! It is just that I do not have the leisure for the drawn-out battle which would leave you sorry. May I close by remarking that five thousand dollars is a demand which Hitler would characterize as non-Aryan, if our parts were reversed? Nevertheless (who knows why) I like you and am loyal.

Sincerely,
DELMORE

/ · /

Look in the back: The colophon of *IDBR* reads: "One thousand copies of *In Dreams Begin Responsibilities* were printed for New Directions at the Walpole Printing Office in October and November 1938."

117. TLS-2   Monday morning
                                             January 25, 1943

DEAR JAY:

Many thanks for the encouraging letter, which comes just at the right time. I will bear it next to my heart forever.

Matthiessen, Van Doren, Berryman, Blackmur,

Aiken and Agee (all of whom have told me that this or that effort of mine was no good) say that this poem is very good. You say it is no good. Mary Colum wrote me that I ought to work longer on it. The score is thus six against two.

You may be right and they may be wrong. Everyone is right once in a while. But for large-scale irresponsibility you have no equal in our time. Why did you not read the manuscript when I sent it to you in October? Answer me that. If you had said then, what you say now, I would gladly have considered waiting until the war was over. (During the post-war period, everyone will forget what has been published during the war, the whole mood will be different, etc. and this work will—with Books Two and Three—be just right.)

PR is going to ask Matthiessen to review it. Blackmur is reviewing it for the *Kenyon,* and Agee *may* review it for *Time*. Kazin is very friendly, Margaret Marshall sends me books for review, and there is a growing tendency to hysterical praise going on, anyway. All you have to do by way of campaigning is to visit Adams and Irita Van Doren, and also, write letters to Margaret Marshall and Fadiman, unless he has told you that he does not like me, anymore. No editor likes to print damning reviews, no editor except Dwight Macdonald; if you warn Adams against Peter Jack and Mary Colum, in tactful terms; if you tell Irita Van Doren what Mark said of the book and that Eda Lou Walton and Babette Deutsch hate me; if you suggest to both of these people that Louis Untermeyer would be above the battle in a way that most poets would not: then everything may turn out all right. The worst that can happen is that they will either not print unfavorable reviews at all, or that they will print them nine months later. The same thing is true of Fadiman; if he does not like the book, he will say nothing; if he likes it, he may take it away from Louise Bogan, who has been preparing to damn it since early summer by making denunciatory general remarks about over-intellectual poets.

Meanwhile Matthiessen is preparing to lecture on it, as soon as it comes out, to his class in modern poetry; although all these delays may make it come out when the course is over, because all the upper classmen will have departed.

The really regrettable thing about all these efforts (which are, let us frankly admit it, neither noble nor honest) is that I may never know who was right about the book, you or Berryman. Melville went to the grave thinking that *Moby Dick* was a failure because the stupid reviewers of the day said that it was. Stupid reviews so inhibited him that he could not write any more.

In any case, I doubt very much that my reputation stands or falls by this book. I am glad you cut down the edition to 1000 copies. If this is the flop you think it will be, then I want the rest of the paper for a new book just like *IDBR,* containing a story, a play, a sixty-page poem, and forty lyrics. The story is "America, America!", which was a big hit.

The play is about an evening in Cambridge in the late Eighties; William and Henry James are trying to elicit, with the utmost gentility, from Henry Adams, the reason why Mrs. Adams killed herself one fine morning; Adams leads them on, teases them, tells them nothing and goes home to burn all his diaries and letters etc. The three great men all talk in their own late styles. I mention all this because a quick follow-up might be good whether *Genesis* is a flop or not. In any case, that paper belongs to me.

But to return to your fears: Look in your files for a carbon copy of a letter you wrote to Cap Pearce in

November 1938; you will see that you told him you were afraid *IDBR* would be a flop. Later, as the reviews appeared, you became very enthusiastic; in fact, the reviews made you so curious you actually read the long poem which was the backbone of the book!

Another thing which puzzles me: the jacket prose is an excellent account of the book, apart from the misuse of the word, "rationalize." Why then do you find the voices so meaningless? They explain the true chain of causes for each important episode: They do so dramatically and emotionally, thinking of their own lives. This dramatic and emotional presentation makes for surprises and excitements which are poetic, or so I have been told by six critics. The last episode is the conclusion of childhood:

> Childhood was ended here! or innocence
> —Henceforth suspicious of experience

And the chorus tells the protagonist that the road-house denunciation will have an important effect on his later life and that the fundamental question or problem in life is, Does God exist or not? The obsession comes in later, in Book Two. What you have, up to this point, is the picture of a child being engendered. It is much less inconclusive than any volume of Pound's *Cantos*.

However, it is pointless to argue with you. We will see. Enclosed are quotations for the back jacket and comment on your blurb. As I said, I doubt that quotations will do any good, but they will, at any rate, save your face, if you are afraid you are disgracing yourself by publishing this work.

Just between the two of us, when did you read the page proofs? The last fifteen minutes before going to sleep every night, after a hard day of insulting letters and skiing? The time to read a new work is in the morning when one is well; but in the morning, as I know, you read your mail.

Now, instead of sleeping at night, I will spend my time arguing with your billet doux. I hope this pleases you.

Sincerely,
DELMORE

P.S. The shift from "he" to "I" on p. 188 was a deliberate device. Hershey is moved to forget his third-person objectivity and speak of himself in the first person by his emotion at that point.

/ · /

Aiken: Conrad Aiken (1889–1973), American poet and fiction writer. ND published his poem, *The Soldier,* in 1944.

Agee: James Agee.

Mary Colum: Wife of Padraic Colum.

rest of the paper: Publishers were assigned limited allotments of paper during World War II.

a big hit: "America, America!" appeared in *Partisan Review,* 7 (March–April 1940), 112–34. (Omitted from the Zucker bibliography.)

Enclosed are quotations: Schwartz included blurbs from Blackmur and Matthiessen, among others. The book's jacket, as published, contained no blurbs; the back was a full-page advertisement for other New Directions books.

118. TLS-1

692 Wisconsin Street
San Francisco, Cal.
April 25, 1943

DEAR DELMORE:

The Progressive Book Club has offered to buy up fifty or so of *Genesis* for 25 cents and use them as bonuses.

Please see the enclosed leaflet for how they do this with Jarrell, etc.

I am for this. It will move some books. What do you say? May I pay you a royalty of a nickel on these 25-cent sales? Let me but know quickly. Hopefully,

J

119. TLS-1   20 Ellery St.
                                Cambridge, Mass.
                                May 20, 1943

DEAR JAY:

Will you, both as a good in itself and as a personal favor to me, give William Phillips one of the Makers books to write? I don't know whether you are any longer interested in personal favors to me, it is hard to think so, although I would like to think so. But in any case, Phillips is a first-rate critic, probably the best of the *PR* boys, and he is stuck in a curious way, he has been involved in a major project which keeps becoming more difficult and ambitious, while his wife has supported him by working at a miserable job. A short but solid piece of work would free his conscience.

I mention this to explain my own interest, not yours. If you want to be sure how good he is, ask Lionel Trilling or Edmund Wilson, or for that matter, Mary McCarthy. You would not have to give him any money, only a contract, and then if you did not like the book, you would not have to publish it.

Will you let me know right off? Phillips is interested in Gide, but there are a dozen other authors he could do as well.

Again, if you are interested, there will be at least

two reviews of *Genesis* with sentences in them such as my first book was given. If you want to, one solid advertisement in the *Times* would do more than a dozen advertisements elsewhere to get copies bought, especially with these quotations. Meanwhile I have a whole throng of letters from strangers and from friends which say how interesting and important this book is, but I hesitate to send them to you, for you may merely quote the house whore and Margaret back at me again.

Goodman, on the other hand, went from place to place to get a review and found only *The New Leader* willing to permit him to vent his jealousy. Will you let me know what you think of this?

I hear that you asked Matthiessen to write an introduction to the stories of James at the same time that you asked me. Let me know also what I am to make of this. Fortunately M. mentioned this to me, before I mentioned it to him; otherwise he should have thought I had taken it from him and I would have lost the friendship of one who gained me my job.

Yours,
Delmore

/ · /

Lionel Trilling: (1905–1975), American critic and professor. ND published his *E. M. Forster* (1943) in The Makers of Modern Literature Series.

Mary McCarthy: (1912–1989), American critic and novelist.

The Stories of James: The aforementioned collection of stories of writers and artists, edited by Matthiessen (1944).

120. TLS-1   Saturday

DEAR DELMORE:

I am glad that you like the poems. I think your idea of printing them in *PR* a good one. I would hate to get the *ND* volume in trouble on account of my personal politics.

But I think it would be important that Dwight should take half destructive and half constructive ones. They compliment each other and either kind without the other give a wrong impression of my position.

I am enclosing a letter for him which you can show him when you show him the poems. As those are my only copies, you probably better not send them off to Nantucket, but just hold them till he comes to you.

No, I don't see any objection to using a subtitle on *Genesis*. We have advertised it already a good deal as *Genesis*, so I wouldn't submerge that altogether. It could be,

GENESIS
Part I
Made in America

Or something like that.

How is it going? When should one anticipate the manuscript? I am more or less resigned to seeing the book out in 1950, but am curious just the same.

We are doing an enormous business these days. It would appear that *ND* has finally "gotten through." Many orders from soldiers in camps.

J

/ · /

the poems: Unidentified. None were published in *Partisan Review*.

a subtitle: The book was published without subtitle.

in 1950: Though undated, this letter was written in 1943; JL is making a joke.

121. TLS-1   June 12, 1943

DEAR JAY:

Here is a suitable quotation from Profound Eberhart to add to the ones I sent you last Sunday:

Genesis represents a triumph and control over time and events, in their inexhaustible meanings, the triumph of an elaborate plan. There is such freshness of perception, such understanding of childhood, such a cohesion and order in the writing, and indeed such splendid areas of poetic feeling, that one acknowledges the satisfaction of a harmonious work of art.

One good ad in the *Times* on Sunday, where I will be writing reviews soon, will repay the expense.

I want you to send me a contract for my next book. My novel is finished, but it is a big thing, it will take time to get ready to print by whoever I give it to, and I want to let it cool off, anyway. The book I want a contract for will have five stories, one hundred pages in all, and an equal number of pages of verse. You have already seen three of the stories, "America, America!", "The Commencement Day Address" (but in a new version), and "The Statues"; one of the others is going to be printed by *Partisan Review* and another one will be in *Best Short Stories of 1942*. The poems are a selection from the hundred written during the past five years, many about America, so that

I think a good title would be, "America, America!" Will you write a contract right off, binding yourself to publish the volume by April 1944? I don't want to have the Matthiessen business occur again, and if you don't want it, I intend to get another publisher for it right now, but in that case I will give you my novel and whether you want it or not, the terms of my contract will have been fulfilled. I don't intend to print the second and third books of *Genesis* until the war and the war books subside. Send me the contract immediately, or a waiver, for I am free of school now for the last time in the next six months, and this is the only time I can go to New York with the manuscript.

Yours,
DELMORE

/ · /

Eberhart: Richard G. Eberhart (b. 1904), American poet. His *Poems New & Selected* was published by ND in 1944, and his *Selected Poems,* also a ND book, won the Pulitzer Prize.

"The Commencement Day Address": When Schwartz published his next collection, eventually called *The World Is a Wedding,* he did not reprint this story; it was not gathered in a book by Schwartz until 1978, when James Atlas included it in the selection *In Dreams Begin Responsibilities and Other Stories.*

one of the others: "New Year's Eve" was to appear in *Partisan Review,* 7 (Summer 1945), 327–61.

Best Short Stories of 1942: "An Argument in 1934," which Schwartz did not reprint.

second and third books of Genesis: They were never published. Sections of *Genesis,* Book II, were included in the revised edition of *Last & Lost Poems* (1989), pp. 122–34.

122. TL-1   August 16, 1943

DEAR JAY:

I'd like to have a new play in verse in the P of M
series, the one about the James boys trying to find
out from Henry Adams why his wife destroyed herself. I have no title yet and also I may be deluded
about its merit, so that you ought only to announce
A New Play in Verse, and if I don't feel as I now do
about it by Christmas, we can use the homosexual-
Faust play you read in the dead days of 1938.

Also I want you to look carefully at a mss by
George Palmer which I will send you in a week. The
poems are certainly worth a pamphlet, and Palmer
will pay the expense of printing up to $300.

Jackson Matthews has translated Valéry's "La Jeune
Parque," which is indeed a great poem, and if he was
willing and you wanted me to, I'd write a short
introduction. The only other possibility who occurs
to me is Alfred Young Fisher. Berryman *does* and
Jarrell *may* have some good new poems.

I can't possibly get the mss. of *AA* to you so soon.
You can see two of the new unpolished stories if you
like, and provided you express no opinion of them.
But I now have to correct 257 papers a week for my
Navy classes, and there will be no let-up until October. In any case, it would be foolish to publish *AA*
before a year has passed. Will you tell me how long
the book can be? The lyrics continue to accumulate.
You will get the mss. by Nov.

Gertrude and I have been separated since March
and it is very sad, but for the poor best. In June, after
one of the best farces in Harvard's history, I was given
a five-year appointment.

The war will be over long before some of my Navy

boys learn how to spell. For my pains, I receive charming notes which read, FUCK THE JEWS, and once a swastika on the placard with my name on it in front of my office.

Faber & Faber are publishing volumes of selected poems by such great lights as David Gascoyne, Vernon Watkins, and Henry Treece. It occurs to me that you might persuade them to publish either *Genesis* or a volume of selections of mine, by offering to pay the expenses or send them sheets and saying that you want to get me started in England. I will give you the money for this, for I've just had a belated windfall, modest but delightful, from my father's estate. If you tell anyone I am involved in this, however, it will truly be the last of your crimes against me, though none will equal the gratuitous denunciation of a new book on the eve of publication, when it was too late to do anything about it. Enclose a sample of the reviews of *Genesis* & *IDBR*.

Let me know about this English business immediately, for I have other things to do with the money.

Auden has been here on weekends, with scenes of comedy hardly to be equalled, the two of us composing verse in parallel rooms and becoming irritable about who was to have the only eraser in the house, or my effort to explain baseball to him. He finds a doubleplay incomprehensible.

I think seriously of taking up with a black girl, like Baudelaire, in order to épater Cambridge. The difficulty is that I don't like black girls, I like girls with an education, pale.

Genesis received quite favorable reviews in *The Nation, New Republic, Kenyon,* and *Partisan,* which certainly means that you ought to keep your promise of tying them together with one big ad somewhere—the *Times* or the *New Republic.*

/ · /

the one about the James boys: Schartz titled this play *Marianne,* mispelling
Marian Adams's (Mrs. Henry Adams) first name. The manuscript has
not survived.

the homosexual-Faust play: Venus in the Back Room.

George Palmer: George Anthony Palmer, R. P. Blackmur's Cambridge
cousin, who published poetry under the name "George Anthony."

Jackson Matthews: Translator and critic. He co-edited (with Marthiel
Matthews) a bilingual edition of *The Flowers of Evil* by Charles Baudelaire, which ND published in 1955.

Paul Valéry: Ambroise Toussaint Jules Paul Valéry (1871–1945), French
poet and critic. ND published *Selected Writings of Paul Valéry* in 1950.

A.A.: America, America! No ND book with this typically Schwartzian
title was published. The title was later used by Elia Kazan for his novel.

since March: Gertrude Buckman Schwartz had left Cambridge—and
Schwartz—and returned to New York.

David Gascoyne: (b. 1916), Contemporary British poet.

Vernon Watkins: (1906–1967), Welsh poet, friend of Dylan Thomas.
ND published five of his books between 1948 and 1968.

Henry Treece: (1912–1966), British poet, novelist, and critic. In 1949,
ND published his *New Romantic Anthology.*

123. TLS-1   Monday

DEAR JAY:

The magazine seems like a very good idea in several ways. For one thing, it is an opportunity to cash
in on all the capital built up by *PR, SR,* and *KR.*

You don't have to pay five dollars a page. *PR* pays
two and does better than the other two. If the whole
thing is a success, the pay can be moved up.

A tentative title would be: *New Europe.* The program would be, in part, the hypothesis that Europe
is through, but that something has to be done to
carry on the greatness of European culture. (Thus,
lively articles on Horace by people like MacNeice.)

But in addition and as the main burden, the program would be to carry on a large-scale attack on

popular culture. Not so much space given to exegesis on minor poems of T. S. Eliot, as detailed criticism of Hollywood, Broadway, popular novels, comic strips, *NY Times* editorials and poems, the prose of *Time* and the photos of *Life*. As a war-cry, one might say, let us overcome the gulf between popular culture and advance guard culture.

Meanwhile one would also continue some of the *KR* and *SR*'s special kind of literary criticism.

But I think with the definite program of taking popular culture seriously, one would have a real chance at success.

The editorship ought to be announced as James Laughlin and Delmore Schwartz, for various reasons, even if you are off somewhere.

For various reasons, including the draft, the fact that I would be quitting my instructorship ought to be kept quiet. If I can manage a leave of absence, it would be much better than just quitting, obviously.

The two keynotes of the business would be that, Europe is the greatest thing in America (a fact dramatized in *Genesis*) but the next greatest thing in America is Hollywood; and between those two large-scale cultural factors, the future of culture lies.

There are a good many other possibilities, even within a forty-eight page issue, but this should be enough as a starting point. The idea would be to announce the thing soon and come out with a first issue in October. Let me know how all this impresses you.

DELMORE

/ · /

The magazine: JL proposed a new publication which did not materialize. Instead, his name was to appear in 1952–56 on the masthead of *Perspectives,* the Ford Foundation–sponsored magazine that was published for four years in English, French, German, and Italian editions; and on *Diogenes,* published by the International Council for Philosophy and Humanistic Studies, in 1952–54 in an English-language edition.

the greatest thing in America: A notion Schwartz explores in his poem "The Greatest Thing in North America." See *Last & Lost Poems,* p. 21.

124. TLS-1   [N.D.]

DEAR JAY:

Do you think you can stop screwing in that relay team long enough to send me a check to come to Romantic Alta? No haggling, I am not interested in fame or fortune or screwing, though I don't intend to turn them down. I *must* come to Alta and see you and I have only ten days.

The enclosed, you will note, is a *Times* review damning three poets. If you have the time to read over Karenina's shoulder, read the Sunday *Times* every week henceforward.

Altabound,
D

P.S. Set aside the best-looking house whore, if I may use your phrase, which will live forever.

I am now what Harry Levin would refer to as a pet Jew, dine only with the Murdochs, and speak only to the Conants, so that you need not think I am of social ambition, nor disagreeable. I want to talk to you, but if you find authors of a difficulty so great, we can write notes and pass them back and forth.

See you soon, unless you are so preoccupied in the Russian that you do not remember how lucky you are to have known me. Note the supreme assurance in this last remark, for a way of determining that I have enough fame, don't care about rivals, have enough money, and can find sex by ringing numbers. I am going through Boston womanhood from A to Z.

/ · /

Karenina's shoulder: Allusion to the fact Laughlin had a Russian girlfriend at the time, Maria Britneva (later Lady St. Just). She was the inspiration for Tennessee Williams's character Maggie the Cat in *Cat on a Hot Tin Roof,* and is a trustee of Williams's estate.

the Murdochs: Kenneth Murdoch and his wife. He was a professor of English at Harvard, who passionately wanted to become president of the university. He lost out to James B. Conant, a scientist.

the Conants: Dr. and Mrs. James B. Conant.

125. TL-2   20 Ellery St.
Cambridge
10.26.43

DEAR JAY:

I am glad that you are curious. It is good for you to be curious, and you will have to wait now with the general public before being enlightened. I was willing to come to Alta, or to meet you halfway in Chicago, but you were too concerned with screwing, skiing, mining and fighting.

Your sentence, "I insist on continuing to publish you" fascinates me. I no longer understand the word, "insist," when you speak or write it. Henceforward you must ask me, politely and handsomely.

You have a contractural right to my first novel and *The Singers* (books two and three of *Genesis*); also *The Imitation of Life,* a work I may not care to publish.

At present, however, I am author of the following unpublished works:

A History of the Boys & the Girls, a beautiful novel, 310 pp.

Eurydice, a short novel, also very beautiful;

The New York Story, a profound work of fiction concerned with life in the big town until the outbreak of the World War to make the world safe for the lesser evil;

America, America!, five stories and one hundred poems;

The World Is a Wedding Day, a book which contains a "symbolic" story, a long poem, forty lyrics, and a play in verse, all composed during the past year.

Marianne, a play about the wife of Henry Adams, in verse, full of brilliant conversation between Henry and William James, Henry Adams, and Mrs. William James. Mrs. Adams appears as a ghost and makes ironic remarks, in verse worthy of Pope, as the others discuss her character and death. "How little they understand," she says, "how little they knew me! Henry was all right for a visit, but I did not care to live with him."

The Irreversible Track, a volume of essays describing the experience of a modern poet who teaches composition and persuades his students to delight in the early works of T. S. Eliot, W. C. Williams, and James Laughlin.

And, since I am industrious, since I write every day, and since I am not a party boy, I have many unfinished opera [sic] which will soon be ready for publication.

Enclosed is the editorial on Pound, which need be only the opening gun. Write your letter as a communication to *Partisan Review* and take as much room as you like. But it occurs to me that to make Pound out as a lunatic might not please either the poor major poet or his family, and if this is just a guess on your part, perhaps you ought to put it quite tentatively. For myself, I'd choose lunacy every time to what is in store for Pound, but who knows how he feels about it? He may prefer to be a traitor.

Child Gertrude left not for the sake of a man, or a woman I must add, knowing your mind; but because she felt guilt about the strain and difficulty she made for me. I don't think you understand or saw her real goodness, despite inadequacies she was unable to do anything about. After all, book-keeping is not the only trial of character.

In your last letter, you say that you merely expressed a negative opinion of *Genesis* privately. But that is just what you did not do; although I asked you to keep your judgement to yourself, you wrote letters all over, saying that you did not like the book but thought it deserved a serious review. I don't know if you were trying to cover yourself, or just not thinking, but surely nothing can do a book more harm than to have the publisher say in advance that he does not think it is any good. So too, you quarreled with Margaret Marshall ostensibly because ND books were not being handled well, actually because your pretended indifference to criticism had been penetrated by a brief remark about yourself in a review of the Pindar translation. Your letter made her very angry and since my book was one reason for the letter, she had to show her independence to you by holding back Jones' favorable review from April until August.

Members of the English department received marked copies of Goodman's review of my book. How do you like that? Was he not an old whore? He is.

One more ad, a new one, with new quotations, in *The New Republic,* and then you will have somewhat kept your promise, and I will be at peace; until the next book.

As postscript to the note about Berryman, if you give him a pamphlet, I can get it for review in the *Times.*

Will you write to Matthews, and suggest that I write two introductory pages on Valéry after you have seen his translation and decided if you want to print it?

If you don't want to be my heir, my feelings will not be hurt; but if you do, it seems that I must write in your date of birth? What is it?

Can it be, do you think, that you have some Jewish blood? Is this possible? Some of your behaviour suggests certain descriptions of—

No, it is too unlikely.

I see that you are now calling Edmund Wilson a drunkard. You really ought to stop fighting. If Wilson omits certain references to his friends and himself in the Fitzgerald, one of his reasons may be simple concern for the feelings of the living.

Letters from fans are mounting now, both in volume and in incoherence, and *IDBR* is being translated into Spanish for the benefit of Latin-America, a country recently discovered by Dudley Fitts, although he cast overboard his sense of meter on the voyage.

Unable to sleep the other night, I read in a periodical that a man in Calcutta has not slept for two years.

/ · /

America, America!: By now Schwartz had dropped the notion of including a play in this ms. *The World Is a Wedding Day* (later shortened to simply *The World Is a Wedding*) was to contain a play in verse plus lyrics. Ultimately the book was all fiction.

"How little they understand": Schwartz must have read or seen Thornton Wilder's *Our Town* (1938). In Act II of that play, Emily, come back from the dead, declares of the living, "They don't understand much, do they?"

what is in store for Pound: In World War II, Ezra Pound broadcast Fascist propaganda to the United States for the Italians and was indicted for treason. He was never brought to trial, however, because he was judged to be of unsound mind, and came to St. Elizabeths Hospital in Washington, D.C., where he remained for thirteen years.

the Pindar translation: Some Odes of Pindar, translated by Richmond Lattimore, published by ND in the Poets of the Year series, 1942.

Goodman's review: Paul Goodman's review, appearing in *The New Leader,* called *Genesis* a "combination of ineptitude and earnestness," and bemoaned its "calamitous lack of language" as well as "inaccurate learning."

recently discovered by Dudley Fitts: Fitts had edited *An Anthology of Contemporary Latin American Poetry,* published by ND in 1942.

126. TLS-4   [Date missing]

[First 2 pp. missing]

. . . It is clear, is it not, that fame and fortune are mine, especially since, if I may improve upon a revolutionary hero of the past, I have just begun to write.

My chief weakness or Achilles' heel is an irrational devotion to you. However, I am even more devoted to my self, and to good behavior, and your conduct during the last year—Matthiessen, duress before publication, spite or insensitivity about publication matters, quarrels with one and all, and your complete lack of responsibility—has done much to teach me how costly it is to be devoted to you.

It is possible for us to continue on a new basis by means of several plans, all of which will have to be confirmed in front of witnesses: (The following need not be in conflict with my new publishing venture):

Plan A: You give me a half-interest in New Directions. This is the best plan of all, but I know that, smart as you are, you are not smart enough to see how profitable this would be for you. Since it does not seem likely that this plan will delight you or impress you with its infinite practicality, I pass on to Plan B;

Plan B: You mail me a check for two thousand dollars as a retainer for my services as editor and author during the coming year. This is not as an advance, just as payment for services to be rendered the publishing house. This plan must be put into effect within eight days or the check will have to be augmented by five hundred dollars. After two weeks have elapsed, there will be no more price rises because it will be too late. I will have gone to New York and transferred my services elsewhere.

This plan, too, does not strike me as being likely to win your approval. If it does not, I do not really care very much, I will prosper with more responsible characters who care less for skiing and insulting sensitive human beings.

Supposing then that you are not shrewd enough to seize upon either of these plans, there remains the question of previous agreements. Since I am an honest person, I am prepared to give you the two books promised you, the work of fiction and the sequel to *Genesis,* once you have kept some of your broken promises and made some new ones of an unfinancial nature.

Thus, *Plan C:* You must send me a complete accounting of my royalties, give me a contract for an introduction to Flaubert's *Three Tales* to requite me for the Matthiessen business, write me a letter apologizing for your reference in various quarters to Gertrude and Emily as "those lice in Cambridge," sign a statement saying that any such unfavorable remarks will void any contractual agreements entered into in the future, and pay me the fifty-seven cents a copy for each copy of my first book above the cost of publication, an item stated in our initial contract which, I am told, you have broken in a dozen ways, many of them stated in your succinct prose which Robert Fitzgerald once compared to Mozart.

I trust that whatever your emotions at the moment are, you will be reasonable enough to consider the fact that your criminal behavior is a matter which can be proven by other human beings and by your own letters. Meanwhile, I really don't demand an adherence to any of these plans. You can just disregard them. Each of them is a request for what is my just due, but I am perfectly content to forget about them. But since you have broken our contract in various ways, I will then have to consider it broken. There is no publisher in the country who would not be delighted to publish what I write, and there are several who are prepared to prove in court that you have broken your contract, if you are foolish enough to start a costly legal struggle in which your method of behavior comes out into the open.

I have not yet signed a contract for *America, America!*, and I do not intend to, unless equity is restored and I have a real guarantee that you will not in the future behave in such a fashion as to make life difficult for me: Such as abusing literary editors, applying duress on the eve of publication by threatening not to publish an already-printed book, losing mss. for months at a time, endangering my relationships with friends such as Matthiessen, insulting my wife (whose inefficiency was less than her predecessor's and who in any case did nothing to warrant your touching tribute), disturbing me with reports of conspiracies, and not promoting a book properly (as in the instance of *Genesis*) because of spite or timorousness or penuriousness or skiing.

All of this is merely a postcript, you will recognize, to the period last March when you taught me a lesson once and for all by writing me of Plans A and B. And all I want by way of restitution is either peace to go my own way, or two, the guarantee that so far as I am concerned, you will recognize and act upon the profound truth that Honesty is the best policy. That is the reason that Plan A strikes me as the most brilliant of the lot.

Our six years' association, so fruitful to you, so fruitful and difficult for me, opened with a letter in which you called me a crook. It continued by your opening a letter to me from Harcourt, Brace, a violation of the laws about the mail. It reached great humiliation when Gertrude and I were unloaded at Baton Rouge so that you might have more room for baggage and a whore. It achieved a height of torment when my translation of Rimbaud appeared, and although you behaved with much kindness then, nevertheless this would not have occurred if I had been with a responsible publisher and if I had not been forced by poverty to live at Yaddo, far from anyone to consult about my translation. Told of this poverty in the early fall, you sent me a check for $150., a handsome reward to an author who had just helped very much to give the publishing house and publisher an immense success. There is no need to continue with these memoirs; my purpose is to see that such episodes do not occur again.

I don't think you have any idea of the amount of ill-will you have accumulated in important places. Thus, the fact that you did little or nothing with Trilling's book is going to keep other critics who might do as well from writing in that series. You can always get the third-rate, but that will do no good, especially since the first-rate authors will write for others. What chance, for example do you think I have for the kind of success my book on Eliot ought to have, if you are too intent on skiing to make provision for new editions? I say nothing of the difficulty of merely buying a book from New Directions, such is the character of your office.

Once again, I refer to the fact that if you had been willing to listen to me, you would have published Karl Shapiro and Eudora Welty. As a perhaps last piece of advice, I suggest that you act quickly in order not to lose a poet, critic, playwright, editor and teacher who has added much to the prestige, prosperity, and character of New Directions. If you look with care through the new list or catalogue, you will see that so far as success goes, half of the credit is just sheer luck, half is divided in equal parts: One, your money and energy and ambition; two, my ideas, or the direction you went in because of my interests as a critic, or my initial success. You ought also to regard the list from the point of view of the possibility of another author, old or young, being capable of my many activities, no matter how much you promoted him. Williams, Patchen, Fitts, even Miller's lucid pornography, or Harry Brown, Paul Goodman, Robert Hivnor, Tennessee Williams, and whatever candidate attracts you at the moment.

As a reward, I've received some fifteen hundred dollars, many psychological attacks, and the news that you speak of my former wife, to whom I remain devoted, as "one of those lice in Cambridge," a remark not made in a moment's emotion, but typed and mailed.

Now if you are really sensible, you will not resort to charm, or anger, or threats, or anything but the decent behavior I have outlined above; which will not cost you anything, if you wish to save money in that pathological manner which leads to many of your worst errors. Don't take the trouble to break away from the pleasures of Utah in order to converse and dicker with me, because within two weeks it will be too late and you will learn as never before that Honesty is the best policy, it pays to be good, and you have cast a pearl away.

I remain devoted to you, although I don't know why. If you want to take the alternative of just calling off all bets, then our friendship can continue and be renewed on an uncommercial and disinterested level, though Utah is quite distant. But the best beginning would be a check and an apology.

Yours affectionately,
DELMORE

/ · /

Robert Fitzgerald: (1910–1985), American poet and translator. ND published his *Poems* in 1935 and *Spring Shade* in 1971.

period last March: It was actually January. See Schwartz to JL, Letter 115, January 12, 1943.

Trilling's book: E. M. Forster by Lionel Trilling (1943).

127. TLS-1   Nov. 2, 1943

DEAR JAY:

How amiable of you to turn the other cheek. Your reply, however, is full of illusions and hallucinations which I do not have time to discuss, except to say that it is necessary for you to send me a royalty statement for *IDBR, SH, Shenandoah,* and *Genesis* without delay; also a statement of how many copies of my first book were published. Include with the statement a payment in full of all arrears. If you hesitate, it will be one more nuisance for me when I visit New York late next week; but it will be far more than a nuisance for you. Or do you insist on digging your own grave? I will come and weep sour nostalgic tears at your tomb.

Your true friend,
DELMORE

/ · /

SH: Rimbaud's *A Season in Hell.*

128. TLS-1   Nov. 20, 1943
                                                    Cambridge

DEAR JAY:

I am glad to read in your letter that you are happy with your hallucinations. Few things are more desirable to me than your happiness, though I wish it might be secured without hallucination. Moreover, the euphoria sometimes becomes dangerous as aficionados of drug and delusion find out in the end.

For example the royalty statements you sent me might, in kindness, be described as sheer impressionism. An enemy might say they were dishonest. I prefer to term them hallucinated. How else can one explain the fact that in the statement of September 1941 you said that only seventy-five copies of my first book remained and no sheets were available; but now there are more than two hundred copies available? A remarkable book and a remarkable publisher; with the passage of time the number of copies sold all told diminishes! This is but one of many remarkable facts which can be found by comparing previous royalty sheets with the ones you sent me, such as extraordinary arithmetic which, however due to a lack of mathematical gifts, succeeds always in keeping more money in your pocket than belongs there. Since life in Utah affords you such happiness, you will not mind my unhappiness about your imprudent and ill-advised dealings, in these and other matters.

What, by the way, is the reference to foreign royalties for *A Season in Hell, 2*? How is it that almost six hundred copies of *Genesis* have been sold without the natural augmentation of the sales of the first book and *Shenandoah*? What insanity persuades you to write that I bought one hundred and sixty-nine dollars worth of copies of my first book? That would mean more than one hundred copies. Do you think that I have lost my mind and memory? I was given twenty copies and I bought perhaps five more. Have you been drinking again? Will you let me know the views on this subject of the house whore and your wife, since you let me know how they viewed *Genesis*?

I enclose a review which may suggest once more what a loss you have endured in losing my services as an editor. Left to yourself, you would by now have published four books by Whiz Bang. Under different cover, I am sending you back mss. you sent me, since I am no longer involved in this; and also two mss. by Alfred Young Fisher which he requested me to send to you.

Your query as to when you will receive the mss. of *America, America!* is interesting. You will receive it when I send it to you. This is undeniable. But if you think I intend to send it to Utah, you are even more hallucinated than I had feared. It is now some other author's turn to have his mss. misplaced for three months.

Ski!
DELMORE

/ · /

A Season in Hell, 2: Reference to the second edition—the revised translation—of Rimbaud's work, which appeared in JL's New Classics Series.
your wife: Laughlin had married Margaret Keyser of Salt Lake City.
Whiz Bang: Kenneth Patchen.

129. TLS-1   August 29, 1944

DEAR JAY:

I don't in the least know how many copies of *Genesis* were printed. Each time I look at the royalty sheets I begin to feel cross-eyed.

Last week, I wrote you, at Norfolk, that *America, America!* was in the process of being typed out, and that the book on Eliot would soon be finished. The sooner the book of poems and stories is printed, the sooner the Eliot book can appear. You might as well brace yourself now for the painful process of inscribing a check for five hundred dollars for the latter, for copies will be bought forever.

How about mentioning some of my books in your ads?

With a little effort, you would be able to get a printer to put out *America, America!* before Xmas, which would be a good and prosperous thing.

Four times during the past year I have forced myself not to comment on certain acts of yours, but as a devoted friend, in spite of all, I will permit myself to say, although you will hate me for it and commit some devious revenge at a later date, that Nabokov's *Gogol* should never have been printed, or at least the references to you should have been eliminated. In unreal Utah you have no idea of how they impinge upon the literary world. Though it is too late to do anything about this now, you ought not to permit such things to occur again.

Yours earnestly,
SCHWARTZ

/ · /

Nabokov's Gogol: ND published Vladimir Nabokov's *Nikolai Gogol* in The Makers of Modern Literature Series (1944). Edmund Wilson hailed it as "one of the best volumes so far in the interesting series," *Classics and Commercials* (New York: Farrar, Straus, 1950), p. 216. Nabokov used to twit JL that there were numerous legpulls at his expense in the text; JL could never find them—although Schwartz apparently thought he did.

130. TL-1   September 17, 1944

DEAR JAY:

The new book consists of 135 typewritten pages; this estimate does not include the title pages for the different parts, however. *IDBR* was 160 pages, if the auxiliary pages are not included. The new book has four stories, which ought to be kept apart, I think; and a long poem or suite of poems. I want the titles of the different parts set in capitals.

Will you please be certain to keep enough paper for the book on Eliot? It ought to appear next summer or next fall. I think that I will get a leave of absence from teaching, beginning next March, and I must count on the Eliot book for the only funds with which to support myself.

If you like, you might review your promise—in a letter in 1942—that you would give me a stipend of $600 a year for my poetry and criticism, if *Genesis* were a success; which, so far as I am concerned, it was. If you don't want to go through with this, then I wish you would arrive with a clear-cut idea of the extent of my obligation to you for future books. So far as I can make out, I owe you the book of critical essays, the sequel and conclusion to *Genesis,* and the advance on my novel; and also the book on Eliot.

I must give the novel, the first version of which is written, to a commercial publisher, if I am ever to try to earn a living as an author. I like teaching very much, but it takes a great deal of time, and other matters in addition to enjoyment are involved. I should think that by this time you would know if I was worth a permanent investment on the part of ND, as a poet and critic; and also you should be able to afford the expenditure. In any case, will you decide before arriving in Cambridge. The question is simple enough to make discussion unnecessary.

Of the two kinds of paper, I like the white vellum better. Most of the poetry is iambic pentameter.

Your preface to the new anthology, which I am reviewing for *The Nation,* inspires in me some perplexity.

Yours,

/ · /

the new anthology: New Directions 1944, which Schwartz reviewed in *The Nation,* October 21, 1944, 476–77.

DEAR DELMORE:

Many thanks for the information about the book. We are coming to Cambridge Sunday, will be at the Commander, and I hope we can have some tennis and general literary discussion unrelated to personal problems.

In regard to your future plans: I don't think you ought to count on any very substantial sums from me. My plans for New Directions during the next two or three years are going to be subordinated to my own desire—and great psychic need—to express *myself* directly in my own writings. Don't laugh, but a good analyst whom I have been consulting tells me that I simply must stop sublimating my interest in writing into other writers. In other words, the idea of sponsoring you as my writing self by a subsidy— which is what we once planned—is just the thing which would be most destructive to my personality and lead to inevitable bad feeling between us.

Therefore I plan during the next few years to concentrate on my own writing. I shall keep New Directions going, but do fewer and perhaps better books. Naturally I want to include some of yours in this number and will give them stronger promotion than I have in the past, because the list will be smaller and more selective.

I think the fair thing to do about the novel is for you to let me read it when it is finished and have me make you an offer which will include two guarantees—the sum which I would guarantee you in royalties and the sum which I would agree to spend on advertising. If these didn't compare favorably with other offers you could then repay the advance and

be free to give the novel to someone else. How does
that strike you?

On the Eliot book, I have the feeling that he may
still write some major works and that it might be
better to hold off for a few years on that. It would
be a shame to have the book put out of date by some
later development in his career. Why don't you concentrate your efforts now on the novel, which will,
after all, bring you in a far greater return than the
Eliot book would.

Best wishes & see you soon,

132. TLS-1   Thursday

DEAR JAY:

Since I have gone to the trouble of doing a great
deal of work on the Eliot book, and since you asked
me to do it some time ago, you might as well decide
right now to give me a contract for it. Otherwise all
bets are off, and it would be foolish for you to waste
your time coming here. You get nothing more from
me until I get that contract, stipulating the date of
publication—you don't have to pay me any advance
until you get the mss.

My book is independent of any great works Eliot
may subsequently write; and this is one occasion when
you are not going to waste my time and work by
your irresponsibility.

Yours,
DELMORE

133. TLS-1   November 1, 1944

DEAR JAY:

I am sorry to be responsible for another delay, but the fourth story, "New Year's Eve," has to be rewritten; and that will take at least two weeks. Can you arrange matters with a printer so that I can send him a mss. directly? I will send you a carbon at the same time so that you can be sure of the innocence of the work.

Many thanks for Rexroth's book. Since you ask for comment, I can only say that though readable, the book seems to me to be a sad rehashing of Poundian method. The passages of description are pleasant to read, but the efforts to versify theory are demonstrably senseless. Rexroth just does not understand the ideas he is writing about. I suspect that he enjoys a spurious feeling of profundity from the very state of *not* understanding the ideas he has found in his reading. On the other hand, a book like this is all right as period poetry: The only thing is, there are about five other younger and far better poets who deserve a volume of their own. It must be friendship and personal charm, and nostalgic associations with Pound, that made you decide to publish the book.

From many quarters I hear of your "charm," "graciousness" and general "amenability." Perhaps you will conclude like St. Francis and Mohammed who also sinned in youth? In any case, good will do New Directions no harm at all.

In exchange for this gratuitous advice, tell me why you thought I ought not to get married: Elena's report? I see no reason why I should not marry at least as often as Katherine Anne Porter.

Please send me back the story I must rewrite and

give my best regards to your beautiful wife. You might tell her that my review of *New Directions* was written before our recent interviews; not that I could have said anything else.

Yours ever,
DIFFICULT

/ · /

Rexroth's book: The Phoenix and the Tortoise, a long poem (1944).

Elena's report: Mrs. Harry Levin.

as often as Katherine Anne Porter: At this time Porter had had four husbands: John Henry Koontz, Ernest Stock, Eugene Dove Pressly, and Albert Erskine. "It was not until their wedding in New Orleans that Erskine, then twenty-six, learned that Porter was nearly fifty." Joan Givner, *Katherine Anne Porter: A Life* (New York: Simon and Schuster, 1982).

134. TLS-1   Jan. 2, 1945

DEAR JAY:

It turns out that I must delay sending you the mss. of *AA* for a period which will, I think, be brief. I trust that you have no objection to a somewhat longer book, longer by no more than twenty pages. This is the reason for the delay. If you're not in a hurry, neither am I. The Eliot book is the one I would like to have put out with speed, since I think it will make money and I need money for my year in New York, which will begin in just six weeks.

I am still trying to translate your Latin verses. Perhaps Life, as heretofore, will in the end illuminate them.

Hurriedly,
DELMORE

/ · /

AA: *America, America!*
my year in New York: Schwartz applied for and received a year's sab-
batical from Harvard since "he had taught more consecutive terms than
anyone else on the faculty" (Atlas, p. 248).

135. TLS-1   Alta Lodge
                                                       Alta, Utah
                                                       [N.D.]

[No salutation]

You speak of going off to NYC. If you have a
Harvard contract I should certainly advise you to hold
on to it. I have some knowledge of those creatures
in the big city and I can tell you they will kiss you
today and cut your throat tomorrow. Strongly I urge
you to recall the wise saying of the folk: All that
which glitters is not true gold. Yes Sir.

Weary not my unhearing ears with tales of Trilling and other miffed or unsatisfied authors. It is true
that things could be conducted a great deal more
actively if I were there, but I prefer to be here, and
prefer a mixed life to a single life. For what is life for
but to enjoy it, and certainly in the scales of happiness a fine day in the bright sun and snow on one of
our mountains here is of more worth than publishing a book by a dyspeptic author. Everything is in
place, I say. A little of this and a little of that and the
whole makes a variety and a pleasure. To take ND
with utter seriousness would be to become soon a
nervous wreck. Is this not true?

Draw what inferences you wish from this letter,
dear Delmore, but believe, I beg you, in my undy-
ing interest in your quaintly abstracted soul and
luminous literatures. And do not fear that I will not

welcome you back to the fold if you have sad and disillusioning experiences in the city for which Babylon is too pleasant a name.

However, one final word. Do not become a cheap writer. Keep up your standards. It is better to be read by 800 readers and be a good writer than be read by all the world and be Somerset Maugham. Alleluia. Who would think that came from Good Time Jack, the barman's delight?

Much snow here,
JAY

/ · /

Somerset Maugham: (1874–1965), Popular English author.

136. ACS-1

Partisan Review
45 Astor Place
New York 3, N.Y.
3 / 3 / 45

I've tried to reach you a number of times. My new address is: 91 Bedford St., N.Y.C. (Between Grove & Barrow Sts.)

DELMORE

137. ACS-1   Partisan Review
                                          45 Astor Place
                                          New York 3, N.Y.
                                          3 / 5 / 45

   Must woo the frigid muse and eat lunch in soli-
tude. How about coming down here and having
dinner in the Village some night this week? You can
leave a message for me at *P.R.*

                                          DELMORE

138. ALS-1   91 Bedford St.
                                          New York City
                                          May 1st, 1945

DEAR JAY:

   Sorry to say that I must postpone the sending of
the mss. for at least one more month. I think this
will be the last delay.
   How are you? I've been ill myself lately. "As we
grow older," says Goethe as he grew older, "our
ordeals become greater."
   What is the meaning of the enclosed clipping?
   Your recent royalty statement was inconsistent
with previous ones, but I have decided to forgive
you everything in the years which remain to us.

                                          With love,
                                          DELMORE

139. TLS-1

20 Ellery St.
Cambridge, Mass.
January 26, 1946

DEAR JAY:

How much time must elapse between my giving you a manuscript and the appearance of the book? I've been asking others to read the fiction I've written during the past year, and perhaps this time I will feel that the book is good enough; or perhaps I won't, as before. But the time between giving the manuscript and the book's being printed is usually an unpleasant waste, and my impression is that now the war is over, matters might be expedited if you wanted to be expeditious.

There is a further question of what I am going to include in the book. It can be a book of ten stories or a book of six stories and a short novel. If you will accept the short novel as a fulfillment of my obligation to give you a novel, then the latter arrangement will do. If not, I had better wait until I see what I can do to the other short novel I wrote during the year and with which I am unsatisfied. When it is repaired, I will then have a book of two short novels and as you doubtless know, short novels are all the cry these days.

The poems I was going to include with the stories I want to keep for a book of poems. As a matter of fact, perhaps I ought to receive the laurel of the New Classics like Patchen and publish a volume of "Selected Poems" next fall, especially since I have new versions of many of my old poems.

Needless to say, I am full of hesitation and I may be dissatisfied with my new pieces when the excitement of writing them is over. But I'd like to know about the above questions right now. The question of the royalty statements can wait, but the fact is, that they make no sense. They ought to be straightened out, if possible, and then we ought to figure out what books are due you, how much money in advances I owe you, and the like.

Yours,
DELMORE

/ · /

20 Ellery St.: Schwartz returned to Cambridge in mid-January 1946.
for a book of poems: This was to become *Vaudeville for a Princess* (1950).

140. ALS-1

20 Ellery St.
Cambridge, Mass.
June 3, 1946

DEAR JAY:

Thanks for your note. I hope to send you a manuscript soon and also to resume our correspondence, your half of which I was rereading with pleasure & new understanding this winter: It seemed to me that we were both perhaps figments of Dostoevsky's imagination, though he never visited Pittsburgh.

When you come to Cambridge, you must meet my cat, Oranges Schwartz, who does the *entre-chat* for Pussy-Willows' sake and is having an affair with the fattest tom-cat I ever saw.

As ever,
DELMORE

/ · /

Oranges Schwartz: This cat was immortalized in a poem by Robert Lowell (1917–1977), "To Delmore Schwartz," in *Life Studies* (1959).

141. TLS-1

20 Ellery
Cambridge 38, Mass.
Oct. 16, 1946

DEAR JAY:

I've finally got a manuscript to the point where it seems satisfactory. It's a volume of two short novels and five stories entitled *The World Is a Wedding*. Will you let me know when you get this letter how soon it can be published? I can come down to New York with the manuscript as soon as you get back to America, and I think this would be the best procedure because there are extra-literary reasons for rushing as much as possible. If you can get it out by early spring, both of us will profit by the speed.

How do you feel about my appearing with two books in one year? The book on Eliot is close enough to being ready, though there is no question of rushing about this.

Yours,
DELMORE

/ · /

back to America: The Laughlins were in France.

142. TLS-1

20 Ellery St.
Cambridge
Jan. 7, 1947

DEAR JAY:

I am delighted more than I would have believed possible that you like the script. Perhaps all the sad

years since 1943 can be traced back to your con-
tempt for my last work. Can it be that your approval
means so much to me? Be this as it may, I hope you
will sustain your liking at least until the date of publication, and refrain from letters to editors telling them
that you don't like the book. My uneasiness is occasioned by the fact that you liked *Shenandoah* very
much until you started to lend an ear to rival authors:
"Your effort is VERY GOOD," you wrote to me, "My
congratulations on this evidence of the increasing
tumescence of your esteemed literary powers."

"Tumescence," that's what the girls like.

I think it would be a good idea to include the story
"In Dreams Begin Responsibilities," not as an
appendix, but just like the other stories. I've been
getting letters asking for the entire book. Is it out of
print? And is *Shenandoah* out of print too?

Can you get the book out by June? The Dial Press,
which is no great shakes, takes only three months
with an anthology of 600 pages. If it appears in June,
I will bet you Elinor Blanchard's address against two
of my roundest, warmest and wettest students at
Radcliffe that Orville Prescott will review the book
in the *Times* and declare that I am almost as good as
John Steinbeck. Is it a bet? But only if the book
appears by June, because it gets hot and Prescott goes
away because he does not like the heat and dear Alfred
Kazin, who might review it on Sunday, will have
departed to France.

How about giving me the introduction to Cocteau's *Selected Writings*? I will do as good a job as
John L. Sweeney, but faster. I also admire Svevo,
Pasternak, and Valéry very much, but more than
anything else I lust for The Almighty Dollar, just
like you.

You can have the page of ads in *PR* for $40, if you

will sign up for six times a year. $40 is $8 less than anyone else. Please advise.

I don't understand what "the Jewish problem" is, so far as my book goes. No reader has ever accused me of providing anti-Semitic ammunition. In fact, I should think that this might well be the link with the gross public of New York, where most of the readers are, anyway.

The enclosures, which please return, are to show you that I always get good reviews. The gross public will love me, if it is given a chance. And now that I am an assistant professor, I am almost as authoritative as Harry Levin, n'est-ce pas?

Yours,

DELMORE

/ · /

the script: Typescript of *The World Is a Wedding.*

my last work: Genesis (1943).

Orville Prescott: Principal book reviewer for the daily *New York Times.*

John Steinbeck: (1902–1968), American novelist.

Cocteau: Jean Cocteau (1889–1963), French writer, artist, and film maker.

John L. Sweeney: Sweeney had edited the ND *Selected Writings of Dylan Thomas* (1946).

Svevo: Italo Svevo (1861–1928), Italian writer whose *Confessions of Zeno* ND brought out in 1947.

"the Jewish problem": JL was having difficulty writing flap copy for *The World Is a Wedding.* See his later letter (no. 145) to Schwartz dated January 31, 1948, in which he articulates the problem.

143. TLS-1   Cambridge
                                              March 23, 1947

DEAR JAY:

What happened about the proofs, which you said would be along fairly soon, two months ago? And who is printing the book? If the printer is in New York, perhaps I can expedite matters by going to see him. Please advise so that our long association can ripen into lasting friendship and no more long distance calls will be necessary.

What do you think of this as a motto for the book? "My Conscience Shall Be My Bride"?

Do you know, I think we would get along perfectly if only you told me what you were thinking instead of telling me just the opposite. For example, in New York in December you told me you were through with Patchen. How was I to guess from this that you cared what I said about him?

One thing I forgot to tell you about, and have meant to for several times: Your book of poems was sent to Dudley Fitts for review. If you read the review he wrote for the Winter 1946 issue of *PR,* you can find out that dear Fitts said in public print that I was absolutely honest.

Please let me hear about the book immediately. I'll be in New York the first two weeks in April.

                                    With love,
                                    DELMORE

P.S. Please return the enclosures which are meant to show that the book can be a real success.

/ · /

who is printing the book?: It was produced by Dudley Kimball at Blue
Ridge Mountain Press, Parsippany, N.J.

your book of poems: JL had no new book of poems in 1947. Schwartz
may have seen *A Small Book of Poems,* which came out in English with
Pound's protégé, Vanni Scheiwiller, in Milan.

144. TLS-2   319 W. 12th St.
                                        December 22, 1947

DEAR JAY:

Berryman tells me that you are unhappy. This may
be merely his interpretation, but anyway I am writing to commiserate with you and tell you that I, too,
am unhappy. What can the reason be? I have reflected
upon the problem and upon a related problem,
namely, Who has slept with more girls, you or me?
The two problems are related because I have a theory that one becomes unhappy because one sleeps
with too many girls. The question then arises as to
who is more unhappy, you or me? If you are more
unhappy than I am and have slept with more girls,
it obviously follows that my theory is correct.

Theories apart, I am sorry I did not get to see you
before you went away, because there were several
things to discuss. One reason I did not see you was
that I was given the impression that you were already
in Europe. When are you coming back? And can you
do anything to get me the page proofs of my book?
I spoke to Creekmore two weeks ago, but he
obviously has difficulties in handling the self-indulgent Kimball. I want to publish one more part of the
book in *PR* just before the book appears as a way of
advertising it. *Gentlemen's Agreement,* which as you
know also deals with the unhappy chosen people in

America, has sold 920,000 copies—which suggests that my book may sell at least 9,200 copies, if handled properly.

My experience at the Gotham Book Mart party was practically traumatic, since you had given me some reason to believe that I was about to meet my blushing bride and henceforth be able to stop hackwork and bundling, both boring. I hope the lady is still unattached when you return.

Please give my love to the beautiful Margaret whom I adore, even though she has done me out of your insurance policy.

Yours,
DELMORE

P.S. Your poste carte arrived just after I wrote the above. Many thanks for telling me about Gloria. I will buy a new suit and take a hair-cut.

I will be delighted to receive your new poem. What about some prose?

You have my permission to draw up a contract for publishing my stories in French. It is time for them to discover that not all Americans behave like Humphrey Bogart.

/ · /

Creekmore: Hubert Creekmore (1907–1966), American poet, translator, and novelist, who worked at ND for several years. ND published his poem, *The Long Reprieve,* in 1946.

Gentlemen's Agreement: Best-selling novel by Laura Z. Hobson (1900–1986), about anti-Semitism in America.

insurance policy: JL had changed beneficiaries after his marriage.

Gloria: Imaginary name for a girlfriend for Schwartz.

Humphrey Bogart: Tough-guy American film star.

145. TLS-1 National Ski Association of America
Alta Lodge
Sandy, Utah
January 31st, 1948

DEAR DELMORE:

I'm sorry that you were distressed to the point of having to phone the other evening, though it was a pleasure to hear your tenebrous voice, defying the snows of the Rockies and the cocktail drinkers of Salt Lake's fast set.

Jarrell will surely burn in hell for a term of years for this latest piece of mischief. He surely knew what he was doing and how malicious an action it was.

If God loves anyone on this evil earth it is surely poor simple cowlike Patchen exuding love in his den. As Cicero says: "The wicked flourish like a green bay tree." That's Jarrell. All that glitter attracts the applause of the febrile horde. But GOD SEES. Let him recall that on his deathbed. AND GOD BURNS THEM. A long roast.

I don't blame you for this. I'm sure you didn't suggest it to him. But I am surprised that you would go ahead and write a review, knowing all the trouble it would lead to.

Well, I only hope that you can withdraw the thing now.

I have not been able to locate your letter, but it will doubtless come up through the mass as I progress downward.

Your stories have been at the printer's for some time and we should have some proofs on them fairly soon now.

You must write the blurb for the book yourself. I cannot handle the Jewish question. If I write that you describe the lives and thoughts of the Jews more lovingly and more observingly than I have ever read before, then there will be people who will resent the fact that I single out Jews as being Jews and not just people. It is all too complex for me. In the case of Klein, I pointed out that he was a Jew and so offended all the crossed-over Jews like Untermeyer, Fadiman, Cerf etc., who like to see Jews succeed in the world but do not like to have them labelled as such. There is certainly no solution to the problem except that everyone should marry a Jew at one time and obliterate the tribe. Is this not right?

J

/ · /

malicious an action: The issue here is unclear. But both Schwartz and Jarrell had gone after Patchen in print before. See Schwartz's " 'I Feel Drunk All the Time' " (review of *Selected Poems of Kenneth Patchen* in *The Nation,* February 22, 1947), 220–22; and Jarrell's review of *First Will and Testament* in *Partisan Review,* 7 (March–April 1940). In the latter, Jarrell called Patchen "a real, but disorganized, self-indulgent, and rather commonplace talent."

the case of Klein: A. M. Klein, Canadian poet whose *Hitleriad* JL published in the Poets of the Year series in 1944. Schwartz called him "Abe."

Cerf: Bennett Cerf. Head of Random House.

146. TL-1   [N.D.]

[No salutation]

In *The World Is a Wedding* Delmore Schwartz has used the Jew as a symbol of modern man subjected to the profound disorders and conflicts of modern life. In choosing such a symbol Schwartz has followed the precedent set by such authors as Mann, Joyce, and Proust. Mann's Naphta in *The Magic*

Mountain, Joyce's Leopold Bloom and Proust's Swann testify to the importance of the Jew as a central figure in modern literature. This volume of two short novels and five short stories should have additional interest in showing how an author of a later generation handles, with extraordinary originality, the preoccupation of earlier modern authors.

Readers interested in the craft of fiction will also be struck by the newness of Schwartz's technique, a technique which makes possible the fascinating and saga-like narration of several generations of life within a few pages, and at the same time permits a swift shift of focus to some illuminating moment or episode.

DELMORE

147. ALS-1

c / o J. Pollet
RFD #2
Saugerties, N.Y.
July 4, 1949

DEAR JAY:

I am here for the summer, enjoying rural & marital contentment. This is two miles from Woodstock, N.Y., & not so far by car from Norfolk, so that if you have nothing better to do, you might drive over with Margaret for any kind of visit.

What has happened to that book?

Did I tell you I thought you ought to take on Burford's novel, even though it is a fragment?

How sad it is to be thirty-five years of age.

As ever,
DELMORE

/ · /

marital contentment: In June 1949, Schwartz had married his second wife, the novelist Elizabeth Pollet. They were honeymooning at her father's farm in Saugerties, N.Y.

Burford's novel: Unpublished work by William Burford. A section appeared in *ND* 11.

148. TLS-1   September 12, 1949

DEAR DELMORE:

Here is your check for that story which was used in the College Freshman text which Dick Smyth has put out.

I am sorry to have been so silent for so long, but it has been a busy summer. I went out to the Goethe Festival in Aspen for nearly a month and as a result, all the work in the office has piled up on me since I got back. I am afraid that I have to confess that I haven't been able to find much time to put in on the revision of your Eliot manuscript. The work which that Canadian girl did was all right, in so far as it went, but it didn't go very far. I am going over it inch by inch myself, trying to retain meanings with absolute fidelity but to reshape your sentences in such a way that they will have more life and bite on the page. When I have more of it done, I'll show it to you and you can let me know what you think about the changes.

Am I to understand from your little note of July 4th that you actually got married? Please inform me on this interesting point, so that I may take the necessary steps.

Bill Burford continues to bombard me with revised versions of his poems, and we are running three of them in the next number of *New Directions,* along

with the fine excerpt from his first novel about when
he comes into his mother's room as a little boy. By
the way, why don't you dig down and find some
poems for me to use in the next annual? It has been
years, I think, since you favored the poetry public.

As ever,
JAMES LAUGHLIN

/ · /

Dick Smyth: Richard Smyth, a friend of JL's, who created a list of six
textbooks for ND in the early 1950s. Most notable was the MacIntyre /
Laughlin translation of Goethe's *Faust, Part I.*

Goethe Festival: A convocation to celebrate Goethe's bi-centennial,
organized by Walter Paepke and Robert Hutchins, which featured such
notables as Albert Schweitzer, José Ortega y Gasset, Thornton Wilder,
and Stephen Spender. JL ran a bookstore for the occasion in Aspen.

149. TLS-1   November 28, 1949

DEAR DELMORE:

Over the weekend I have been doing a little research
in the list of Turgenev novels which you kindly sent
me. My set of Turgenev does not have the same
translation which you have been using. My translation is the Hapgood version. It is definitely a stinker,
and I hope that the Garnett one is better, though
from conversations with Nabokov, I would gather
that none of them are much good. However, it is
out of the question to go to the extent of having new
translations made. Have you checked whether there
are any better ones available in England?

How did you go about choosing the material? Did
you read all of the stories, or just take someone's
advice? As closely as I can estimate it, the eight short

novels which you have listed in your table of contents will total about 281 thousand words. How long does your introduction run? If we use the same style layout which they used in *The Short Novels of Dostoevsky,* we would get an average of about 450 words to a page. I estimate that we would have a book of somewhere around 640 pages. Composition and plating on such a page would run about $3, so that we would have nearly $2000 of investment before we even started buying our paper. So this proposition has got to be studied carefully. What other commitments would there be? How much do you owe to Dial in the way of an advance? And exactly how much must be paid to Macmillan for the use of the translations?

I must say that I don't think much of their jacket. It looks awfully trashy to me. There would also be the question of whether the plates could be remade to eliminate their imprint and their series title. I would prefer to pass up the jacket unless they wanted to give us the plates for a very small sum indeed.

I am, on the whole, pretty enthusiastic about this project, as Turgenev has always been one of my favorite writers, and if we can get the expenses into line, I think that we definitely ought to go forward with it.

With best wishes,
JAMES LAUGHLIN

/ · /

November 28, 1949: This was the first letter addressed by JL to 75 Charles Street, where Schwartz and his wife had moved at summer's end.

Turgenev: Ivan Sergeyevich Turgenev (1818–1883), Russian novelist.

Hapgood: Isabel F. Hapgood.

Garnett: Constance Garnett.

enthusiastic about this project: The book was not published by ND. Schwartz, however, was to write an introduction to Turgenev's *Fathers and Sons,* translated by Constance Garnett and published in Harper's Modern Classics Series (1951).

150. TLS-1   75 Charles St.
                                                New York City 14
                                                April 3, 1950

DEAR JAY:

Since you are away, I've taken the liberty of post-poning my book of poems until fall. The chief reason is that I want to include another part of about 30 pages because the book as it is looks incomplete to me. I've spoken to Jacobs about it and he says that the delay makes no difference to him, as long as it is all right with you. He says there will be no additional expense at all.

Please forgive me. I know what a nuisance it is, but since the book will be better, you should be pleased in the end and perhaps as soon as next Xmas. I should have seen the need for another part before giving you the manuscript, but teaching at N.Y.U. and Princeton, and working on *PR* to arrive at the lordly reward of forty-one dollars a week, does not conduce to a clear-eyed view of one's literary productions.

Will you write to Jacobs, stating your approval? I will probably be done with the new part by June 1st at the latest. Between May 10 and June 1st I will be free of all but my editorial duties, thus permitting me to pull everything new together. After June 1st, I depart for Kenyon College to teach why the short story is short for six weeks. This would have resulted in a stunning rise in worldly goods, except that on June 1st, my *PR* wage is cut in half because we then become a bimonthly, thus bringing me down to thirty-nine dollars a week. Still and all, I do not feel I have any reason to kick, since in twenty-eight years I will be eligible for an old-age pension and can then devote myself exclusively to the Muse. Provided I am still alive, of course.

You may remember that there was a like delay with my first book and the results were pleasing. You were in Rapallo, I think, and bemused by a girl named Lulu, or something like that.

Existence has been very cruel of late. The little black cat died last week of distemper. The mother cat is still sick and may not recover. My brother, after driving my mother to wild excitement by leaving his wife, has now reduced her to melancholy by returning to the lady. There is not enough water in New York. They are thinking of aiding nature by dropping ice in the clouds, but the inhabitants of Dutchess County are against it. Truman is bound to be reelected, and the cultural implications of his last election have still not been understood by the intelligentsia. With the defeat of the Spanish Armada, English became the language of the sea. In the same way, as the sale of radio sets increases, Danny Kaye, Brooklyn's gift to Brooklyn, will replace Lord Tennyson, thus paving the way for me, I hope. . . .

Please write to me, even if enraged.

Yours,
DELMORE

/ · /

my book of poems: *Vaudeville for a Princess.*

Jacobs: S. A. Jacobs, designer of the book, which was to be printed in an edition of 1,600 copies at the Golden Eagle Press, Mt. Vernon, N.Y.

Rapallo: Rapallo, Italy, site of Ezra Pound's "Ezuversity," which JL attended.

Lulu: JL met Lola Avena in Rapallo while studying with Pound in 1934–35. She was the subject of JL's poem "In Another Country."

my brother: Kenneth Schwartz (1916–1990).

Danny Kaye: Popular American comedian admired by Princess Elizabeth of Great Britain, hence the book title, *Vaudeville for a Princess* (1950).

151. ALS-1   Monday, July 23, 1950

DEAR JAY:

Maybe the enclosed copy is better than the one I sent you yesterday. However, I think it might be best if you wrote the jacket yourself—it's more becoming or something, but you know what I mean.

Best,
DELMORE

This is Delmore Schwartz's first book of poems since 1943. It is a remarkable book in many ways, but perhaps most of all in its richness of emotion and subject-matter.

Subjects such as Existentialism, famous men, automobiles, promiscuity, marriage and divorce, Hamlet and Iago are the starting points for profound excursions among the extremes of emotion: Hope, joy, suffering, innocence, guilt and forgiveness, sorrow, excitement, and exaltation.

And Mr. Schwartz's style, which moves freely and exactly through the modes of wit, irony, narrative and analysis, is an extraordinary poetic fusion of colloquial speech, Elizabethan form, the imagery of the theatre, and the conflicting points of view of modern thought.

152. TL-1   [1950]

[No salutation]

Delmore Schwartz's new book of poems, his first collection of verse since 1943, may be compared to a concert and a carnival.

In the poems it is a concert of the heights and depths of the emotions: Joy, Sorrow, Innocence, Guilt and Forgiveness, Excitement and Exaltation.

And in the prose interludes it is a carnival or *Mardi Gras* in which Automobiles, Promiscuity, Existentialism, Famous Men, Marriage and Divorce, Hamlet, Othello, and Don Giovanni appear in new masks and new costumes as strange beings.

The reader will be delighted by the music, the wit, and the richness of an awakened mind.

153. ALS-1   RFD #2
                                          c / o Pollet
                                          Saugerties, N.Y.
                                          Aug. 21, 1950

DEAR JAY:

We're staying here for the next few weeks, though I have to drive to New York once a week for *PR*. And perhaps you and Margaret might drive over some afternoon and stay for dinner to view the rural scene—which long nourished the imagination of the budding novelist. On the maps it looks like a drive of about 50 miles from Norfolk. I think you'd find it pleasant, if you're not too busy.

Philip, who certainly knows the publishing racket, thinks that considerable opportunity is being lost by not using a bigger and more glamorous photograph of Elizabeth on the jacket. It's a beautiful jacket, but the photograph is not the kind that will make some readers buy the book because they want to find out more about the girl, the way that Mary McCarthy's did in *The Company She Keeps.* Is it too late or too costly to do anything about it? I think it might make a vast difference not only in sales but in the attention the book gets from the vulgar press.

Best,
DELMORE

/ · /

Philip: Philip Rahv.
Elizabeth on the jacket: Laughlin was about to publish Elizabeth Pollet's novel, *A Family Romance* (1950).

154. ALS-2

RFD #2
Saugerties, N.Y.
Sept. 8, 1950

DEAR JAY:

There are about six errors in my book, and several of them make a difference in the sense—for example THOUGH, on p. 77, is printed as THROUGH, and at another point, NOT turns the meaning of a sentence upside down. I suppose it is too late to do anything about this, unless you want to insert a list of *Errata,* which is a lot of trouble, of course. I'll be back in New York by next Wednesday or Thursday, and you can let me know then. I'm extremely sorry about the errors, as I was quite careful, I think. But I can't read proof of my own work as proof should be read, and I guess most proof-readers are not very good with poems.

I should also have done something about a new photograph just in case someone wants to use the old ones taken in the last half of the 14th century, which never looked like me anyway. I have a good one taken on the Kenyon campus just after I took another set from Arthur, but unfortunately I'm unshaven. I'll bring it down with me next week, but I suppose it's too late to do anything about this too.

My brother-in-law Sylvester asks me to tell you that I ought to be billed as Bernie Schwartz. He thinks this would increase sales. I pass this advice along to you without comment.

I can't make head or tail of the review list for Elizabeth's book because I don't know much about the many newspapers on the list, nor about how you handle novels. There are about eight people who might make some favorable comment and who are not on the list. Is that what you want?

Best,
DELMORE

P.S. On second thought, I'm enclosing the photograph and the list of critics for E's book.

/ · /

Arthur: Arthur Mizener.
Sylvester: Sylvester Pollet.
Bernie Schwartz: Real name of screen actor Tony Curtis.

155. ALS-1   75 Charles St.
                                                Oct. 11, 1950

DEAR JAY:

Have you received any payment for the 2 new anthologies which use some of my work? One is Matthiessen's *Oxford Book of American Verse* and the other is *The Story* by Mark Schorer (Prentice-Hall). There is no acknowledgment of permissions in the latter. Also is it not true and just that I should receive copies of each work? Please let me know so that I can continue my struggle with inflation.

To the recent biographical data on the flowering blonde novelist you might add this: "Miss Pollet recently remarked to her aging husband, 'I thought I was marrying the prize bull, but now I find myself on the horns of a dilemma.' "

I don't know what this means, but it is unquestionably unfavorable, I know. In reply I had to quote The Talmud: "Who is a hero? He who can suppress a wise-crack."

                                                Yours,
                                                DELMORE

156. TLS-1   November 19, 1950

DEAR JAY:

Please send me only favorable reviews and comments for the time being. I wish to live in a fool's paradise for the time being, which is until I finish what I am trying to do now. This does not apply to Elizabeth's reviews, since she is stronger or more modest, or more curious than I am. This request is prompted by the note from Pearn, Pollinger & Higham announcing that Lehmann has turned down my book. I suspect that the references to the English royal family, perfidious Albion, and the like may make them say the book is "not quite (!) suitable for the English market," and though this may be false, such practical considerations interfere with my native candor, honesty, and goodness of heart; and anyway once a poet feels that he cannot be a bull in a china shop, he is through, don't you agree?

I saw John Slocum the other day and like him more than I had before and was much bemused by his concern with Joyce. What does it all mean?

Is it true, or has my memory deceived me again, that at Elizabeth's party, when Kirgo or someone said that bookstores were offering $10 for *IDBR,* you replied that the book was not very good in your opinion? Well, anyway, you were always a fickle fellow, and some day your former feelings may revive.

After a long argument with one of the strongest New England consciences of our time, I have finally persuaded Elizabeth to promise that in the likely event that I predecease her, she will not marry nor even hold hands with anyone but her children. I figure that I will know that they are really mine when they start to kick. This promise makes it possible for me to be less concerned about my health.

How about going with us to Princeton for one of the Princeton seminars in literary criticism? They are on Wednesday evenings. They are quite exciting. Last year Helen Blackmur came to one of my seminar meetings and afterward, when they asked her how she liked it, she said that it was just like being at home except that no one was allowed to interrupt Delmore for the first hour. She was right, since as soon as I shut up, Blackmur and Berryman began arguing with each other and Berryman maintained that I had been vilely insulted by Blackmur, much to my surprise, since I was too depressed to understand what anyone was saying, and when Stauffer compared me to Cardinal Newman for objecting to the fact that the Royalist Eliot bragged to Kazin that he had voted for the Labour Party, I decided that Stauffer had lost his mind, or I had lost mine, or both.

See you soon,
DELMORE

/ · /

only favorable reviews: Schwartz's *Vaudeville for a Princess* received mixed reviews, whereas Pollet's novel, *A Family Romance,* was well received and sold briskly. It went into a mass-market paperback edition.

Pearn, Pollinger & Higham: British literary agents.

Lehmann: John Lehmann (1907–1987), British author and publisher, who brought out a U.K. edition of *The World Is a Wedding.*

John Slocum: John Jermain Slocum, Laughlin's Harvard classmate, who with Herbert Cahoon prepared the definitive bibliography of James Joyce.

Kirgo: A rare book dealer with whom Schwartz was friends.

Stauffer: Donald Stauffer, who held the Christian Gauss Chair at Princeton.

Helen Blackmur: Wife of R. P. Blackmur.

Cardinal Newman: John Henry Newman (1801–1890), English churchman famous for his leadership of the Oxford movement.

Royalist Eliot: T. S. Eliot had declared himself to be in turn "a classicist, royalist and anglo-catholic" (Preface to *For Lancelot Andrewes,* London, 1928).

157. TL-2   RD1—Box 230
                                     Pittstown, N.J.
                                     Feb. 1, 1951

DEAR JAY:

I tried to obey your command in your last comnuniqué to relax and I did relax for half an hour, but
there is no rest for the wicked. We bought a new
used car on the 21st, after extorting a loan from a
friend, and I thought, "Now I can relax in this brandnew used Buick 1941, 90-day guarantee, even though
first gear is not all that it might be; especially since
Elizabeth, who was once the quiz kid of Canada and
mastered the calculus (although she can never figure
out what age she is) had learned how to drive very
quickly." So there I was, seated next to my serene
wife, driving to Princeton in the early morning and
admiring the pretty countryside which, with the thin
lines of the trees and the snow on it looks just like
Brueghel, and some Japanese prints. But Elizabeth,
who was born in the New England conscience, had
begun to speed for fear of being late, and in her moral
haste she passed a school bus unloading and the state
police was upon us again with a thirteen-dollar ticket.
I tried to argue out of it by pointing out that Elizabeth had almost been arrested as a blonde bandit and
that our power lawn mower had been stolen a month
ago without any reparation on the part of the police,
but all in vain. The crooks steal our property and the
cops take away our (borrowed) money. I drove to
New York the next day and received a fifteen-dollar
ticket for parking on the wrong side of the street for
ten minutes while trying to extricate an old kerosene
stove from our cold water flat on Hudson St., and
bring it out here so we won't freeze to death in the
sub-zero weather; twenty-eight dollars in twenty-four

hours for the sake of Elizabeth's lordly stipend: Fifty dollars a week. I never expected to be rich nor until recently desired to be, but this is going too far in the other direction.

Nevertheless, it is truly darkest just before dawn and the next day Elizabeth received an air mail cable from Marguerite Caetani accepting seventy pages of her short novel, *A Cold Water Flat,* which you read last December. Now if you tell the lady how hard-up we are so that she will pay Elizabeth twenty dollars a page, and if we can keep the news from the state police, we may, D.V., be able to buy a new power mower which we will hide ninety feet underground all winter.

Please send me news, news, all the news, if you can. I feel as if this were an extra-inning ball game, and you were Bobby Thomson.

Did I remember to tell you that Milton Katz knows and admires Meyer Schapiro very much?

P.R. raised exactly $500, despite a two-month campaign and an exciting party at which I met Victor Weybright, who seems very nice and certainly seems to like to drink.

After much careful study of the financial situation, I came to the tentative conclusion that this is the time to borrow money, since inflation is likely to continue and when you have to pay the money back it will be worth less than it is now.

/ · /

Brueghel: Pieter Brueghel the Elder (1525–1569), Flemish painter of landscapes and peasant life.

darkest just before dawn: Schwartz was to echo this sentiment in his 1961 poem, "This Is a Poem I Wrote at Night, Before the Dawn," in which he proclaims: "It is always darkness before delight!" (*Last & Lost Poems,* p. 3).

Marguerite Caetani: Princess Caetani was a wealthy American woman married to an Italian prince. She published the international literary magazine *Botteghe Oscure*.

Bobby Thomson: New York Giants baseball star.

Milton Katz: Professor at Harvard Law School and an associate director of the Ford Foundation.

Meyer Schapiro: Professor of Art History at Columbia and erudite author of works of art criticism. Schwartz dedicated "Seurat's Sunday Afternoon Along the Seine" to Meyer and Lillian Schapiro.

Victor Weybright: Head of New American Library, the publishing firm.

158. ALS-1

75 Charles St.
New York City 14
February 22, 1951

DEAR JAY:

Many thanks. Elizabeth and I are very touched by your solicitude, and we are suffering, as you noticed, from cabin fever, but right now both of us are tied to the city by our jobs. Maybe you can ask us again, when we are not tied down, and everyone has gone away.

I've discovered, I think, one of the most important secrets of matrimony. I give Elizabeth all incoming income, such as it is, to deposit in the bank. And the other day, I had occasion to give her a fresh green $100 bill. My only purpose was to save myself the nuisance of going to the bank, but Elizabeth seems to feel that this, more than anything else, testifies to marital devotion. Does not this response—in so pure and unworldly a heart—show how deeply our society has been corrupted by The Almighty Dollar?

Best,
DELMORE

P.S. I'd like to read Brossard's book. I can come up to the office and get it, if that'll save trouble.

/ · /

solicitude: JL offered the Schwartzes the use of his Norfolk home during his absence, to give them a break from the city.

Brossard's novel: Chandler Brossard, whose novel about Greenwich Village, *Who Walk in Darkness,* was published by ND in 1952. He later became an editor at *Esquire.* The novel created a scandal because it portrayed a well-known Village writer, Anatole Broyard, later a staff member of *The New York Times Book Review.*

159. TLS-1

75 Charles Street
New York City 14
April 10, 1951

DEAR JAY:

Many thanks for letting me read Brossard's novel. I cannot sincerely say that I think it is any good, but perhaps I am wrong again.

Your poem is supposed to appear after six previously accepted verses have been published, but if you feel impatient, let me know. There is never room for much poetry in any issue, and when we shifted from monthly to bimonthly publication, everything was slowed up.

I am sorry to hear that you are bored by skiing. I personally have been bored since 1942 when my first wife, little Miss Gertrude, declared that no girl could be interested in me. Pure curiosity as to the truth of her remark made me engage in operations which soon demonstrated that anyone who wrote poems was regarded by the entire female sex as an impersonation or incarnation of Phoebus Apollo. This discovery of the extremely literary character of the female libido destroyed my *joie de vivre* and since then I have been bored.

Elizabeth did not get a Guggenheim, so I have been trying to sell my soul, but with little success, since so many other souls are for sale. I've thought of becoming a banker like Uncle Tom, just so I might be near money, or a big-time gambler. Gamblers are very interesting. Did you read how one of them answered an innocuous question put to him by Kefauver? "Probably yes," he said, "and probably no." In how many other fields of endeavor does such politeness and effort at exactitude show itself?

I encountered Oscar Williams on 8th St. the other day. He was carrying four anthologies by other anthologists and he explained to me what must be a new concept: The plagiarized anthologist. He thinks the other anthologists have been stealing his ideas. I suggested that he retire as an anthologist, since he now holds the world's record, and he said he meant to retire after just one more which was to be entitled: *From Thomas Wyatt to Dylan Thomas.* How about, *From Beowulf to Virginia Woolf?* I asked him, but instead of answering me, he rushed uptown, so I guess Scribner's may have to come through again.

I can't keep after Elizabeth to do her work. If I merely ask her politely how she is getting along, I feel for the next two weeks that I am living with Dracula's sister. However, expressions of interest on your part seem to have a very good effect.

I've misplaced your newspaper clipping, but it is certainly in the house and I'll send it to you as soon as I find it.

Best,
DELMORE

/ · /

Uncle Tom: T. S. Eliot worked for a time at Lloyds Bank in London.

Kefauver: Estes Kefauver, senator from Tennessee, who conducted a much-publicized investigation into organized crime.

160. TLS-1

75 Charles St.
New York City 14
May 8, 1951

DEAR JAY:

I can't find your last letter at the moment, but will try to answer it from memory.

You mention your poems, but I thought you just gave me one, entitled "Step On His Head." However, if there were two or you have another one you want to publish now, please send it to me at the above address.

Unless I am mistaken, which is likely enough, you may have taken my remarks on money in my last letter as a kind of hint, naturally enough. But I merely meant to report on what preoccupied me, which is the only way I can write letters, and I sincerely yearn for the day when our friendship is so pure that all my royalties can be assigned to some charitable cause such as a society for making it clear to the American people that MacArthur is an unspeakable ham.

I have decided not to be a bank clerk, after all, since I would probably be paralyzed by the conflict between my desire to steal money and my fear of doing so.

It was pleasant to learn that you expected our correspondence to be read in the international salons and boudoirs of the future. Do you think they will be able to distinguish between the obfuscations, mystifications, efforts at humor, and plain statements of fact? Will they recognize my prime feelings as a correspondent—the catacomb from which I write to you, seeking to secure some word from the real world, or at least news of the Far West—and sigh with compassion? Or will they just think that I am nasty, an over-eager clown, gauche, awkward, and bookish? Will they understand that I am always direct, open, friendly, simple and candid to the point of naiveté until the ways of the fiendish world infuriate me and I am forced to be devious, suspicious, calculating, not that it does me any good anyway? And for that matter, what will they make of your complex character?

It develops that the juke-boxes in bars now have an item entitled Silence, which costs a nickel, just like Music. This can only lead to drunken disputations between those who want Silence and those who will be goddamned if they can't have a little Music with their beer.

The Giants, after losing eleven straight and thus preventing me from buying the newspaper for eleven days, defeated Pittsburgh twice in three days, which made me reflect on the fact that I have been a Giant rooter for thirty years: The expense of spirit in a waste of games.

Did you see that MacArthur called his wife "my best soldier" and told the D.A.R. that they were the advance-guard of American society? Maybe you ought to invite him or them to appear in the next New Directions annual?

Probably I've forgotten something you mentioned in your letter, but I'll check up when I locate it.

Yours,
DELMORE

/ · /

expense of spirit in a waste of games: Schwartz paraphrases Shakespeare's Sonnet #129.

MacArthur: General Douglas MacArthur (1880–1964), Commander of the Allied Forces in the Southwest Pacific during World War II, and commanding general during the Korean War, which was taking place at this time.

D.A.R.: Daughters of the American Revolution.

161. TLS-3   75 Charles St.
                                                                                    May 28, 1951

DEAR JAY:

I was delighted to get a postcard from the Mallarmé of Nevada. It suggests a new literary theory to me which is roughly as follows: In *Commentary* last December I was called the Brooklyn Lucifer, or rather Lucifer in Brooklyn; eleven years ago, when you had a more hopeful view of my future, you addressed me as the twentieth century Goethe. Lucifer equals Mephisto, who is of course one of Goethe's leading characters. So if you are the Mallarmé of Nevada, as well as the Lenin or Roosevelt of American Literature, we have quite a theory to work with, but I won't elaborate on it right now since I have a serious, literal matter to ask you about, except to say that I've always suspected that Mallarmé and Mephistopheles were in cahoots.

The serious practical matter is this: I've been trying to get in touch with my brother for the past month. He has not written me for more than a year. One letter, sent to his last address, came back with "NO FORWARDING ADDRESS" on it. My second letter was sent to the last address he had when he was still living with his wife (to whom I thought he might have returned). It has not come back. Both addresses are in San Francisco, and it was the fact that your postcard was marked San Francisco which made me think you might have a chance to find out where my brother is and perhaps also how he is. My second letter was sent to 1559 Pine St., San Francisco, Cal., and there must be some knowledge of his whereabouts there. It's quite possible that he may not be working in San Francisco right now, but in any case someone at that address should know what the forwarding address is, and probably his wife still lives at the address. It would be a great kindness, if you were able to get me some information. I don't know anyone in San Francisco except authors rejected by P.R. who do not tend to be cooperative or eager to please me.

So I agree in return to help you to find your brother, if ever you want to know where he is. I must remember to tell you how I once had to track down Berryman in Brattleboro, Vermont, in 1943, when Peruvians wanted him to become a professor at the University of Peru, or somesuch place, and had to have an answer in four days. It all ended with Berryman's refusing the job and denouncing the insolence of South America, but I had a lot of fun making phone calls, and it reminded me that it was not an accident that I idolized Sherlock Holmes when a boy.

Someone said that Tony Bower said that you and Margaret were getting divorced, which makes me feel sad, if true. I've been unalterably opposed to divorce ever since Gertrude Buckman's departure, and the fact is that nowadays, I don't even like Elizabeth to leave the house. Anyway, is it not true that existence would be less difficult if a few more people were less unhappy?

Yours,
DELMORE

/ · /

Sherlock Holmes: Famous private detective who figures in works by Conan Doyle.

Tony Bower: An editor at ND whom Laughlin transplanted in 1948 to a chalet in Klosters, Switzerland, where he did editorial work for a year.

getting divorced: JL and Margaret Keyser were divorced in 1952.

162. TLS-2   405 East 7th St.
Bloomington, Indiana
June 26, 1951

DEAR JAY:

My brother was finally located in Seattle. The pursuit had narrowed down to some place between Los Angeles, San Francisco, and the Canadian border when at last Kenneth—a man of few words—wrote me that he had returned to the aircraft industry as a tool engineer, giving up household appliances because of credit restrictions. This illustrates once more a truth I have tried to force on the American reading public—the international character of our lives; I wonder why I seem to be the only one who finds it fascinating. However, many thanks for offering to put Marie Rexroth on the trail.

Elizabeth and I want to buy a house which we saw last week in Flemington, New Jersey. It has six acres, three bedrooms, two sheds, a barn, a Bartlett's pear tree, two peach trees, a vegetable garden, a wonderful rooster, and among other valuable assets, a bathtub, for which I have yearned these last four years since leaving Cambridge. We have raised all but one thousand of the four thousand and five hundred dollars necessary to the purchase of it (the total cost is nine thousand, but half is a mortgage), and I wonder if you can lend us the one thousand we need, for a period of two years? You might lend the money to us either as a personal loan, or as an advance of five hundred to Elizabeth and five hundred to me, on books which ND published within the next two years. I will probably have a new book of short stories ready to show you by fall, and that with the addition of Elizabeth's second novel, ought to cover the advance. If it does not, then we will be able to repay you the loan at the end of two years, because both of us will have to take full-time jobs by the fall of 1952 unless we manage to make more money than we are making now. We figure that by getting the house and living in the country as much as possible, we will be able to get more work done during the coming year. I have the promise of a good teaching job for 1952–1953, and unless I succeed in writing for the slicks during the coming year (as I have been trying to do for the past month), I will have to teach anyway, the fall after this, since there will be no *P.R.* salaries after next December.

The house appears to be a good investment and the kind of a place we need very much, as you seemed to have noticed last winter when you suggested that we use your place in Norfolk during your absence and thus get rid of cabin fever. It is just an hour and a half from New York, neither too near nor too far, it is entirely rural, and it is just right for the young novelist and the ageing poet's declining years. I am sure that we can pay you back at the end of two years. However, if you are hard-up for cash or hard-pressed in one or another way, we will naturally understand, since we know how many other needs you have to handle. But do let us know as soon as you can.

We arrived here last Sunday and today I began to teach Yeats and Eliot at the School of Letters, which is the new name of the Kenyon School of English. It is very pleasant, but very hot. Arthur is here but he cannot play tennis with me because his doctor says that he is against it, so I am playing with Francis Fergusson who, as he confesses, is so eccentric a player that his eccentricity becomes a form of power. I never can tell—anymore than he can—what he will do next, while Arthur, while powerful, was entirely predictable. If Francis were but ten years younger, what matches we might have! Tate is here too; he has just become a Catholic and attacks Cardinal Spellman with a vigor he formerly reserved for Robert Hillyer. All in all, it looks like a pretty hot six weeks, and I wish you could come out and inspect the little boom in culture. Next week I lecture to the entire congregation on television and literature, and what chance there is that any sensible and sane portion of the reading public will ever open a book again once they get used to the television scream. As Shakesbeer said, "Some rise by vice, and some by virtue fall," and the main thing is just to keep swatting the ball.

We passed through Greenfield, Indiana, on our way out, and it turned out to be the former home of James Whitcomb Riley, which made me think of Marguerite Young, since the dear girl is writing a book about the great bard. The heat and the strain of driving for three days was such that I was moved to compose the following masterpiece on the spur of the moment:

> Who's your Hoosier poet?
> Pure corn entirely?
> Marguerite would know it!
> James Whitcomb Riley!

As Tears Eliot remarked, and he ought to know, poetry is a mug's game—but if one is born a mug, one might as well accept the fact.

As ever,
DELMORE

/ · /

Marie Rexroth: Kenneth Rexroth's second wife.

Cardinal Spellman: (1889–1967), Francis Cardinal Spellman, Archbishop of New York.

Robert Hillyer: (1895–1961), Boylston Professor of Rhetoric at Harvard, who led the campaign against the award of the Bollingen Prize to Ezra Pound in 1948.

James Whitcomb Riley: (1849–1916), Known as "The Hoosier Poet."

writing a book about the great bard: Schwartz is mistaken or making another of his jokes; Young's *Angel in the Forest* dealt with Utopian aspiration in New Harmony, Ind.

163. TLS-1   June 30, 1951

DEAR DELMORE:

I was very glad to hear from you and get the news about life in the upper reaches. It must be very intense. Here in Norfolk we have the venerable Chauncey Brewster Tinker giving the literary lectures at the music school, and he is very SLY about A. E. Housman.

I think that is fine about the house in the country, and I hope you can get it, but would you be able to commute to the college where you are to teach? The way things are going in general in the literary world, I can't see how any serious writer is going to make a living just by writing. I think publishing as we know it is going to collapse in the next five years, with the 25-cent people taking over direct relationships with popular novelists and new book publishing being limited to How-to-Do-Its and He-Did-Its.

Business has been worse in the past year than anyone can remember and all except those who have had at least three best sellers or Books-of-the-Month are preparing to shoot themselves. As for me, I shall simply retire to the country, eliminate all overhead, and practice the pure essentials—printing books, selling them to the really interested by mail, and bypass the prodigious waste of advertising-promotion-sales pressure, all of which is now revealing its complete futility to even the great minds who invented it. A book of poetry, after all, is in its essence not the same as a bottle of mouthwash.

Thus the literary future for you, Delmore, seems to be one of austerity. After all, Mallarmé taught English and wrote descriptions of ladies' dresses. But I see no reason why Elizabeth cannot sail right into the pocket books without much compromise of quality. After all, if they were not frightened by the first book they are not likely to be put off by the later ones—which will be, I judge, increasingly gay, now that Pollet is pitching for Branch Rickey's Amazing Pirates.

I wonder whether you are still a Giant fan now that they have become the rage of Negroes, barbers and Durocher: This is the team that fits the spirit of the age. As Maglie "shaves" Campanella the blood of the polloi pleasantly rises and all those animosities against their mothers which Henry Luce seeks to vent on the Chinese are released as healthfully as bubble gum. We must have a look at all that when you get back.

Well, don't be mean on the court—let the great minds hit a few back so they don't get complexes—and tell Elizabeth that a page a day keeps Canasta away. Can you find out if Arthur is doing anything about the Conrad book he promised me, or is he now writing for the *Saturday Evening Post*?

See you soon,

J L

/ · /

Chauncey Brewster Tinker: Yale Professor of English and a popular lecturer.

A. E. Housman: (1859–1936), English poet and classical scholar. Tinker's "sly" approach was most likely avoiding references to Housman's latent homoerotic subjects.

the 25-cent people: Reference to publishers of paperback books, called pocketbooks then, which sold for twenty-five cents.

Henry Luce: American publisher, founder of *Time, Fortune, Life,* and *Sports Illustrated.*

Branch Rickey: Owner of the Pittsburgh baseball team.

Durocher: Leo Durocher, manager of the Brooklyn Dodgers.

Maglie: Sal Maglie, a Dodgers pitcher.

Campanella: Roy Campanella, catcher for the Dodgers.

Canasta: Popular card game during the 1950s.

Arthur: Mizener.

164. TLS-1   405 E. 7th St.
                               Bloomington, Indiana
                               July 16, 1951

DEAR JAY:

Your last communiqué was rather on the enigmatic side, even to the point of being sent to Ohio instead of Indiana, but since existence is so full of mysteries, I am content to accept a few more, now and then.

I asked Arthur about Conrad and he appeared to be somewhat piqued about a contract he was supposed to receive two years ago. Unless I misunderstood him, he now no longer feels obligated to produce the book.

I am sorry to hear that business is not good, and that you are moving toward austerity. I must insist that I have been living in austerity for the past fifteen years, and certainly not in the lap of luxury, teaching English just like Mallarmé and if not describing ladies' dresses, doing my awkward best to find out what is beneath them.

Bloomington continues to be very interesting. Among my students I've been trying to develop the idea that it [the city of Bloomington] was named after Leopold Bloom. Glenway Wescott has been here and he has lectured on the modern novel, describing Henry James as a Fascist who appeased English aristocracy and American plutocracy, and Dostoevsky as the apostle of pure evil. Joyce moreover committed the sin of pride by trying to invent a new language, and Willie Maugham—as he called him—his dear good great friend, is a very great author. It was also revealed for the first time that Henry James left France because when he went to see Gustave Flaubert, Flaubert was not wearing shoes, just carpet slippers, which embarrassed Henry so much he immediately moved back to London.

The other night I met Dr. Kinsey, who looks like a somewhat bemused rhinoceros, and when I learned that Wescott had been doing research for him for the past two years, I warned him of the coming victory of heterosexuality, a prediction which made him sufficiently curious to invite me to his house next Friday and inspect his library and files. I will send you a full report, if you want one.

My new book of stories is finished and I am just letting it cool off a while before sending you a copy. It contains the best sentence of all my efforts:

"Although ordinarily not thought of as such, the mind is the first of the erogenous zones."

Did you know that Villiers de l'Isle-Adam had a novel in which the hero is Thomas Alva Edison, who is very sad because he was born too late to make phonograph recordings of all the great sounds of history—the fall of Jericho, the Flood, the opening of the Red Sea, and the like? An Englishman in love with a very beautiful and very stupid opera singer commissions Edison to make a dummy automaton who looks just like the singer and sings like her, so that he will be free of his infatuation. Edison does, and the two ladies meet and it is all quite profound, in its way. Maybe you ought to get the book translated and published?

I thought you were going to England this summer?

Yours,
DELMORE

/ · /

Leopold Bloom: The hero of James Joyce's Ulysses.

Glenway Wescott: (1901–1987), American novelist.

Dr. Kinsey: Alfred Kinsey, biologist who conducted research on human sexuality at the Institute of Sex Research in Bloomington, Ind.

My new book of stories: Not published by ND. Schwartz's next collection, Successful Love and Other Stories, did not appear until 1961, from Corinth Books.

Villiers de L'Isle-Adam had a novel: Apocryphal.

165. TLS-3   RFD Pittstown, N.J.
                              January 10, 1952

DEAR JAY:

I am writing this on a public typewriter ($10 for thirty minutes) in the Princeton Library and in a state of over-excitement and exhaustion, so please use this as the context for whatever I say.

With regard to the enclosed unsigned mss., I cannot deduce very well at present, and the best I can do is to suggest that the piece was either written by William Candlewood, Hiram Handspring, and yourself in collaboration, or was composed by someone intent upon your public utterances in *ND* annuals and the like. The handwriting, it is true, shows no resemblance to that of Handspring or Candlewood, but they both know French and French girls. If I had the nervous energy to go and look for a Connecticut Baedeker, I could determine how near Middle Haddam is to Norfolk, not that that would prove anything, since you move about so much and so fast. However, if I assume that you have as little nervous energy now as I have, it becomes extremely unlikely that the work is a product of your mind, and it is statistically probable, given the number of authors in Connecticut other than yourself and the number of authors who study your opinions or are unconsciously influenced by them, that it was written by someone else of great gifts. In any case, it is as you say very fine, and if it is not you, the gent ought certainly to be tracked down and persuaded that he ought not to be hiding his light under any bush except the proper improper one.

I will resume my investigations as soon as I quiet down somewhat. My life at present consists of an imitation of all the difficulties encountered by Laurel & Hardy, Abbott & Costello, Hercules, John Berryman, and anyone who was ever drafted into the army. I must rise at 5:30, drive 33 miles with Elizabeth to Princeton's Art Museum where she is employed (I started out as an author and I am concluding as a chauffeur, the fate you predicted for yourself in one phase of your war novel), waste my

diminishing life and day gassing away with the literati all day while my wife works for our food, gas-
oline, and kerosene, lunch lavishly at Princeton's most
expensive restaurant at my own or my wife's expense,
since the installed literati won't eat anywhere else and
think it rude of me not to go with them, etc. At 5, I
drive Elizabeth back to our country estate (I don't
know for sure if we are landed gentry or poor white
trash, but I'm sure I would not recognize the difference at this stage), and when we get home after driving over unfamiliar country roads in the dark I am
so enervated and exasperated and exacerbated by all
that has occurred that I get good and drunk, which
makes me feel untroubled by the fact that the pump
has broken down every other day, the windshield
wiper on the car does not work, there is no heater in
the car, and I am not in all truth a native country
boy.

However, it is a lot of fun too, and I would feel
entirely happy if I did not feel oppressed at the
thought that I might be writing now and am not.

The previous page was written last Thursday. Now
it is Sunday (except that authors have no Sundays)
and I am back upon my fief, which I have decided
not to name Mix-and-Mingle, New Jersey, because
Elizabeth does not like that name, nor Ho! Ho!, New
Jersey, nor Good Night, N.J., nor Good Morning,
New Jersey.

On Wednesday I gave someone at your office
Elizabeth's number in Princeton, which is Princeton
2300, Extension 760. In case of something really
urgent you can try the corner store, at Baptistown:
The phone number there is Frenchtown 22212. I will
be in town next Thursday and will try to get you
again. Some of those who answer the phone at AL5-
2204 do tend to give the impression that you are there
but cannot be disturbed, which does not offend me

but does make it difficult for me to prove that I am not entirely cut off from New York.

Shortly after trying to call you on Wednesday I learned that my grandmother had died the previous weekend and I had missed her funeral, which I had been preparing to attend for the past thirty-four years. She was eighty-eight years of age, born in the same decade as Whitehead and Yeats, but she had, if I may say so, a better heart and a superior mind. In my most euphoric moments (which become more and more infrequent) I suffer from the delusion that if I live long enough I may be half as good as she was at 50. She was the only woman I ever loved (don't repeat this) except for Elizabeth, who is probably largely a disguise or substitute for her. Of her wisdom, which was five thousand years of age, let me give you one example: During the five years between my first and second marriage she often urged me to marry a good non-Aryan girl with a great deal of cash, and when I countered by proposing marriage to her, she turned away in disgust at my decadent sense of humor, but then, seeing that my feelings were hurt at her inability to laugh at some of my desperate jokes, she reassured me by saying that I should come back to New York and depart from Cambridge because in New York there were more people, more girls, more Jewish girls, more moreness, more everything! "The best is none too good for you," she added, and you can see how and why I loved her very much when I add that she always said this to me from the time we first met.

I am touched that you are sad that we no longer live at Charles Street. You must come out here soon, bringing Gertrude or whatever other beauty is on duty. The plumbing broke down again last night and I feel as if I had known the plumber for years, he is here so often. In Princeton I am known as Squire

Schwartz, to which I reply that I am really Squatter Schwartz. They are mystified, and they are too polite for me to explain to them that I have a new interpretation for Uncle Tom's great lines, "The jew squats on the windowsill / The owner." The gimmick is the breakdown of the plumbing. There have been quite a few visitors here and I imagine a certain amount of Aryan squatting also.

Please let me know how things go in Pasadena. George Kennan, the new Ambassador to Russia, is still in Princeton and still on the Ford Foundation, I think. I don't know him, but he is an old friend of Dr. Gruenthal (whom, you may remember, is my godfather), and since it is quite likely that all friends of the good doctor are sympathetic to adopted sons and daughters, I might be of some use to you if any enemies get through to Hutchins, Hoffman, Katz or the Trustees.

If I seem frantic in tone, or too intense or insensitive, disregard it. I will calm down as soon as I don't have to move around so much. Since Thursday I have accumulated a whole set of deductions and over-deductions with regard to the anonymous prose-writer, including several which have to do with the hand-writing. But I will save them for a more serene state of mind. Elizabeth sends her love to you and was pleased that you sent yours to her.

See you soon,
DELMORE

P.S. Did you know that William James said, "God may forgive, your friends may forget, but the nerve-cells will record it forever." What a thing to say, even if true!

P.P.S. If Mr. Anon. is not W. Candlewood, will you let me know soon so that I can call off the police dogs running around in my mind? And if you have already found out who he is, will you tell me?

/ · /

William Candlewood: Doppelgänger of JL, who answered difficult letters of complaint to ND under that name.

Hiram Handspring: Another JL doppelgänger, this one a comedian. A third pen name was Tasilo Ribischke, who wrote arcane Surrealist pieces for some of the early *ND* annuals.

my grandmother: Hannah Nathanson.

Whitehead: Alfred North Whitehead (1861–1947), English mathematician and philosopher who became a professor at Harvard.

Gertrude: Gertrude Huston, art director at New Directions, later to become Laughlin's third wife.

Uncle Tom's great lines: Schwartz quotes line 8 of Eliot's *Gerontion*, "And the Jew squats on the window sill, the owner."

Dr. Gruenthal: Max Gruenthal, Schwartz's psychiatrist.

in Pasadena: JL was traveling to California to confer on Ford Foundation business.

Hoffman: Paul Hoffman, one-time head of the Ford Foundation.

Katz: Milton Katz.

166. TL-1

RD1, Box 230
Pittstown, NJ
January 1, 1952

DEAR JAY:

One of our intelligence agents, whose reliability I don't yet know, says that Mary Lou Aswell is starting a fiction magazine for Hutchins & Ford. If so, this suggests, does it not, a poetry magazine, a theatre, an opera house, a publishing house, a university, and a Ford version of *Time, Life & Fortune*? Hutchins must have been studying the methods of Branch Rickey, for the boy wonder emeritus is using the whole of American culture as a farm system of minor league clubs. He chooses people who have already proven that they are star managers in the minor leagues. Mary Lou Aswell, for example won the pennant on *Harper's Bazaar,* and you have won a series of pennants with the Norfolk club, the Brooklyn club, the St. Louis–Tennessee Williams club, etc.

When you see him, you might say that I hit .400 in the unconscious-conscious league twice: One in 1938 when you published "In Reams Begin Responsibilities" (and "reams" is no misprint, if you remember the season we spent in hell in 1940 because I trusted and overestimated Will Barrett's knowledge of French and my first wife's ability to look up words in a dictionary); and the second time I hit .400 was in 1948 when you published *The World Is a Wedding* (or *I Want to Get Married Again*) and wedded the princess Elizabeth (who has a mind like radar) in 1949, which I expected to be the second edition of the gold rush, but which turned out to be the second version of Chaplin's *The Gold Rush,* with me in the lead role in a Chicago stock company. I am sometimes hopeful that I will hit .400 at least four more times and sometimes afraid that I will never hit it again. As Uncle Tom says in one of his prayers, "Teach me to care and not to care," and as I say in my perhaps almost-finished book about him, "Teach me to hope and not to hope."

Joking aside, how hopeful can I be about a job on the new review? When you see Hutchins, you might point out to him that if you give me a job, you are buying someone who was trained for eight years in Cambridge and educated by the task of teaching freshmen to make myself clear to the most unlettered and interested freshman. You are also getting someone who had eight years of training on *Partisan Review,* but who is a poet and not a politician, and who is sometimes thought of as the one soft touch of the four editors.

Forgive me for bragging, I don't really feel very good, seeing that Elizabeth has to work instead of writing novels and next fall I will have to teach instead of writing poems and stories. I can do editorial work with much less strain than teaching. The Almighty Dollar has knocked me out of the ring just as Firpo knocked Dempsey out of the ring and into a sports-writer's lap in the first round of their fight (in New Jersey!) in 1921. But you will remember that it was not long after that that Dempsey knocked Firpo out of consciousness and won the fight. And in 1922, just thirty years ago, the Giants, led by John McGraw, otherwise known as The Master Mind and the Little Napoleon, won the pennant and beat the Yankees in four straight games in the World Series, a feat which has not since been repeated. Perhaps, since it is 1952, it is high time that my thirty years' war with the Almighty Dollar. . . . [Letter incomplete]

/ · /

Mary Lou Aswell: Magazine editor; she did not edit a magazine for the Ford Foundation.

Hutchins & Ford: Robert Hutchins was an associate director of the Ford Foundation.

"Teach me to care and not to care . . .": From the fifth stanza of Eliot's *Ash-Wednesday:* "Teach us to care and not to care . . ."

I will have to teach: He was to take over the creative writing department at Princeton in the fall of 1952, in R. P. Blackmur's absence.

a job on the new review: Schwartz's campaign to win support from the Ford Foundation is recounted in Saul Bellow's novel, *Humboldt's Gift* (1975).

Firpo and Dempsey: Famous professional boxers.

167. TLS-2 Pasadena, California
February 9, 1952

DEAR DELMORE:

Be sure to tune in again next week, same time, same station, for the next thrilling chapter of our story, "A Country Boy in the Land of the Kind-hearted Tycoons"—but meanwhile, please accept the following brief digest of events here.

At the end of one of the more nerve-wracking but fascinating days on that Great Stage which is This Life, your old friend ended up as president of a corporation called Intercultural Publications Inc., of which the directors are one banker, one corporation lawyer, one publisher, one industrialist, one college president, and one public relations expert.

He also finished the day as "publisher" of a magazine called *Perspectives USA,* which will be edited by teams of guest editors, and which will have an advisory board so large that it will be impossible to hold meetings in any place smaller than Madison Square Garden, and from which meetings it seems likely that the bodies of outraged bards will be carried forth in quantity.

As president of what Hutchins is already calling Intervultural Publications, may I invite you to become a member of the advisory board of *Perspectives USA*? Salary nil, but lots of free meals and stamped envelopes.

As publisher of *Perspectives,* may I invite you to serve at some future date as member of a team of guest editors for an issue of the magazine? Salary for this work to be a share of a budget per issue for editing of $2500. If you learn to play the zither before I get back East you can obviously edit the music section as well as the rest and thus spare the expense of a musical colleague.

As publisher of *Perspectives* may I also invite you to accept the part-time position of confidential literary consultant to the publisher at a salary of $100 a month? Your duties in this role would be to screen American magazines for outstanding material, which the publisher should call to the attention of rotating editors, and also to screen such manuscripts as are sent to the magazine, even though such submissions will be discouraged. Should anything really remarkable come in, it could be shown to an appropriate guest editor, since there is no reason the magazine cannot run new material, even though much of its contents will be reprint. Should the duties of this office become onerous, the salary for it would rise. But at the outset it should be fairly easy, and you read most of the magazines anyway. One day every other week in town should cover it, plus answering the telephone when the publisher needs to find out what some great mind means by something expressed in a noble style.

If you would care further to supplement your income beyond these proposals above mentioned, I see no reason why the now ghostly editor of New Directions should not offer you the ghostly privilege of returning to their authors with a soft-hearted kind word the manuscripts which come into the office at 333 Sixth Avenue. You wouldn't have to read them as there are more books already on the schedule than we have the funds to print—just change the envelopes and send them back, though screening out for me to read anything that is short which might do for the annual. This could be done, I should judge, in one day in town a week, with anything of interest to be taken home to the squirearchy for perusal. Perhaps $100 a month from ND for this.

I hope you will not feel that the way things have worked out here is the most abject piece of back-stabbing on record. There is no question in *my* mind you would do a better job on this magazine than I can, but it simply was not possible from the point of view of practical politics here. The trustees would have liked to have someone like Ted Weeks. They were willing to settle for me because I came from Pittsburgh and looked like a business man. I felt I had to get the thing tied down quickly before they did get ahold of somebody who would pull the thing down to a lower level than where we want it to be. I hope you will understand all this and be willing to give me the help on the brain level I will need to handle the rotating editors efficiently.

Please don't say anything about these matters to anyone until the Foundation puts out its formal press release. I shall have to write to Blackmur, because he needs some money right away to pay his taxes, but I will ask him not to talk about it, either.

And, as we said before, swallow this paper before they knock at the door. I'm going up to San Francisco on Sunday and will go to Alta in the middle of the week. So write me at Alta Lodge, Sandy, Utah.

See you soon,

J

/ · /

Ted Weeks: Edward Weeks, editor of the *Atlantic Monthly,* and an old friend of JL's from Harvard days.

168. TLS-2

RD1, Box 230
Pittstown, New Jersey
February 10, 1952

DEAR JAY:

Your hot communiqué from Pasadena was hilarious. But I had Great Expectations when it arrived and left it unopened, thinking perhaps that in it you announced that you were bringing back not only the bacon, but the prize pig ($, *in hoc signo vincit*). So my joy in the jokes was mixed with letdown and disappointment.

I will obey your command of silence. I do have a tendency to blab when I am not particularly instructed to be silent. But once instructed, I imitate tombstones and Trappist monks. Besides, when I blab, it is so mixed up with free associations, far-fetched metaphors, and desperate puns, that anyone who is attempting to pump me ends up in a state of mystification, if he or she is conceited, and in a state of deception, if they take me too literally or too seriously.

If you feel like passing along a piece of well-meaning advice to King—(as you call him: I take it you mean the Prince of Peace), you might tell him that it is my considered opinion, for whatever it is worth, that he will never be made Pope. He might become President of the U.S.A., however, if there is a split in the Democratic Party, as there might very well be in 1956. You remember, it was a split in the Republican Party in 1912 which made it possible for college president Woodrow Wilson to become Chief Executive and subsequently to be royally f——d like Isabel Archer and Daisy Miller when he went to Paris and dealt with those arch-seducers Clemenceau and Lloyd George.

Speaking of Presidents, it does seem as if we may be living through the last days of the great republic, for if Eisenhower is the megalomaniac some say he is, it will be Julius Caesar all over again, and even if Thomas E. Dewey plays Brutus and assassinates him, and tries to take power himself, one of Eisenhower's nephews, Octavius Augustus Eisenhower (now a student of Blackmur's at Princeton), will win out after Dewey falls madly in love with Lana (Cleopatra) Turner (Topping!). Anyway, history certainly sometimes repeats itself, and existence frequently imitates Shakespeare.

Personally, I think I will vote for Truman if he is senseless enough to run again, on the grounds that a politician who tolerates the petty thieves of mink coats and deep freezes is preferable to any five-star general who has convinced himself that he can do no wrong. That's what Eisenhower said on D-day when the reporters wanted to know what he would have done if Rommel had been permitted to drive him back into the nasty water. He said something like, "You can't do something like that (invade Fortress Europe) if you think you might not succeed." The ego-element here, I think, is "If I want to do something very much, I am bound to succeed," and this is, is it not, a very dangerous view for a President to maintain. First thing you know, he may decide that either he or Stalin has to be the first real emperor of the entire globe. I don't like either-or guys because they conclude by saying neither-nor, except for me.

Speaking of Stalin, they have just drafted Willie Mays, which is obviously the result of Stalin's lust for Korea, and the rest of the world, and though they have also drafted Don Newcombe, the Giants' pennant chances are seriously weakened, unless Durocher can find an intelligent thought in his head, namely to put Bobby Thomson back in center, Hank

Thompson on third, and get Laraine Day Durocher to find a high yaller girl friend for Hank Thompson—one who will convince him that high yallers are the best of two worlds which they probably are, I am told. The newspapers said that Thompson, who is very gifted, has "personal problems." This can mean only one thing: He must set his bed in order.

I came upon one glitter of hopeful interpretation in your passage reading, "They are wetting down the oubliette for you in a certain Embassy on Connecticut Avenue. The lady you wrote those jokes about is now a Queen." If I interpret this with wild optimism, it may mean, a cradle is being prepared so that Elizabeth can bring a poor child into this grave new world. I feel that in such an eventuality, the second Elizabethan period has a chance of surpassing the first.

What does M.F.H. mean after my name on your envelope? My Friend Hersey? My Frantic Henchman?

You say that I was seen without a necktie in the Huntington Library. This is untrue. I was wearing one of my three neckties that day.

It has been a sad week. I wrote a piece of 4200 words in the hope of being paid 10 cents a word by *The Reporter*. The only thing I've heard so far is that Phil Horton, to whom I sent it, took sick the day after he received it. No news may be good news, but it is also nervous-making.

Please let me know of further roulette convolutions and convulsions, as H—— passes the Buck in Pasadena. And write me collect if you have won the Peace Sweepstakes.

> Messieurs, faites vos jeux!
> Les jeux sont faits!

> DELMORE, A.A.A.

P.S. I better get away from French: It's unlucky. Did I ever tell you my version of the last two lines of *Faust:* "The eternal frau (fiancée, bride) / Can get it up."

P.P.S. If the former boy wonder thinks that all roads lead to Rome, he is really wrong. Stalin thinks all roads lead to Moscow. He is wrong too. Nor do all roads lead to Washington, though more and more will (e.g., the Jersey Turnpike). All roads, I feel at the moment, go in a vicious or benign circle, since all roads lead nowhere or to Inferno, Paradiso, & / or Purgatorio. Perhaps we can hold a post-mortem on the subject some day in Purgatorio. It is pretty cold in this house and I could do with a little more fire.

P.P.P.S. If a guest editor will get $2500 for an issue, should you not get $2500 for the pilot issue?

/ · /

King: Possible reference to Robert M. Hutchins.

Isabel Archer and Daisy Miller: Heroines of Henry James's international novels, *Portrait of a Lady* and *Daisy Miller*.

Clemenceau: Georges Clemenceau (1846–1921), premier of France during World War I.

Lloyd George: David Lloyd George (1869–1945), prime minister of Great Britain during World War I.

Thomas E. Dewey: (1902–1971), Twice an unsuccessful Republican candidate for the U.S. presidency.

Lana Turner: Hollywood film star of the 1940s and 1950s.

Rommel: Irwin Rommel (1891–1944), German field marshal in World War II.

Stalin: Joseph Stalin (1879–1953) was head of the Communist Party of the Soviet Union for a quarter of a century.

Willie Mays, Don Newcomb, Hank Thompson, Leo Durocher: Famous figures in baseball.

Laraine Day Dorocher: Film star and wife of Leo Durocher.

M.F.H.: Usually Master of Fox Hounds; a reference to Schwartz's bucolic setting in New Jersey.

Huntington Library: The great scholarly and rare book library in Pasadena, California, founded by the railroad tycoon Henry Edwards Huntington (1850–1927).

the last two lines of Faust: The Bayard Taylor translation, in the original meters, reads: "The Woman-soul leadeth us / Upward and on!"

Inferno: The three books of Dante's *Divine Comedy:* Hell, Purgatory, and Paradise.

169. TLS-1

RD1, Box 230
Pittstown, New Jersey
February 12, 1952

DEAR KING JAMES:

Or perhaps I should say, President James?

So you really did it. This is one of the biggest coups since Drake defeated the Spanish Armada and gave the British Empire its power to rule the waves. Fitzgerald was wrong: *You* are the last tycoon! Long live the last tycoon!

Just exactly how old are you? What is your date of birth? I feel that a little astrology is necessary at this point. All of this is written in the stars, they say. But leave us not forget the remark I put in my last book of poems, which was not written by Hamlet: "Those whom the gods would destroy they first make successful." A rush of *hubris* to the head is natural, and you deserve all the fun you must be feeling right now. But this is the time to move slowly, as you well know most of the time, and I put it in only because you must be naturally very excited and delighted, and it is just at such times that *I* make the most catastrophic errors, to wit, I spend a season in Hell, to show that one is after all responsible for one's reams and dreams. In the same way last season it was when the Dodgers had a lead of thirteen-and-one-half games that they began to skid. So with

Napoleon: It was when he was most victorious that he made the errors which brought him in the end to Waterloo.

Leave us profit from the lessons and lesions of history. History does not necessarily repeat itself.

Who are the other assistants on your cabinet? A president, as you well know, has to have a cabinet. Does Intercultural Publications mean that you are president of a brand-new publishing house?

Elizabeth is sick and in bed today, we ran out of kerosene in the middle of the night—*mea culpa*—so I can't write at length today. But Elizabeth also is overjoyed by your feats, despite her sore throat and exhaustion.

I'll write as soon as I hear from you. When are you coming back? We ought to have a celebration. And to show you how pleased I am, I will drink only Pepsi-Cola, since pleasure can be my champagne.

You can be the international hero if you are careful not to be the International Nero. (See Suetonius when in doubt, and then read the Four Gospels.)

Please write soon, if you can. Let's have a coronation day.

Now I see what Greeley meant when he said, "Go West, young man, until you reach the new Klondike, Pasadena."

Yours,
DELMORE
(A Red Letter Day)

/ · /

Dear King James: Schwartz is responding to the news in JL's letter of February 9.

Fitzgerald: Reference to F. Scott Fitzgerald's unfinished final novel, *The Last Tycoon.*

Suetonius: Caius Suetonius Tranquillus (A.D. c.69–after 122), Roman historian, author of *The Lives of the Caesars.*

Greeley: Horace Greeley (1811–1872), American newspaper editor.
Klondike: The most famous gold-mining region in Alaska.

170. ALS-1   RD1 Box 230
                                                Pittstown, N.J.
                                                March 21, 1952

DEAR JAY:

I've been to see Dr. Gruenthal (whom I've mentioned to you on several occasions) and he would
like to speak to you and perhaps see you. His number is TR7-6058, and you'll find talking to him
interesting in itself, I think, as well as being a favor
to me. The sooner the better, if possible.

                                                Yours,
                                                DELMORE

                          / · /

Dr. Gruenthal: JL called on him as requested to check on Schwartz's
increasingly manic state.

171. ALS-4   RD1 Box 230
                                                Pittstown, N.J.
                                                September 10, 1952

DEAR JAY:

Joy was unrestrained in this obscure plot of New
Jersey when your news arrived. Elizabeth (Barrett
Browning Pollet) Schwartz sat up in her sickbed,
color rose to her cheeks, and she finally inquired as
to whether we could now purchase the pop-up toaster

which has been the apple of her eye for the past eight months.

I won't embarrass you with the clinical details of our difficulties of the last few months—but we're both more grateful to you than you could possibly imagine without knowing the details. I've read the piece by E. M. Cioran on Scott Fitzgerald and cannot say that it seems very good to me. There is something dreadfully off-key—at least to me—in writing about Fitzgerald's "Pascalian experience" and thinking about him in terms of Kierkegaard and Dostoevsky. Nothing that Cioran says is particularly wrong (though much of it is a sumptuous intellectualized paraphrasing of the obvious), but the point of view is such that the next step would have to be *John O'Hara and St. John of the Cross,* or *Walter Winchell and Thomas Aquinas' Doctrine of the Angelic Intelligences.* Pascal, Kierkegaard and Dostoevsky should seem to apply to Fitzgerald, since they spoke of the universal human situation, but the intermediate steps are missing. I may be wrong and I would guess that European readers would not know what is lacking in the piece while Americans probably would not read it at all. Since the typescript is a carbon, I'll send it back to your Ford office.

I wait impatiently for orders to proceed with the digest. I suppose the first one should be ready for the January issue.

I see that the Ford Foundation is tinkering with the intellectual level of television. This seems to me a profound error to judge by my impressions of the new art-form garnered at the village saloon where I irritate the bartender by drinking only Coca-Cola: the dramas on TV have an effect hitherto unknown in any literature or art. Their representation of existence appear to be so awful, banal, vulgar and pointless that the "viewer" returns to his own life with a feeling of *escape*. Instead of escaping from life's pain by means of literature and art, we now can enjoy escaping from TV drama into actual existence. To improve TV would be to lose this new and important experience. If Dante were able to revise the *Inferno* he would have the new form of damnation an eternity in which one looked only at TV.

Yours,
DELMORE

P.S. Have you listened to the utterances of Adlai? Perhaps it is time for you to choose between literature and the G.O.P. (War has broken out at *Time* magazine; T. S. Matthews has discovered, after 20 years, that *Time*'s stories are *slanted* [!] [he is a Stevenson man].) It is also reported that the Old Possum himself has said that although it would be improper for him to express any view with regard to our domestic problems, if he were an American (!), he would vote for Stevenson.

/ · /

the piece by E. M. Cioran: "Physionomie d'un effondrement," on Fitzgerald's *The Crack-up,* which appeared in *Profils* (October 1952). Cioran was a contemporary Swiss critic and essayist.

Kierkegaard: Søren Kierkegaard (1813–1855), Danish philosopher and religious writer.

John O'Hara: (1905–1970), American realistic novelist.

St. John of the Cross: (1542–1591), Spanish mystic and poet.

Walter Winchell: (1897–1972), American gossip columnist for *The New York Mirror* beginning in 1929.

Pascal: (1623–1662), Blaise Pascal, French religious thinker and author.

the digest: Synopses of important articles from literary journals for *Perspectives USA.*

T. S. Matthews: An editor of *Time.*

Adlai: Adlai Ewing Stevenson (1900–1965), governor of Illinois and twice unsuccessful Democratic candidate for the presidency.

G.O.P.: Grand Old Party; i.e., the Republican Party.

an American: Eliot adopted British citizenship in November 1927.

172. AL-2

Princeton University
Princeton, N.J.
[N.D.]

[No salutation]

Unfinished Narrative Poem about Ethel Schwartz

In nine short months, the cat Ethel
Has had nine kittens!
In nine long months, I have only written
One short poem, and it is not at all as well-constructed
As the least of the kittens, which the reader can see
By direct inspection . . .

Unfinished Narrative Poem about Buttons Schwartz

My cat Buttons
Is far superior to Barbara Hutton.
She is poor but sincere,
While Miss Hutton is probably neither poor nor sincere,
And is probably just as much of a glutton . . .

/ · /

Barbara Hutton: American heiress.

173. TLS-1

RD1 Box 230
Pittstown, N.J.
December 21, 1952

DEAR JAY:

Enclosed is a revised carbon copy of my digest. I left a clean, proof-read copy with Carruth on the 15th as requested. There are 21 new items and I could have made it 80, since I read more than 400 articles for the piece. I was much surprised that you were not entirely satisfied by my first effort, since I tried it out on a number of people in Princeton, and in addition Blackmur, who did not know I had done it and who was sent a copy as the editor of the issue, said that it was very good. However, I can make it whatever you want it to be, as soon as I know exactly what you want. It is much easier to do an index than a commentary, obviously, but the problem, I think, is that it will then not be particularly interesting; and there is an *International Index of Periodicals*. As soon as possible, I will send you specimens of the magazine digests in European periodicals, so you can see what Europeans want or, rather, so you can see what I modelled myself upon.

Carruth will send the good copy to the printer as soon as he hears from you. I have many other matters to tell you about, but can't write much of a letter today since Elizabeth is ill again. I should be able to write you during the week and I hope very much that you can spare me two or three hours of your time as soon as you return. Perhaps we can set up a rapid system of communication; that would help a lot I think.

The first issue of *Perspectives* was a big hit in Princeton and even Edmund Wilson expressed approval and a desire to write for it. But he wanted to give an essay on Sartre's book on Genet, which *The New Yorker* would not print because it was too "scabrous," so I put him off until I could find out what your policy is. This is one of the things I mean by the helpfulness of rapid communication. Which reminds me that one of the sentences in my piece is a quotation from Tate on Hart Crane as "an extreme example of the unwilling homosexual." Please advise on this and let me know when you are coming back.

Yours,
DELMORE

P.S. I sent a carbon to England. No one was sure of just where you would be.

/ · /

Carruth: The poet Hayden Carruth (b. 1921) was working on the staff of *Perspectives.*

Sartre: Jean-Paul Sartre (1903–1950), French Existentialist philosopher and novelist. ND published his *Stories,* his study of Baudelaire, and his novel *Nausea* (1959).

Jean Genet: (b. 1910), French dramatist and novelist.

quotation from Tate: The phrase appears in Allen Tate's "Crane: The Poet As Hero," subtitled "An Encomium Twenty Years Later," which was printed in *The New Republic* in 1952.

Hart Crane: (1899–1933), American poet.

174. ALS-1

DEAR DELMORE:

The quality of this material is *excellent.*

But some of the little pieces are still too long. None should be more than 100 words and the closer to 50, the better. Will you try to boil these long ones down and let me have them by January 7th at the latest?

No time to lose. I hope you have also boiled down the other batch.

3rd request! When typing please put periods and commas *inside* quotes. Thus, ." ," That is our style.

I think Tate's remark about Crane would get by on the basis of taste, but what about libel? His mother is still alive and could sue, I think.

Wilson on Genet would not go down well with the Brass, I fear.

I hope Elizabeth is feeling better. Best wishes for 1953!

See you soon,
J

/ · /

That is our style: Schwartz's punctuation style in the letters has also been changed to W. W. Norton house style passim for this edition.

---

175. TLS-2
RD1 Box 230
Pittstown, N.J.
January 4, 1953

DEAR JAY:

I've been working day and night since getting your latest communiqué to cut the copy. I'll certainly get it into the Pierre, where the elevator boys seem to think that I am an agent of the Mafia, bringing opium to the patrons, by Wednesday. I sent the old batch, cut, plus the new batch of entries to you in Zürich as well as England, and Carruth or Mary Cox has a copy of the old and new batch of entries, both of which I will try to pull together, proof-read, and tidy up when I get to town on Tuesday.

When you have the time, which I suppose you don't have now, I'd like you to compare my uncut and my cut entries to see the difference which condensation beyond a certain point makes. Some condensed author may yelp that the entry does not do justice to his epoch-making insights. Perhaps you don't care, and if you don't, I certainly don't. But please advise when you have the leisure. Also, when you have more time, I'd like you to inspect the European abstracts of periodical reviews on which I modelled mine. Again, if you don't think it is of the essence of this part of *Perspectives* to give the European reader what he wants, or which he will think useful and interesting, if it is, on the other hand, more a matter of giving fair and comprehensive representation to American periodicals, please let me know. It is less trouble to summarize 100 articles in 50 words than it is to write an interesting and informative summary of the articles which are really good in 100 to 150 words. I can do it either way or we can have what Aquinas sometimes called a *synthesis* of longs and shorts.

I take it that you agree that it is best for the digest to be unsigned and officially anonymous, just like the listing of books (I've taken over some of the books for the next listing, at Carruth's suggestion).

I have not been as efficient as I am sure that I will be, partly because I am still not entirely clear as to what you want and partly because the teaching at Princeton, which will end in the spring, has involved me in a great deal more work than I expected. Since Blackmur is away, I am supposed to be in charge of the Creative Arts Program, and this takes up a lot of time, to say nothing of energy. But the worst part is over and by the end of May, I will be entirely free.

Last week I suggested to Carruth, who thought that the idea would be agreeable to you, that I spend at least half a day a week, and longer if necessary, in the *Perspectives* office as a way of routinizing my work. Which leads naturally to the question which has been perplexing me more and more: How does a literary consultant consult? I have dozens of notations of suggestions for you—some or many of them doubtless cockeyed or unfeasible—and I have held off in sending them to you because I figured that you were probably preoccupied with Yogi and the Upanishads in little old Calcutta. Some of these suggestions might be of use to you, or for that matter might not—I don't have the dimmest idea which— since they are based in part on the comments I've heard about the pilot and first issue. Most of the comments were extremely favorable, but some of them involved the assumption that it would be likely that each guest editor would tend to print his friends mainly, and since they are all editors for only one issue, disregard the chief purposes of *Perspectives*. I know that you want to keep yourself down to a minimum of interference with the guest editors, but if you don't want to give them complete *carte blanche* in the choice of material, but instead a certain amount of discreet guidance at certain junctures, *before* they have launched out on their choices, then I think the method of sending them memoranda, which has already been used, could be practised some more, and I don't think it need involve much extra work for you, apart from your deciding on what suggestions were wise and to whom.

Which makes me remember that some of the guest editors have caused some gratuitous ill-feeling by making long lists of what they wanted to publish— longer than any issue could possibly contain—and then subsequently announcing that they could not keep their promises because they had been mistaken as to the amount of space available to them. I suppose that a certain number of such incidents, which result in disappointment and even debt, are unavoidable; but some of them certainly could be avoided.

I have a great deal more to consult with you about, but will restrain myself until I am sure you are not preoccupied with other problems, an impression I got from Carruth. Will you and Gertrude have time to visit us in our rural seat some weekend when you return from Pasadena, and inspect our version of post-urbanism? I can hardly wait to hear Gertrude's impressions of India. In return I will tell her of the alarming incidence of the rape of men by women in Princeton. Please advise.

Yours,
DELMORE

P.S. What about the notes on contributors? We have not yet done anything about eliciting the necessary information.

P.P.S. Would you kindly favor me with your candid, confidential opinion as a friend on the enclosed article, which is certainly going to rock Morningside Heights.

/ · /

the Pierre: The Pierre Hotel on Fifth Avenue, where *Perspectives* had its office.

Mary Cox: Copy editor for *Perspectives.*

Upanishads: Hindu scriptures dating back to 900 B.C. Laughlin would soon be going to India to work on a Ford Foundation project.

Gertrude: Gertrude Huston.

enclosed article: Draft of "The Duchess's Red Shoes," an article later published in two parts in *Partisan Review* in 1953. It was an attack on Lionel Trilling's critique of "the liberal imagination." Schwartz was at odds with Trilling's exclusive concern "with the ideas and attitudes and interests of the educated class."

Morningside Heights: Location of Columbia University, where Trilling lived and taught.

176. ALS-2   In Flight with American
                                            [N.D.]

DEAR DELMORE:

It seems to me that it was very inconsiderate of your friend Swann to upset his friends by talking about his health, which is bad manners anyway, when he knew they were in a rush to go out and eat.

Do you *enjoy* writing pieces like that? I enjoy them when you are being cute, but being cute is not exactly the full realization of the "promise" of the author of *In Dreams*. The serious part just seems to me a lot of fooling around with language. (Will return proofs separately.)

Isn't it really time for the whole *PR* crowd to disappear? It strikes me all as a kind of hardening of the arteries. I don't know exactly what is to replace it, but as long as Philip keeps flogging that old horse, the wagon is not going to deliver the milk. (This figure is not entirely clear, but you know what I mean.)

It's a pity that Harry Brown took to Hollywood. He was funny enough to dispose of Barrett & Co. You should cut loose from them before they ruin you. Your "cuteness" is perhaps your reaction to their sterility but still within the frame of snobbism they impose. Break loose from them and maybe you will become really creative again. Is this what you wanted to hear?

I had to rush off to Pasadena before I could re-read your shortened versions of the magazine guide paragraphs, but I left them with Mrs. Cox to forward for translation. But you *must* do your own typing. We do not have the funds to have your stuff retyped. You are expected to supply 5 sets of really clean script, carefully copyread. And remember—quotes *outside* the periods.

Have you written to Roger Caillois about *Diogenes*? He needs suggestions for American contributions and also American books to be reviewed. Who is there at Princeton in the social sciences or the humanities who is doing something new and significant?

It is very cumbersome to try to direct the guest editors. I think they are doing a good enough job to be left alone. Maybe I will do another issue soon myself, to fill in the principal gaps which they have left—American dance, industrial architecture, a short play, Wallace Stevens, Marsden Hartley, something on history—most of the issues are a bit too literary. It's a pity that Meyer Schapiro is too busy to do one. He had some very different leads. But I haven't the time to push people. Whatever became of *your* issue? Any thoughts about that? Try to be *un*-literary.

I suppose I'll be a week or ten days in the West. Then when I am back perhaps I might get down to see you and Elizabeth except that my new girl friend—whom you will not like—has no automobile. I suppose we could take the train to Princeton.

Love to Elizabeth,

J

/ · /

your friend Swann: Laughlin refers to a point in Schwartz's essay on Trilling, when Schwartz alludes to the critic's attitude toward a famous episode in Proust's *Remembrance of Times Past.* The character Swann has gone to see his close friends, the Duc and Duchesse de Guermantes, to tell them he is dying. But they are in a hurry to leave for a dinner party and haven't time to hear his news. The Duchesse does, however, find time to change her black slippers, which her husband objects to, for red ones.

being cute: Schwartz's style in this essay is as personal and chatty as in his "bagatelles," published as *The Ego Is Always at the Wheel* (ed. Phillips, 1986). At one point in the Trilling piece, Schwartz declares, "Yes, we have no bananas. But all God's chillun got shoes."

Philip: Philip Rahv.

Harry Brown: Poet, Harvard graduate, and friend of Robert Lowell.

Barrett & Co.: William Barrett and the other editors of *Partisan Review*.

Roger Caillois: Paris-based editor of *Diogenes,* the journal published in four languages by the International Council for Philosophy and Humanistic Studies.

Marsden Hartley: (1877–1945), American painter.

177. TLS-4

RD1, Box 230
Pittstown, N.J.
Jan. 16, 1953

DEAR JAY:

I was sorry to miss you last week when you were in and out of the Pierre, but I had to get down to the *P.R.* editorial meeting to find out what the Machiavellian Trilling might be doing by way of responding to my piece on Diana's Red Shoes. Besides, you were having lunch with your mother and others appeared to be on the waiting list to see you and I had already written you three letters requesting an interview, in addition to asking Hayden to arrange for an audience with you. And all in vain, so, having recently studied good manners, I felt I might be forcing myself on your sacred presence while preoccupied with what Trilling might be insinuating ubiquitously by means of that evil invention, the telephone, which permits him to be any number of places in an hour's time.

But I do think that we ought to confer. Do you have an appointment on the Ides of March? There is a bar on Third Avenue where, if we speak only English, no one will know what we are saying. I am free to come hastening to your summons on all days but Wednesday and Thursday, when I have to be down in Princeton.

Also I hope that you are serious when you say "perhaps I might get down to see you and Elizabeth, except that my new girl friend—whom you will not like—has no automobile." You don't need a car, it just takes an hour from Penn Station to Flemington (I am enclosing a train schedule) where I can pick you and the lady up at the Junction. I am disturbed to hear that I will not like your new girl friend. Don't you like her? I don't expect her to admire me or know Dante by heart, all I require of any lady friend of yours is that she like you. Besides, I like everyone, at least to begin with, and foolishly, for I suppose that if I were less fond and naive, at the start, I would get kicked in the face less frequently. (This is, is it not, what it is to be an American: To expect everyone to love you, admire your works, reward you with friendship, and esteem your automobile and cat.) Seriously, however, do try to come for a weekend when you get back.

Your comments on *P.R.* have been made by others, including Dr. Gruenthal, the Pope of 81st Street. And even if no one else had made them, it would have occurred to me that being on *P.R.* has many disadvantages, including the not unimportant one of making me feel, after some editorial meetings, that the only sensible thing for me to do would be to go home and cut my throat since—I won't try to make a detailed list of what is wrong. I stay on partly because I don't want to leave a sinking ship, and partly because, given various personal disabilities, it is a way of keeping in touch with people and having friends, however trying. After all, I do have a hard time knowing people, since I am often utterly lacking in social initiative, depressed, etc. and who else is available? You are never around, or when you are, only briefly (it is eight years since last we played tennis with the late Boylston Professor, who is unquestionably giving cocktail parties now in the other life). The Village and like places are choked with fairies with whom I can never quite feel at ease, no matter how nice and intelligent they are, etc. There is always Berryman, of course, but being friends with Berryman is like being friends with a volcano. I exaggerate, but you can see what I mean. I now number several psychiatrists among my acquaintances but here too relaxed friendship is difficult because they are all afraid that I am psychoanalyzing them, when I am not afraid that the reverse is taking place. However, I did move to the country partly to break out, somewhat, from the *P.R.* circle—circle is good, if it suggests the *Inferno*—and I intend to get away entirely as soon as it seems proper, and sensible.

You can judge my feelings about some aspects of *P.R.* when I report that they won't let Elizabeth review books, although they know very well that she is an excellent critic of fiction. The reason advanced is that since she is my wife, the other wives will be jealous! So you can see why at times when I feel like calling *P.R.* a snake pit, I hesitate only because to do so would be to insult snakes. None of the other wives are authors. On the other hand, snake pits are sometimes useful, if only to cure maniacs.

Many thanks for your candid comments on "The Duchess's Red Shoes," which you conclude with, "Is this what you wanted to hear?" I can't pretend that I basked in pleasure on reading "being cute is not exactly the full realization of the 'promise' of the

author of 'In Dreams.' " But I am really grateful that
you felt like saying it, if only because it is the first
sign of interest, in three years, from you in literary
production on my part. Moreover, I wish you would
resolve to vent any disappointment, irritation, or
negative feeling of which I am the cause directly to
me without sparing my feelings, since I am bound
to profit by knowing what your impressions are, and
bound to find out things which I ought to know and
can't find out for myself. I don't like to hear that I
have not fulfilled the promise of my youth, but almost
everyone else is too polite to tell me and left to myself,
I tend to put all new poems and stories in my filing
cabinet and forget about them. Hence, in view of
the fact that we have now been friends for some fifteen years, it is, I think, your *duty* as well as your
privilege to say what you really think. I would prefer
that you say it in a pleasant tone, but I'd rather have
the tone unpleasant than be left in ignorance and self-
delusion.

It may be self-delusion, but I have really been more
productive in the last two years than ever before.
The only trouble is that it no longer seems important as it did in my green and acne'd youth to appear
in print as soon as a poem and story are finished,
especially since I discovered that I do actually improve
whatever I write by revision over a long period of
time. What does seem important is to write the poem
and the less I think of publication, the more freedom
and energy I have in writing. However. You may
not find this news of the most urgent interest. I will
conclude this topic by saying that I often feel convinced that you and the Widow Schwartz will gain
vast sums when the contents of my filing cabinets
are finally published and I am in the cold, cold ground
or perhaps trying to wangle an invitation to or crash
one of Theodore's divine cocktail parties. And long

before I have departed for a far, far better world, I think you will agree with me that *Tales from the Vienna Woods* is the best book I have written and justifies the long periods of not publishing anything creative, for the sake of patient revision.

Which reminds me to ask if you have given up the novel in three parts (Germany wins, America wins, it is a stalemate) which you told me about in 1942. If so, I would like to borrow one of the ideas, the one about Christ returning to earth, for a story. I will make full acknowledgement of the source. Please advise. Needless to say, the idea of the novel is as good as new, with the mere substitution of Russia for Germany, and your new lady friend for Margaret, and I would ask for a loan of the idea of the entire novel, not the lady friend, except that I am afraid that I lack the globe-trotting and transcontinental touring which seems necessary to its realization.

I will reserve questions and answers about literary business for another page.

In Princeton I am considered quite a "sport." A well-stacked young lady named Kitty Morgan inquired, after listening to me for a time in perplexity: "Where do you come from originally?" "Bohemia," I said, and when she still looked perplexed, I recited this new paraphrase poem:

> I shall not rest from mental fight
>   Nor shall my glass slip from my hand,
> Till I have built Bohemia
>   In Jersey's green and pleasant land!

My students are also very curious. The Firestone boy asked me, "Sir, have you anything against humor?" I told him that I certainly did not and asked him if he knew a few good jokes. But when he told me his most cherished joke, I admitted that perhaps

I was not as much in sympathy with humor as I had supposed. Two weeks after, I yielded to temptation when he arrived for a conference about his manuscript—a satire on the idle rich—and remarked bashfully, "Mr. Firestone, I just had a flat tire." *He* thought this was very funny, no matter what *you* may think. And one other student made me think that a new era had truly begun in literature and among young writers. He had just shown me so good a manuscript that I told him I might be able to help him get it published if the whole thing was as good as the first part. "Sir," he said, "I have two more years at Princeton and two years in the army. I do not want to be published prematurely!" Has this *ever* happened before? I mean, among young would-be authors who have never appeared in print? His name is Dabney, a name to remember, he is a Virginian, his chief pride is his sporting car, and he has only one serious fault as an author, a tendency to . . . [last line of page torn off] in no position to warn him. Then there is an earnest unshaven boy named Fletcher who decided to write about the seduction of a young girl, but felt that he did not know enough. I told him to ask his older sisters, if they were married and if they were hospitable to such questions and discussions, what it was like to lose one's virginity if one were a girl. He said he would and they would be glad to tell him and regarded the suggestions as excellent, but instead, being impatient about his literary research, and since his sisters live elsewhere, he "dated" two "rough" girls during the Xmas vacation, persuaded them to bed, and questioned them in detail about how each had felt during the loss of their respective virginities. Both replied that it was just a "kick," nothing else, leaving him quite at a loss for the emotional validity he was seeking. When he reported the worthless results of his research to

me after the Xmas recess, I became alarmed by the—
would you not agree?—over-zealous way in which
he sought literary material. So I told him that if he
had ever had a wisdom tooth extracted or an appen-
dicitis operation, he probably knew enough about
pain to describe defloration.

But only last week when another boy named Put-
nam expressed distress because he had written a story
about a little girl and did not know enough about
little girls, I carelessly thoughtlessly told him that
there were pictures of little girls in *Life,* all over
Princeton, in the park and on the street: "Mr. Put-
nam," I said to him bashfully, "the entire universe is
your research assistant." Hours after, thinking of
Fletcher's over-zeal, I became tense with anxiety and
resolved to go back to advising all the would-be
authors to use their imaginations and shun experience as banal and trite and distracting.

Is it not a Dantesque punishment for my sins, that
wishing to write manuscripts, I am condemned to
read manuscripts? Please advise.

I may get to that Boylston divine cocktail party
sooner than you think and than I want, if the fog
and the ice on the safaris between Princeton and the
farm do not abate. So if you don't confer or visit me
soon, you may never see me again, but anyway then
you can dedicate the next *ND* annual to me and speak
more favorably of my mind and character than heretofore. But write to me soon just in case my worst
fears are delightfully wrong.

Yours,
DELMORE

P.S. *Please* return this carbon copy, since I sent one
to Pasadena and one to N.D.

/ · /

Diana's Red Shoes: Trilling's wife was named Diana.

studied good manners: He had been reading Amy Vanderbilt on etiquette.

the late Boylston Professor: Theodore Spencer.

Tales from the Vienna Woods: Early title of collection which became *Successful Love and Other Stories.*

green and pleasant land: Schwartz is parodying the last stanza of William Blake's "Jerusalem."

"a flat tire": The joke is funny because the young man to whom he told it was heir to the Firestone Tire and Rubber Company of Akron, Ohio.

---

178. TLS-2   February 9, 1953

[Letter from Robert M. MacGregor]

DEAR DELMORE:

I should have brought this up the other day when we had lunch, but I wanted first to talk to J., since he of course has made the arrangement with you. However, I gathered that you were sensitive to my concern and my feeling that a more business-like arrangement should be worked out.

I may have the facts quite wrong, and I hope in that case you will correct me, but my understanding of your arrangement with J from the beginning was that New Directions would pay you $25 a week to come in for one day a week to read manuscripts and make recommendations. Certainly I interpreted the fact that you read very fast and could judge the worth of a manuscript quickly to mean that you should not be expected to spend a whole day with us each week. However, I must confess that I looked longingly at you from time to time, and $25 a day on a five-day week would of course mean a $200 a week salary. I also realized that there would be times when you couldn't make it at all.

I am sure that you would resent any suggestion that this payment was a subsidy or handout, or that you were not earning what you were getting. But I feel that many things have happened to modify the original situation. For one, there really weren't as many manuscripts coming in as both J and I expected. So many had piled up in that period when J was planning *Perspectives* and getting the pilot issue out, that we got a quite cockeyed idea. And you, of course, turned out to have a good deal more work to do at Princeton and at Intercultural than you had expected. I would also gather from what you said the other day, that you were being adequately compensated at both places, and am guessing therefore that you are not actually dependent on the $25 a week from New Directions.

Because there hasn't been quite so much work, but also because you have been very good at it, you have of course managed to keep things pretty much up-to-date, even when you haven't been able to come in for two or three weeks running. (Incidentally, I have kept track of your visits since sometime in August, but do not propose to look up that record now.) I will admit, however, that I was beginning to get upset when recently five weeks in a row went by without us seeing you. I would gather that you realized I was upset.

What I would like to propose seems to me to be called for by the several sides of the situation. The plan would be that we would pay you on the same basis, for the actual times that you come to us, but which, however, would be no more than twice a month. As much as possible, Delmore, I would like to have these two days spaced out, so that no more than three weeks ever go by without manuscripts being read, and the rejected ones being dispatched back to their authors. I would of course be delighted to have your help from time to time on other matters, but will certainly not expect it. I would certainly like to feel, and have you feel, that the situation is malleable, and subject to changing conditions, dependent on your time, the amount of work to be done, and any other factor.

I trust you realize that I say all this without any criticism of the excellent work you have done, and with appreciation of the help you have given all along.

Yours ever,
RMM:bjm   ROBERT M. MACGREGOR

/ · /

Robert M. MacGregor: Managing director at New Directions, who took over when JL went to work for the Ford Foundation.

---

179. TLS-3   RD1, Box 230
                               Pittstown, N.J.
                               February 14, 1953

DEAR BOB:

I am sorry that you did not mention your letter of February 9 yesterday, when I spoke to you in the office, since matters of the kind you take up in your letter are less likely to lead to misunderstanding when they are dealt with in conversation. I am also perplexed by your having been silent or forgetful about February 9's letter since you did take up the next letter you wrote me.

In your letter you say, "I may have the facts quite wrong, and I hope in that case you will correct me." I must take you at your word, for you have the facts entirely wrong. My arrangement with Jay as stated

in a letter he wrote me last March was that I was to
come in once every *two* weeks and not for a whole
day but merely for as long as was necessary to do
the work that had to be done. Subsequently, in September, Jay, realizing that I was under a considerable
strain because of my wife's illness (which is of course
not a matter for you to be concerned about) and
because of Princeton, told me to tell you to send me
a post-card every time the manuscripts piled up
instead of coming to the office regularly. I did not
report or act on Jay's suggestion because I felt, perhaps wrongly, that you might resent such an
arrangement. Of this fact you were of course
unaware, I suppose.

You do, however, mistake or misunderstand the
facts about the manuscript situation, since I was given
the job of taking care of it. You say: "There really
weren't as many manuscripts coming in as both Jay
and I expected." Jay's expectations, as stated in his
letter of last March, did not anticipate any great
increase in the rate of contributions to *New Directions;* on the contrary, he expected the number to
diminish, since he was not going to publish very
many novels. Furthermore, the rate has remained
fairly constant, as Betty's records will show, since I
took over. You may have been misled by the fact
that soon after taking over, I cleaned up the enormous backlog and since then have kept any new and
large backlog from piling-up.

You say that I am "being adequately compensated
at both places, and I am guessing therefore that you
are not actually dependent on the $25 a week from
New Directions." This is untrue for a variety of reasons; one, that my job at Princeton ends in May; it
is only a one-year appointment. Two, that as a result
of my wife's illness I have not only had additional
expenses, but I have had to become involved in new

and continuing expenses such as hiring a maid and the like, which again is of course no concern of yours, except insofar as your unawareness of my situation has made you come to an entirely inaccurate conclusion about what I am dependent upon for a bare livelihood.

I hope you will understand that I have no wish to offend you when I say that I am extremely perplexed by the fact that you said nothing to me about your dissatisfaction with my work, and chose instead to wait for months and to write me instead of speaking to me. Unless my experience has been entirely misleading (and it probably is not, since I have taught at five colleges, worked for three publishers, and worked for years on several magazines), the customary practice when an employer is dissatisfied with an employee is to give him what I believe is known as "fair warning," and thus a fair chance to revise his behavior in the light of what he has been told is wanting or defective. If you want me to come in once a week for reasons of efficiency, office morale, and the like, I will do so. After May, when the term ends at Princeton, it will be no hardship for me, as it has been since September, to come to your office once a week. And I must confess that I cannot understand why you did not speak to me or write to me sooner about your feelings in the matter. I did notice that you were upset from time to time, but there are so many reasons why any human being may be upset, that I had no way of knowing that it was the infrequency of my visits to the office which upset you. I assumed that the only criterion was whether I got my work done; you say in your letter that I "have been very good at it" and that "I read very fast." You also say: "I trust you realize that I say all this without any criticism of the excellent work you have done," a remark which is hardly consistent with your previous statement: "I will admit, however, that I was beginning to get upset when recently five weeks in a row went by without us seeing you." Your records are inaccurate, I am sure, because although I did miss several weeks around Xmas, it was not five weeks. And no such omission will occur again, particularly since my work at Princeton will diminish during the spring term and terminate in May.

Perhaps I ought to discuss the matter with J, rather than with you, since he knows more of the facts than you do—for example, that my salary, as he told me about it and then wrote me, was in part what you call "a subsidy or handout," and which he felt to be in part help to an old friend and aid to a New Directions author and his wife, also a New Directions author. Will you let me know immediately if you would prefer that I discuss the matter with Jay and explain to him why I think your proposal is in every respect unfair and unjustified, and would be the breach of an agreement between friends? Your proposal would, in addition, make so much a difference to me in terms of my financial obligations (and I assure you that I am not living on any basis other than the minimal one) that I would have to go to the bank and borrow money in order to pay my bills, something which I have had to do twice during the fall.

> Yours sincerely,
> DELMORE

/ · /

Betty's records: Betty Malino, JL's secretary at New Directions.

180. TLS-1   RD1 Box 230
                               Pittstown, N.J.
                               April 12, 1953

DEAR JAY:

You make all my dreams come true, hence I will call my next book of poems, *In Dreams Begin Realities* and dedicate it to you or President Hutchins or the Ford Foundation.

Saul Bellow visited me yesterday to tell me that Princeton, through the good offices of Carlos Baker and Lawrence Thompson and Dean Brown, wants me as a permanent resident lecturer. I really want the job very much, so please help an old friend or someone else will, I am sure. Don't you think I ought to get the offer in writing immediately?

Being in Princeton will enable me to be just as helpful to you, and probably more helpful. It will also help my health which is a little on the sullen sloe gin side.

See you tomorrow, Monday, unless I have to go see the doctor or visit Dudley Johnson or Carlos Baker or Dean Brown or Erich Kahler in Princeton.

Have just received what appears to be a mysterious indirect communiqué from Old Possum. It is called David Jones.

Was all this a secret plan of yours, you Young Possum? or Hutchins? It was certainly not Blackmur's idea.

                               Yours,
                               DELMORE

/ · /

Carlos Baker: (1909–1987), Princeton professor and biographer of Ernest Hemingway.

Lawrence Thompson: (1906–1973), Originally Curator of Rare Books at Princeton University, and subsequently a member of the university's Department of English. He was the official biographer of Robert Frost.

Dean Brown: Slater Brown of Princeton University.

Dudley Johnson: English professor at Princeton.

Erich Kahler: Princeton professor.

David Jones: Schwartz had received a copy of Jones's *The Anathemata,* which T. S. Eliot published at Faber & Faber in 1952.

181. TLS-1

MY DEAR DELMORE:

I want to apologize for losing my temper with you this morning on the telephone. I think you must in all honesty agree, however, that you provoked me. Your statement that I was not trying to help you struck me as one of the most extraordinary remarks that I have ever heard.

Over the years at New Directions I have continued to publish your books, although not one of them has ever been really profitable. When some years ago you told me that you needed money for doctors' bills I gave you the largest advance ever given by New Directions. And I think you will agree that I have not hounded you about this advance, even though you have made little effort to complete the book in question.

When a few months ago you told me that you needed money for your wife's medical bills, I helped you get a job with Intercultural, and I have continued you in that job, even though your performance has been irregular, because I sensed that you were under great nervous pressure and that your work would soon improve.

It seems to me, after reflection, that the best thing for me to do in your case, since my most sincere efforts to help you seem only to have made you resent me, is to separate myself entirely from all decisions affecting your status.

I plan, therefore, to leave all problems connected with your relations to Bob MacGregor, and all matters connected with your work at Intercultural to Hayden Carruth. I will not attempt to influence them for or against you. Both are reasonable and honorable people, and I feel sure that they will judge you entirely on the basis of the quality and regularity of your work, or the fairness of your proposals.

With best wishes, as always,
J

/ · /

largest advance: For the critical book on Eliot that was never completed.

182. TLS-1   April 14, 1953

Mr. Delmore Schwartz
R.D. #1, Box 230
Pittstown, New Jersey

DEAR DELMORE:

I hereby release you from any or all options on future books of yours which may be held by me or by New Directions.

Yours very truly,
JAMES LAUGHLIN, PRESIDENT
NEW DIRECTIONS

183. TLS-3

RD1 Box 230
Pittstown, N.J.
May 22, 1953

DEAR JAY:

As a result of deliberations in which everyone was consulted except the College of Cardinals, the Supreme Court, the Board of Health and Oscar Williams, Princeton has decided that I would be a valuable addition to the faculty. The proposal, which was unanimously affirmed by the full professors, the Dean, and President Dodds, is as follows:

I am to be appointed resident lecturer for three years and my duties are limited to teaching a course of my own, Advanced Composition, which makes a total of six hours a week and which would not interfere with what I have to do for *Diogenes* and *Perspectives*. In return for these efforts I am to receive $5000 a year which Princeton would like the Ford Foundation to pay, although it was indicated quite clearly that if anyone else wants to do so, that will do quite as well. In addition, Princeton would like the Ford Foundation to pay $300 more a year to cover my annuity, but if there is any question as to this additional sum, Princeton will be delighted to show how desirable a teacher I am by paying the annuity from the university funds. The procedure, or protocol, or whatever it is, which must be followed is that the Ford Foundation communicate its willingness to pay my salary to President Dodds. If this could be done quickly, it would be helpful indeed to everyone, and I would be overjoyed. The limitation of the appointment to three years is a mere formality, since "the presumption" is that the appointment will be renewed every three years, provided that I do not commit "moral turpitude," which I would have to commit on Nassau Street during Alumni Week, to judge by various episodes which I will not dwell upon now.

The advantages to you as publisher of Intercultural Publications are fairly clear, I think, particularly in connection with *Diogenes,* where, in dealing with professors, I will certainly be better able to correct the style of the learned gentry and speak with authority if I am part of a university faculty. In addition, it is quite likely that this kind of permanent job would help me be more efficient in regard to *Diogenes* and *Perspectives* by lessening the anxiety about money which has crippled me in recent years. And then there is the further possibility, in which I am not sure that you are passionately interested, that our hurly-burly friendship might achieve exalted regions of disinterested benignity which death alone will surpass.

There is a further link between Princeton's proposal and the Ford Foundation which I am not sure ought to be dealt with right now, and about which I would like to write to Hutchins in detail, if that is all right with you. I don't think that this link is necessary, and in view of all that will have to be done when I become active on *Diogenes,* it would obviously be wiser to postpone anything which would increase the amount of work I have to do immediately.

However, if a further tie-up with the purposes and objectives of the Ford Foundation is necessary, and since you said the money would probably be forthcoming from the Fund for the Advancement of Education, my course could be used as a kind of research into the reasons that so many intelligent and trained human beings write English so poorly, and misunderstand or are baffled by serious literature. Since it is my own course, and it is a course in composition, I can direct it partly toward getting some concrete data on this truly important problem, in which I am interested, anyway. You remember, this was the official reason given for the Rockefeller Foundation's paying of I. A. Richards' salary at Harvard for more than ten years, and had much to do with two of Richards' most influential books, *Practical Criticism* and *Interpretation in Teaching*. And the Rockefeller Foundation has supported Blackmur, and F. R. Leavis for doing things of a similar kind at Princeton and at Cambridge.

I won't try to outline the project in full now, particularly since I'd like to write Hutchins some sort of prospectus, and also because I don't want to embark on it during the coming year, unless I have to, in order to get the Ford Foundation's support, which is all I need for the job. But the general project can be illustrated by some of the key problems:

1) Why do intelligent human beings have so much difficulty in reading and in writing intelligently?

2) Why do people who can speak very well write lifeless and hackneyed prose?

3) What are the effects of mass culture—the radio, the newspapers, and the films—upon the intelligent reading and writing of English?

4) What is the effect of a training in the classics, and in logic, upon the reading and writing of English?

And the like, of which these questions are only a sample. There have been any number of efforts to explain the semi-illiteracy which prevails, but they all seem superficial or wrong to me. For example the secondary school teaching of English is blamed, but this merely begs the question as to why the high school teachers of English have been so poorly trained themselves. And then it is said that if only Greek and Latin were required subjects, people would read and write as well as they once did. But this is foolish too, since Greek and Latin teachers also write poorly, as most scholars do, and there is no significant difference between students trained in the classics and those who are not, when it comes to any real skill in reading and writing.

This is a rough and abbreviated formulation of what would be, I think, a very useful project about which I could write the kind of report or reports which Foundations seem to love.

As a special supplement, I would gladly deal with the fascinating topic: The strange English of Dwight D. Eisenhower; and advance reasons or hypotheses to explain such of his pronunciations as *Career* when he is speaking of *Korea,* and his virtually unfailing inaccuracy in the use of demonstrative pronouns—for example, "these Republicans," he said recently, speaking of the Republican party.

Seriously, however, will you let me know as soon as possible how matters go forward and if you think it would be proper for me to write to Hutchins directly, since, as you said, Princeton's proposal is not within your ordinary field of operations?

Yours,
D E L M O R E

P.S. Rereading what I wrote on the second page, it looks a little too general. To try to be more concrete, what I mean is the kind of thing I encountered when a student who spoke fluently in answering a question suddenly became tongue-tied—halting, choppy, and wobbling in delivery—as soon as he was asked to read a passage of prose aloud. Or students who wrote beautifully and lucidly about some subjects but wrote very poorly about other subjects. And the like. But I won't try to say any more than that the whole situation can be made quite vivid by using all the instances I accumulated during my long years in the vineyards of English freshman composition.

P.P.S.: Please don't mind my sending this to you Special Delivery; it won't get to you any sooner, but nevertheless Special Delivery expresses my feelings. P.P.P.S.: If the toils and travails of the Ford Foundation seem trying, you might find much solace and reassurance in Allan Nevins' new biography of John D. Rockefeller. There is a full account in the second volume of what happened during the first years of the Rockefeller Foundation—which is to say, it has all happened before.

I enclose an announcement of a serious rival of *Perspectives*. Don't you think that the acceptance of original contributions is an advantage over and above the accompanying disadvantages?

/ · /

in connection with Diogenes: JL had no active role in the publication of *Diogenes,* which had its own staff of editors in Paris. Intercultural Publications merely reprinted an English-language edition with assistance for translation and printing costs.

I. A. Richards: Ivor Armstrong Richards (1893–1979), English literary critic, psychologist, and aesthetician.

F. R. Leavis: (1895–1978), Influential British literary critic and editor of the magazine *Scrutiny.*

184. TLS-2
Intercultural Publications Inc.
2 East 61st Street
New York 21, N.Y.
May 28, 1953

DEAR DELMORE:

Thanks for your good letter of May 22nd. I would have answered sooner, except that I was working up in Boston and Cambridge for a couple of days. Albert reports that English department meetings now end at five-fifteen, instead of six, now that Harry is no longer there to clarify moral issues. Otherwise everything seems about the same.

I talked with Dr. Hutchins today on the telephone, at great length, about the problem raised by your letter, but he was not at all optimistic. He expressed total surprise at the idea. Apparently you had not gotten it across to him that assistance would be needed at Princeton when you talked to him here some weeks ago. Certainly I for my own part had no inkling that this would be necessary. When you first talked to me about it, I assumed that Princeton was prepared to take care of the monetary arrangement.

Dr. Hutchins is well disposed toward you, but he points out that the Fund for the Advancement of Education has never supported a "chair" of this kind and that questions of precedent would probably be involved.

I think that your proposed project, for studying communications at the level of prose style, is very interesting. Here again, however, the Fund for Advancement has not set up any mechanism for handling things of this kind. They have, as you know, given certain annual fellowships to college professors and instructors, which have, as their objective, to make the teachers teach better. That is, they are not supposed to use the money to get a degree, or to write a book, but to do some kind of travel or experience which will give them new insight into teaching. For example Brewster Ghiselin has had one of these, and I believe he went around and sat in on a number of composition courses at different colleges. Possibly this idea of yours could be developed on that level. They have already chosen their applicants for the 1953–54 season, I think, but I believe they hope to have another similar program the following year.

I am awfully sorry if I gave you any false encouragement on your Princeton project, but you simply did not make it clear to me at all.

I see that the Giants are beginning to win ball games. I will be looking forward to your explanation of this phenomenon.

As ever,

J

/ · /

Albert: Albert Erskine.
Harry: Harry Levin.
Brewster Ghiselin: (b. 1903), Professor of English at the University of Utah.

185. TLS-2

RD1 Box 230
Pittstown, N.J.
Oct. 9, 1953

DEAR JAY:

I should have sent you a copy of my letter to Hutchins. Thanks for sending me a copy of the one you wrote him. I am sorry to have to say that it is you who are inaccurate, not me, and on both points your inaccuracy is a matter of written record. The record so far as an appointment goes is either in your hands, for you made a note of it at the time, or the Ford bursar has it, for you explained to me that he would have to know the reason that a salary increase was being given. Furthermore, it is absolutely inaccurate and false that you told me you "thought" I "could do a better job than I had been doing," and you added that I was hard to reach out of town and you hesitated to summon anyone from out of town. Certainly you never suggested that I had not been doing as good a job as possible, and you clearly behaved at all times as if the less you saw of me in the office, the more delighted you would be, excluding me—whether deliberately or not I do not know—from any of the kinds of work which I can do and Carruth was doing badly.

The Cornell matter is also a written record, since I had to reply to the people at Cornell in May when I was not burdened by "the condition of anxiety" which you kindly attribute my inexactitude to. In any case, it is quite obvious on the face of it that if I was going to do anything with *Diogenes* to make it more lively, I could not do so without being in New York several days a week. You said at the time that I was going to have my hands full of work. You did say, it is true, that if a permanent job should be offered me, I would be wise to take it, since my work on *Perspectives* was merely for my own benefit, etc., which was hardly consistent with what you thought my job on *Diogenes* was going to be, but let it pass, let it pass.

Since you say that you are "sympathetic to Schwartz's problem and certainly don't blame him at all"—an overwhelming and extraordinary statement to make in a letter so full of hostility—perhaps I should report that I have been told repeatedly that it is customary for Foundations to honor the commitments and obligations in which you engaged and that it was amazing to hear you made no effort whatever to get me some other place in the Foundation, of which I was told there were many, to tide me over at a time when I was penniless and in debt and until a new academic year made a teaching job possible. This was also regarded as very strange behavior on the part of a friend, but let us definitely define this as maudlin sentimentality.

I think I can extend a little more sympathy to you with regard to your problems, and perhaps the unpleasant information may even lead to sensible action: The generally known fact that the Ford Foundation pays MacGregor's *New Directions* salary is viewed as a scandal and the last two numbers of *Perspectives* are regarded, in New York at least, as entirely banal, mediocre, and a shameful waste of a wonderful opportunity. If this seems the inaccurate report of one suffering from a condition of anxiety, perhaps you ought to consult a few intelligent people and request that they tell you the truth, however painful and unpleasant.

I don't yet know whether I will write to Hutchins or send him a copy of this letter or stop bothering him. If you don't want me to, or if you would prefer that I be silent for the time being, let me know. But the clear implication in your letter that I did not do my work well and the explication that a condition of anxiety was capable of making me a liar is not the kind of thing that will help me get a job, which I have so far been unable to do, August being the worst month for a teacher to find himself suddenly and unexpectedly unemployed. Please permit me to add that I did not write to Hutchins until after five weeks had passed and I had been told that Hutchins undoubtedly did not know all the facts and knew that foundations and institutions in their very nature honor their commitments and do not proceed like big business where the avowed aim is a profit.

Yours,
DELMORE

/ · /

pays MacGregor's . . . : The Ford Foundation made no payments to MacGregor, and never made any commitment to provide a job for Schwartz.

the Cornell matter: Arthur Mizener had mentioned a job possibility for Schwartz at Cornell University. Nothing came of the offer.

186. ALS-1   RD1 Box 230
                                              Pittstown, N.J.
                                              Dec. 9, 1953

DEAR BOB:

I've been bedded down with jaundice for the past week and though it is quite unserious, I am supposed to stay put and rest for the next two weeks, so if it seems all right to you, suppose that the manuscripts are sent out here at least once and if necessary twice, at my expense of course, so that there won't be too much of an accumulation. And we might have the same sort of arrangement next summer if I should go off to teach somewhere for six weeks. . . . Do let me know.

Jaundice, if you have not had it, is an entirely uninteresting disease—and invites boredom and enervation. And all I can say in its favor is that at least I understand what is meant by looking at matters with a jaundiced eye.

                              Yours,
                              DELMORE

P.S. Jay and I operated in this way for more than two years between Cambridge and Alta, Utah, and the only manuscript ever lost in transit was a book-length one of mine!

187. ALS-2

RD1 Box 230
Pittstown, N.J.
Jan. 27, 1954

DEAR JAY:

If you have not yet secured another hack, I will swallow my pride—what is left of it—in order to have other things to swallow. The cause of this abasement is the income tax, which of course is based on the income I no longer have and requires a sum I will have to borrow. Don't you think it would be dignified to make it a round sum like $10 a review instead of the $8.33 which your letter suggests? In any case, will you let me know immediately if the "position" has been filled or not, because I'll have to get that money somewhere by March 15th.

Though pleased to learn that you have struck up a friendship with a gifted Brooklyn girl, I am disappointed that Gertrude is not with you, for I had hopes that she and the Pope would converse, thus giving the latter a more wholesome outlook on life.

There is little news here apart from such things as that Philip Rahv acts as if he had lost his mind and Auden appears to be infatuated with J. Edgar Hoover and Molotov, inquiring of all whether they think those chaps are queens.

Yours,
DELMORE

/ · /

not with you: Laughlin was traveling in Italy.

J. Edgar Hoover: (1895–1972), Director of the Federal Bureau of Investigation from 1924 until his death at the age of seventy-seven.

Molotov: Vyacheslav Mikhaylovich Molotov (1890–1986), Soviet statesman and diplomat. He held the post of foreign minister from

1939 until 1949. After Stalin died in 1953, he resumed it until his quarrels with Nikita Khrushchev. He was dismissed in June 1956.

188. TLS-1   Val d'Isère
                                                Feb. 26, 1954

DEAR DELMORE:

I'm sorry that your letter acceding to bargain rates
for short reviews did not catch up with me until I
had already told them in New York to farm them
out with some girl. But I am sure that if you com-
municated your change of heart to Mr. Freelander at
any time, he would accommodate you.

Today's epistle is on the subject of pride and money
and their relationship. Or, to put it more succinctly,
are you of a mind to "front" an issue of the magazine
into which would go—to please various powers—a
number of things which you might not like?

The position at present is that the powers do not
want a literary magazine, but one of subjects and
fields, so to speak. If I had the time, I could put them
together exactly as they like, but I don't have the
time to do it every time. Hence this query to you.

Let me know how you feel about it. I dare say that
40% of the contents would be superimposed on you.
Of the 60% which you might first assemble, perhaps 20% would be eliminated as being too special
or too literary or too advanced.

The task, I can assure you, is not a joyful one, but
it would bring you in a further $2000, beyond the
$500 advance you had, provided that it were done
on time—that is, in the next two months, and in the
most complete dead-pannedness. As I shall be here
and in Japan, you would have to check things with
me by mail.

Of the material to be superimposed, there would be some of the following: A picture piece on American sculpture; an excerpt from the works of the late departed Fred Allen; an excerpt from the works of Bernard DeVoto; a piece about Iroquois Injuns by Carl Carmer; a piece on Federalism by Professor Freund up to Harvard; a nature piece.

You would thus have to find some poetry, a story, a sociology or preferably an anthropology piece, something philosophical–literary, something colorful about the American scene, the book reviews, etc.

How does this seem to you? How is your time fixed in March and April? I suggest you shoot me a cable on this, the address being Hamisham, West-kent, London, or if you prefer to write, c / o Hamish Hamilton, 90 Great Russell Street, London. But I do suggest you cable, because if you don't want to tackle this piece of pliancy, I will have to find another victim ready to lay down his honor on the block of gold.

There is not enough snow this year in the mountains, but there are other things.

And what is your interpretation of Mr. Eliot's play? A strange work.

Best to Elizabeth,

J

/ · /

Mr. Freelander: Ronald Freelander, JL's assistant in the operation of Intercultural Publications.

Fred Allen: Frederick Lewis Allen (1890–1954), American social historian and editor of *Harper's* magazine. In 1953 he was elected a trustee of the Ford Foundation.

Bernard DeVoto: (1897–1955), Writer on literature and history, and editor of the manuscripts of Mark Twain.

Carl Carmer: (1893–1976), American writer, folklorist, and historian.

Professor Freund: Paul Freund, a professor in the Harvard Law School.

Hamisham: The London office of *Perspectives* was a room in the offices
of Hamish Hamilton, publisher.
don't want to tackle: Schwartz did not accept this offer. Rather, he assisted
other guest editors.
Mr. Eliot's play: The Confidential Clerk (1954).

189. TLS-1   RD1 Box 230
                                      Pittstown, N.J.
                                      August 27, 1954

DEAR JAY:

Many and profound apologies for the lateness of
the enclosed, which was due to unforeseeable and
unavoidable causes. The chief of them was the virus
which overtakes first Elizabeth and then myself nearly
every August, which I suspect is due to the drought
and use of rainwater. In addition, both typewriters
broke down just as a Woodstock one undid another
scoundrel, Alger Hiss; and the character of pro-
vincial life, which undid Madame Bovary, caused an
absence of onion-skin paper, in our province. And
finally, the shakiness of the virus was intensified by
a desire to assassinate Durocher for trying to prove
(in seven games which were lost) what a great genius
he is by not walking the batter who came up before
the pitcher with the winning run on the bases (yesterday again, in Chicago).

I am aware that the review is about eight or more
pages than you requested. I have not only cut it down
from sixty pages in the first draft (which I would
like you to read some time) but omitted many
excursions—which at the time seemed quite original—on the relation of Faulkner to Schweitzer,
Bergson, Malraux, Uncle Tom, Gandhi, Tolstoy,
Erich Maria Remarque & Marlene Dietrich, to say
nothing of the extent to which I had to forbid myself

to discuss the great novelist's view of the Negro and the attitude he is likely to adopt when he hears how much Willie Mays is paid in 1956. . . .

As you know, it is very hard to write this kind of review, since it means forgoing self-expression and sticking to the book itself very closely. I did so because the reviews are all so stupid, the book is wonderful, and everyone around here says that they can't read it (everyone of the Indian tribe resident in Bucks County and named the Martinis, but I gather the same is true elsewhere): the enclosed clipping is further evidence.

If you've read the book, I don't think you'll want to cut the review at all. And if other changes are necessary, please summon me and I'll arise from the melancholy of middle age and journey to Babylon on a moment's notice, despite the fact that twenty-seven days' toil over the review is twenty-five longer than I have ever before given to any review.

Yours,
DELMORE

/ · /

the enclosed: Schwartz's review of William Faulkner's novel, *A Fable*, which was published in *Perspectives USA*, 10 (1955), 126–36.

a Woodstock one: At the time of the trial of Alger Hiss, his Woodstock typewriter was in the news. It was proved, from the type, that Hiss had typed copies of certain documents on it.

Albert Schweitzer: (1875–1965), Alsatian theologian, musician, and missionary in Africa.

Bergson: Henri Bergson (1859–1941), French philosopher.

Malraux: André Malraux (1901–1976), French novelist, art historian, and statesman.

Gandhi: Mohandas Gandhi (1869–1948), Indian political and spiritual leader, one of the fathers of Indian independence from the British.

Tolstoy: Count Leo Tolstoy (1829–1910), Russian novelist and philosopher.

Erich Maria Remarque: (1897–1970), German novelist.

190. TLS-3   RD1 Box 230
                                              Pittstown, N.J.
                                              Nov. 2, 1954

DEAR JAY:

   Please excuse me for not writing you before now,
since I was so pleased that you were satisfied at least
with my review. You may not be aware of how
pure—and how rare—my delight was, unless I add
that this is the first expression of the sort in four
years, and the third in ten for any literary effort of
mine. I was also pleased that you seemed, in your
letter, to be more cheerful than you had for a long
time. Unless intuition deceived me, your melancholia between the lines was without precedent & of
such intensity that I wondered if the offer of some
few pints of blood, not entirely free of melancholia
too, & all that I have of negotiable goods, would be
of any use.

   I may be a little late, but I cannot pass over the
great World Series victory and add that I now feel
free to welcome you to the inner elite of loyal Giant
fandom. When you first announced your conversion
last spring, I was pleased, but nervous—the latter on
a purely personal basis, namely, that all ventures in
which we have been united have appeared to begin
very well and then to bog down disastrously, to rise
again in triumph which also ceased precipitately,
resembling in this respect the course of American
capitalism, but tempting me, at times, to think that
your fickle affections had an important role. However, clearly there can be no question of the overwhelming effect or coincidence which has
accompanied your first year as a Giant fan. Shall we
agree, tentatively—in case you are in Europe or Asia
at the time—to attend the first game of the 1955 sea-

son together? Personally I prefer most of the time to watch on TV, since I can address whatever remarks occur to me to Durocher without any harm other than scaring and turning the neighbors' cows' milk to vinegar. I must add that your contention & the prevailing view that Willie is a primitive spontaneous being was shown to be untrue during Cleveland's Armageddon; he was asked if he thought that he had a chance to throw out some Cleveland base runner and his answer was: "*If* you stopped to ask yourself questions like that, you *never* throw anyone out." This is, I think, the insight of a highly intellectual being who realizes the limitations of the intellect & introspection very much as Bergson did.

To pass from the sublime to—Eisenhower, I think I now know why Dwight hangs out around Gettysburg so much: He goes there to work out the way he would have directed hostilities had he been Meade or Lee. If you know any of the Texas oilmen who, though so concerned about states' rights and the like, are engaged in invading the rights of other states, such as Illinois, by enormous campaign contributions, it would be no less than an act of friendship, such as friendship requires, to pass along my view that instead of trying to buy elections and favors so wastefully, they ought to do something simpler and less expensive. They ought to build an enormous aircraft carrier, place upon it a golf course which is incomparable, sail it up the Potomac, & present it to Dwight: Would this not be an incomparable proof of friendship and please Dwight very much? Not only that, it might be the last anyone ever saw of him.

These suggestions may seem idle, but I cannot forget how I wrote you last winter in Rome, thinking that Gertrude was with you and expressing the thought that it would be an excellent idea for you to arrange an interview between that noble lady and

the Pope, which might well lead to a more wholesome view of life upon the part of his Holiness. Little did I know then how prophetic this project was.
Gertrude was not there and soon after Pacelli took
to his bed, was sick for months, and will probably
never enjoy good health again.

Yours,
DELMORE

/ · /

Meade: George Gordon Meade (1815–1872), Union general in the Civil
War.

Lee: Robert E. Lee (1807–1870), General-in-chief of the Confederate
Army in the Civil War.

Pacelli: Pius XII (1876–1958), Roman-born Pope named Eugenio Pacelli,
successor of Pius XI and predecessor of John XXIII.

191. TLS-1

RD1 Box 230
Pittstown, N.J.
December 27, 1954

DEAR JAY:

I enclose the clipping on the off-chance that it might
somehow be usable in *Perspectives* (as a springboard
for the kind of symposium in your last issue, for
example, which I thought very good).

I was sorry to read of your uncle's death. I never
met him, of course, but I did meet his wife once—
the only time anyone has ever looked at me as if the
dog pound were about to be summoned—but he has
long been an endearing figure in the life of this recluse,
by virtue of his encounter with Oscar Williams,
comments on Alger Hiss, admiration of Franco and
Thomas Mann, and other reports you have provided.

Your recent silence combined with the non-appearance of the season's greetings naturally suggests preoccupation or disaffection. It is true that last year Rahv destroyed the Xmas card you sent me at *PR,* so he may have done so again (he acts thus on principle with regard to mail addressed to his fellow-editors from those he regards as important people: it makes him feel that he is still a revolutionist, outwitting the Federal Government and emulating Stalin's way of dealing with the Politburo). If this be the reason, or if you are otherwise preoccupied, will you let me know. I will assume that continued silence means that our long Dostoevskian friendship has now trended toward the brink of permanent estrangement, much to my sorrow. However, I will be brave and make the most of my rich memories. It is just fifteen years to the day that we set out for New Orleans to meet my sister, Hemingway, Katherine Anne Porter, and—as a windfall or dividend, so to speak—Elinor Blanchard. I never did meet my sister nor Hemingway but then, Moses never met Marlene Dietrich or Katherine Anne Porter. Still and all, I must admit that I feel at times the presence of a pattern of destiny in my not having met my sister—it is a symbol, even if it is equally likely that you found my company extremely oppressive after four days. After all, most chaps do get to meet their sisters.

But enough of sentimentality and nostalgia: I was younger fifteen years ago, but I was far less intelligent and my wife then far inferior to the present incumbent. At the moment I have an abscessed jaw which makes me look like a sagging pigskin, but on the other hand also is the reason for the presence of a lot of delightful novocaine in my nervous system, the intrinsic pleasure of which is increased by a new light on the late Mrs. Possum, who is reported to have begun the easy descent to Avernus after a dental visit which led to an infatuation with ether.

Happy New Year,
DELMORE

/ · /

Oscar Williams: JL's uncle, George Lister Carlisle, once returned late to his stately home to find Oscar Williams sleeping on the doorstep.

Thomas Mann: (1875–1955), German novelist and scholar.

My sister: Standing joke between Schwartz and JL. The poet had no sister. When JL was on the road selling books in the 1930s, he met an attractive girl in a Milwaukee bookstore called Schwartz's (it is still in existence today) and she accompanied him to Chicago for a weekend. She later pretended to be Schwartz's sister so she could travel with them to the MLA convention in Baton Rouge.

Mrs. Possum: T. S. Eliot's first wife, Vivienne, who suffered from mental problems.

192. TLS-1

RD1 Box 230
Pittstown, N.J.
March 2, 1955

DEAR JAY:

I can't answer your last letter without suspending for once my resolution not to burden you—or anyone else—with my economic difficulties. Since it has to be suspended, it might be a good idea to say that these difficulties are the reason that I did not accept any of your kind invitations last spring and summer to watch the Giants; and the resolution is the reason I have refrained from explanation. I've seen nothing of almost anyone else I know for the past year and a half, the result being that some think I am avoiding them and others that I am brooding over some slight. But a trip to New York costs at least $5 and to have people here costs even more, so it's impossible to do anything about it very often on an income which averages $25 a week.

Three years ago we borrowed $3000 from Elizabeth's sister, who is a widow with three children and quite poor too. I needed the money to get central heating installed in the house, which cost $1700, and it was necessary because Elizabeth had been quite ill, as you may remember—to pay the medical bills and go get a used car good enough to drive the sixty miles to Princeton and back three times a week. At the time I supposed with some reason that I would be a guest editor in the fairly near future and I certainly had no idea that the policy would change. I also thought I would remain on the *Perspectives* payroll, so I cannot help but conclude that what has occurred was no fault of mine. In addition, I did do all the work necessary to put together an issue.

Elizabeth's sister has waited with a gradually declining patience to be repaid, and since it has been clear that there would be a delay, we have been paying the interest on the money she would otherwise receive. But now she needs the money for the ordinary expenses of life. That's why when I had dinner with you in January, I said that we would probably have to leave for Guatemala soon, and expressed profound relief when you said that I would be paid, passing along the pleasant news to Elizabeth's sister immediately.

Since your last letter we've tried to borrow the money elsewhere, and have been quite unsuccessful for the obvious reasons that my only reliable source of income is the $50 a month I get from N.D. Since a second mortgage also is out of the question, the only alternative is to sell the house, which in addition to being a serious disruption would involve a considerable loss, assuming that it can be sold at all:

we've been unable to keep it up properly, so that, for example, it needs to be painted, and some of the plumbing replaced.

I'll be glad to do a guest issue anonymously; or provide any guarantee of whatever aid I can give which seems possible, though I am perplexed and unable to understand why you should think a guarantee is necessary. Perhaps you can lend me the sum on a written contractual basis in which I assign the monthly payments to you—a proposal which occurs to me only because, in trying to understand your proposal, it occurred to me that some budgetary problem was involved. Will you let me know soon, however, since the entire matter is extremely painful and embarrassing—to such an extent that it's very difficult for me to concentrate on Hemingway or anything else. I really am sorry to have to trouble you with the entire matter.

Yours,
DELMORE

/ · /

on Hemingway: Schwartz was writing "The Fiction of Ernest Hemingway," which would appear in *Perspectives USA,* 13 (1955), 70–88.

193. TLS-1   Intercultural Publications Inc
                               477 Madison Avenue
                               New York 22, N.Y.
                               April 4, 1955

DEAR DELMORE:

I think that your Hemingway piece is impressive. It is one man's interpretation, of course, but I think it makes sense and hangs together as a good lawyer's brief might hang together. Doubtless some people will disagree with it and I hope that we will get a good letter in from one of them which we can print in reply.

The piece may be a bit too long—I doubt if we saved that many pages for it—and so may have to be cut a bit, but substantially I think it is good.

Some hasty readers may think that you repeat yourself a good deal; but actually, when you analyze it, you don't, because in each seeming repetition there is a slight qualification. Now it may be that so much shading is out of place in a short essay, and takes away from the clear-cut impact, but for those who want to read it carefully, a lot of meat is there.

I imagine that you would probably like to have some money on it as soon as possible, and I will suggest to the very kind-hearted Miss Peters that she send you down a check for $500 on account, with the balance to be adjusted when we see how much has to be cut and how many copies of the issue will be printed.

As I shall be getting off to India for a month about April 20th, you had better let me know before that date whether you want to take us up on the offer I made to you in a recent letter.

With best wishes,

As ever,
J. LAUGHLIN

/ · /

Miss Peters: Eleanor Peters, a member of the Intercultural Publications staff.

194. ALS-1   4/9/55

IRENE:

Sorry to miss you. Have been missing myself also.
All of these are worth at least another reading.
Everything in the red chair (in the other room) is
worse than junk.
I've taken home "Le mauvais mari" by Charles
Dutt.

DELMORE

/ · /

Irene: Irene Glynn, business manager at ND's New York office. Schwartz
used to complain that her eyes were too far apart.
Charles Dutt: Unidentified. There is nothing in the ND files to indicate
he was ever published by the firm.

195. ALS-2   RD1, Box 230
                                                Pittstown, N.J.
                                                April 11, 1955

DEAR JAY:

I'll accept the arrangement you suggest, despite
the difficulties it involves, if you will write me that
you regard my doing so as an act of pure friendship
on my part. I couldn't answer you until now because
I couldn't know, until I heard from you, if it was
possible to add the total sum for the Hemingway
piece to the reduction of my long overdue debt. As
a result of the various recent changes of arrangement, I've had to take on an added burden of hackwork, which is the chief reason that my piece was
so late and also that I have been too exhausted much

of the time to be able to send in the requested constant flow of suggestions. It's not to your interest—*qua* editor of *Perspectives*—and certainly not to mine to engage in this arrangement, but if it makes you less unhappy than you usually appear to be, I'll regard it in that light. You might also let me know a little more of your intentions in future issues of *Perspectives*—and tell me if I am wrong to think that there is an immense difference between merely not upsetting the trustees and really pleasing them.

I'm supposed to be getting an "absolute rest," so I don't know if I'll get in to see you before you depart, but if I don't, would you send me your Hindustani address and write a poem for *The New Republic* as well?

Yours,
D E L M O R E

/ · /

The New Republic: Schwartz had become the magazine's poetry editor and regular film critic early in 1955.

196. ALS-1   Darband Hotel
                                Darband s / Tehran
                                4/28/55

DEAR DELMORE:

Would the poem on the other side be suitable for the *N.R.*? Or do you require something more chaste? I suppose you could render it harmless to the virgins of DuPont Circle by removing the first 2 words of the last line, but actually I think they are necessary to the figure. Two real broken-up pieces of old bronze—only one eye left in each face—but where the lips were conjoined. Powerful impact of hot venery amid all that cold dead stone.

But please don't print without letting me see proofs, as the lines may need to be tinkered with when set in type. (Address: 9077, 32 Ferozshah Road, New Delhi.)

The Persians are *real* nice. They have put up statues of the bards in the squares. And the young learn in school what the Koran says they may say to a camel driver if the camel kicks them.

> Hope you are feeling ok,
> J

In the Museum at Teheran

A sentimental curator has placed
two fragments of bronze Grecian
   heads together boy

& girl so that the faces black-
ened by three thousand years of
   desert sand & sun

seem to be whispering something
that the Gurgan lion & the wing-
   ed dog of Azerbaijan

must not hear but I have heard
them as I hear you now half way
   around the world

so simply & so quietly more like
a child than like a woman making
   love say to me in

that soft lost near and distant
voice I'm happy now I'm happy oh
   don't move don't go away.

/ · /

In the Museum at Teheran: Not published in *The New Republic.* The poem appears in JL's *In Another Country* (1978).

197. TLS-1 November 4, 1955

[From Robert M. MacGregor]
DEAR DELMORE:

I am sorry to have been so long in answering your query about your status in regard to options and contractual obligations to New Directions. I asked Jay soon after we talked, but then both thought we ought to see all the contracts involved. This took some digging in Connecticut.

Anyway, after surveying the situation Jay said, as I told you I thought he would, that he would willingly release you from all obligations to New Directions if one of the other publishers who want to take you on would repay New Directions for the outstanding advances that have not been earned. I gather you know what these amount to.

Your query about further monies due from Harcourt, Brace & Co. for the new edition of Louis Untermeyer's *Modern American Poetry—Modern British Poetry* has also taken some time, because the permissions copy of this book was sent to Norfolk by mistake. I have still not seen it, but Harcourt, Brace tells us over the telephone that there were no earlier poems by you reused in this edition. If you have evidence to the contrary, we will look into the matter deeper and prove them wrong, if this be the case. You will recall that in the check Irene and I gave you the last day you were in was included $13.50 for the use of "The Ballet of the Fifth Year," for which a new permission was given for this new edition.

Sincerely yours,
ROBERT M. MACGREGOR

198. TLS-2   November 9, 1955

[From Robert M. MacGregor]
DEAR DELMORE:

Rinehart & Company had gotten in touch with us, asking for a good deal of information and a good deal of work on our part in looking up copyright notices and such things on poems by you. In the process, Mrs. Wilson here discovered that fully half of the poems were from *Vaudeville for a Princess* and therefore we called Miss Lanning at Rinehart, since she had stated that they had received permission from you and all fees would be paid to you.

Actually what had me angry at first was that they expected us to do about half their research. But in the process they said and I now have a letter from Prof. George P. Elliott, editor of the anthology they will be publishing, stating that he had a letter from you dated January 11, 1955, in which you gave your permission and stated, "I own the copyrights and anthology rights on all my poems." What keeps?

I thought that our agreement was that we were to handle all anthology rights for you, withholding 10% as an agent when the books were out of print and keeping the usual fee for books that were in print. I can't understand your having forgotten this.

I can of course point out that this sort of action is not to your own best interests. You will recall that as far as the Untermeyer anthology is concerned, no further money was forthcoming to you because of a reuse of your poems in his new edition—because you had not properly protected yourself about this when you gave the original permission years ago. Rinehart intimates that you gave a blanket permission this time, as well, which allows them to go on using this poem or that in any revised edition edited by Mr. Elliott.

It also has Rinehart all worked up and caused us a great deal of extra trouble.

Yours ever,
ROBERT M. MACGREGOR

/ · /

Mrs. Wilson: JL's secretary at Intercultural Publications. She later went to New Directions.

anthology they will be publishing: Titled *15 Modern American Poets,* edited by George P. Elliott (Holt, Rinehart & Winston, 1956). Elliott (1918–1980) was a fiction writer, poet, and essayist teaching at Syracuse University, where Schwartz eventually would take his last teaching post.

199. TLS-2   RD1 Box 230
                                                            Pittstown, N.J.
                                                            Nov. 15, 1955

DEAR JAY:

The enclosed *billet doux* to MacGregor is sent to you rather than to him because, upon reflection, it seemed to me that it would cause needless trouble without accomplishing any purpose. Moreover, MacGregor's stupidity is so extreme that he might once again do what he has often before to others, exercise his natural enough resentment in a way which he was deluded enough to suppose would be unfortunate to the innocent bystanders. I doubt not at all that the enclosure will make unpleasant reading for you, but I hope not too unpleasant, and certainly less unpleasant than the deterioration which will continue unless you correct him, as you alone can, since he fears you more than death.

Before going on to other and related matters, I should say again, as in the enclosure, that each item and many more I do not mention, is a matter of simple verification. Thus someone who, I imagine, you respect a good deal and who is not an author at all, spoke of M. as "the stupidest man in New York." This seemed extreme to me, in view of the competition, just as the tendency to refer to him as the modern Robin Hood—stealing from the poor to help the rich—was inaccurate in another way, his benefits are directed to you alone and his depredations know no distinction of class, kind or economic rank. However the real point is that you may not believe me and you need not if you don't want to, since it is more desperate than I have represented and combined with your resistance to what you do not want to hear (a habit which you either did not have or concealed in the past), no one is going to tell you freely and without the assurance that you will not resent them rather than the culprit. The authority to whom I refer is someone you respect, for example, responded so violently to M. that you incurred a loss, the extent of which I do not know, but it probably would not seem desirable, in any case, apart from the matter of money; as things are now, you are not likely to be entirely held responsible for what occurs downtown—nor known, while uptown, by the character of the hirelings you employ. But the worth of ND is something again.

The two MacGregorian letters which deal with matters I answer—perhaps unclearly to you—are such as to suggest that you may very well have encouraged his rather uncharacteristic insolence of tone, either explicitly as a way of expressing your own displeasure indirectly or implicitly as a result of your habit, which we have in common has proved perhaps the sturdiest bond between us, of making snide unfavorable or condemnatory remarks about others when they do not represent your total attitude toward others, and even if they did, you would hardly want to base a course of behavior upon that attitude. MacGregor is too stupid not to misapprehend such expressions of mood and temperament whether directed at me or anyone else.

I was going to write a good deal more but the effort is quite tiring and the typing has to be done in bed, and besides you may not want to hear what I have to say, though I meant to dwell upon my feelings of admiration and love for you as well as other matters. At the moment I feel that if I persist, I may not only be wasting time by oppressing you with a hectic and intense emotion which is due to physical causes. I will say more unless requested; and pin my expectations on a time somewhere in the future, perhaps not too distant, when our friendship, which has been more and more inactive, can flourish without the corruptions of the world, the publishing world, high finance and low bank accounts. Though I think you must know, at times, how devoted I am to you, and though my devotion is very often reciprocated by an attitude the old timers must have had toward their favorite cuspidors, I forgive you as I would not another. . . . [Rest of letter missing]

200. TLS-1   December 9, 1955

[From Robert M. MacGregor]
DEAR DELMORE:

I think that you will agree with us that the situation has become patently absurd. It has been three months next Tuesday since you've been in to read manuscripts, and that day you were in for slightly less than an hour and a half and evidently didn't get finished the manuscripts that had been accumulating for two months since the week following the Fourth of July.

All this time, with what seems almost ridiculous patience, we have been sending you $25 every second week for work that just hasn't been done. Whatever your reasons, and I know that you have good ones, I am sure you will understand that New Directions cannot continue to pay out this money. You would be the first to admit that no other organization would have continued it so long.

When you are well again and organized to work regularly, I hope sincerely that you will be willing to come back and help us out. In the meantime I've had to make other arrangements.

Needless to say, Jay knows I'm writing this letter.

Yours ever,
ROBERT M. MACGREGOR

201. TLS-1   December 9, 1955

[From Robert M. MacGregor]
DEAR JAY:

I gather that Gertrude will have told you that I had the lock going in to New Directions offices changed today, and she has a new key for you as well as one herself. As you know, I didn't have it changed when we thought maybe it was a good idea some months ago, because the situation that seemed to call for it was eased. I had found out then that all one had to do was have the locksmith change the combination inside the lock and make new keys.

Gertrude particularly was of enormous help today. The locksmith couldn't come to the office, and when

Louis, the super, offered to remove the lock, she carried it to the locksmith, saving us several dollars I gather.

Throw your old key away if you can identify it. We turned ours in but didn't get more than a few pennies for each.

Needless to say, I did this right now because Delmore has a key.

B O B

/ · /

the situation: According to JL, there was never any thought that Schwartz might take something from the office. But his unexpected visits were often disruptive.

Gertrude: Gertrude Huston.

202. TLS-1
Gambier, Ohio
July 23, 1956

DEAR JAY:

I'm in the doldrums deep, so the enclosed is the best I can do. Sorry not to be able to be more helpful and hope to see you as soon as we get back.

Yours,
DELMORE

P.S. Have you ever thought of reprinting in the New Classics Kenneth Burke's *Toward a Better Life*? It's a wonderful piece of eloquence (somewhat like *Nightwood*) and Burke has an unpublished short synopsis of the narrative situation which would add a good deal to it. It came out in 1932 when everyone was too bewildered to pay attention to it, but now a reprint might get the recognition which the book deserves.

/ · /

Gambier, Ohio: Schwartz was teaching at Kenyon College School of Letters.

the enclosed: Contents unknown.

Nightwood: Novel by Djuna Barnes, first published in 1937, republished by ND in the New Classics Series (1946), with an introduction by T. S. Eliot.

203. TLS-1   February 3, 1961

[From Robert M. MacGregor]

JAY:

Robert Lowell had a footnote to the party at which Norman Mailer stabbed his wife. Seems Delmore was there, along with 200 others, and for several days he went around expressing outrage and the firm belief that Mailer had done this especially to harm Delmore's reputation.

Lowell evidently sees Delmore often, considers him one of his oldest and best friends, and suffers along with all this. Says it takes a lot of time, too much, in fact.

And a footnote to Delmore: A young man whose name I never remember but who came to see us about a job and got one at Doubleday and took over on the Schwartz poems after Jason left, told me at a party that Delmore became almost more than Doubleday with all its receptionists and personnel resources could handle. He was convinced, he said, that they were withholding money due him, and would appear threatening this young man or begging pitifully.

Finally when he yelled in a full reception room that he was being evicted because of their criminal cheating, they gave him a check but had him sign a letter that this was an advance against future earnings.

BOB

/ · /

Norman Mailer: (b. 1923), American novelist who allegedly stabbed his wife, Adele, at a party given by the Mailers in 1961.

the Schwartz poems: Schwartz had negotiated with Doubleday to publish his selected poems. The book appeared as *Summer Knowledge: New & Selected Poems, 1938–1958,* in 1959. At this time he was estranged from JL.

Jason: Editor Jason Epstein.

204. TELEGRAM-1   Syracuse, New York
                                       February 11, 1963

JAMES   LAUGHLIN,   PHONE   IMMY,   REPORT
DELIVERY
NEW DIRECTIONS 333 6 AVE NYC
HOW ABOUT SMOKING THE PEACE PIPE WITH ME
HERE IN SYRACUSE
DELMORE SKYLINE APTS JAMES AND LODI STS
SYRACUSE PHONE GR4-5311 APT 705

/ · /

Syracuse, New York: Schwartz was Visiting Professor of English at Syracuse University from 1962 to 1965, teaching fiction writing and courses in literature, including a seminar on Eliot and Joyce.

CODA

In his last years, Schwartz's drinking increased, his neurosis deepened, and he collapsed into paranoia. The latter state centered on claims of intricate schemes against him—usually involving usurpation of his wife, Elizabeth Pollet, by both Governor Nelson Rockefeller and President John F. Kennedy. Pollet left Schwartz in 1957 and obtained a divorce. Schwartz lived alone in a Village apartment. With the help of a friend, Elizabeth Reardon, he managed to assemble and submit a volume of selected poems to Doubleday, titled *Summer Knowledge*.[1] (New Directions was later to issue a paperback edition, which currently is in its ninth printing.) In 1961, Schwartz put together a second collection of stories, *Successful Love*. Still estranged from Laughlin, he offered it first to Farrar, Straus, and then to his friend Ted Wilentz of the Corinth Press, who published it. (That book has also been reissued in paperback, by Persea Books.)

Always in need of money, Schwartz was evicted from his apartment and was borrowing from friends. Finally, in 1962 he took his last teaching position, at Syracuse University in upstate New York. But he soon began to disappear sporadically. One such occasion was in January 1963, when it was announced that Robert Frost had died. Schwartz, whose first semester of teaching was not yet completed, ran into the English Department office, threw all his student papers on the desk of Chairman Sanford Brown Meech, and declared, *"You'll* have to correct these! I'm off to Frost's funeral!"* What "funeral" Schwartz attended is not clear; there was a private memorial service for Frost in Appleton Chapel of Memorial Church in Harvard Yard on January 31, two days after the poet's death.[2] The public memorial service was not held until February 17, in Johnson Chapel of Amherst College. In any case, Schwartz did not return to campus until the spring semester was well under way. His classes were covered by colleagues.

It was during this absence that Schwartz took a taxi all the way from Providence, Rhode Island, to Cambridge, Massachusetts, to drop in unexpectedly upon John Berryman at eight in the morning. He told the cab to wait while he paced Berryman's living room.

"Schwartz talked wildly about Nelson Rockefeller and about other unintelligible matters," according to John Berryman.[3] The reason he had come was obscure. "He was so *high* that he refused a drink—no drink was needed. He walked up and down the room shouting, 'Literature doesn't matter! The only thing that matters is money and getting your teeth fixed!' " After about an hour, Schwartz left by cab. He called Berryman at midnight that night—from New York City!

At Syracuse, Schwartz's teaching often was indifferent. As told by David H. Zucker, then a graduate student and teaching assistant, "He would come to class most often looking tormented, sallow, bloated, shuffling, and read aloud in a passionless voice, stalling for time and glancing repeatedly at his watch."[4]

Outside the classroom there were episodes of a threatening nature. That same January he called Victoria Bay, his latest woman friend, in Syracuse to tell her, from Cambridge, that "someone was coming to kill her."[5] She called Schwartz's office mate, Professor Donald A. Dike, for help. He and Dr. Meech went to her apartment house and while the stately, plump Meech guarded the lobby in case Schwartz appeared, she and Dike hastily packed her belongings. Then they drove her to the airport. Another day Schwartz chased the middle-aged secretary of the English Department, Elizabeth Allen, around her desk while he brandished a knife, accusing her of stealing from his office the manuscript of his new book of stories. There was such a manuscript; several colleagues had seen it. Where it went is unknown. Certainly, kindly Mrs. Allen did not take it; she would not have known what to do with it. She used to answer the office phone by saying: "English Department. Yah, this is her."

Eventually colleagues at the university urged Schwartz to commit himself to Twin Elms, a psychiatric center, where for a time he was helped. Schwartz did not pay his bills to Twin Elms, however, despite the fact that he was making a good salary—$16,000 a year in 1962—and had nearly $4,000 in his bank account. He paid for his drinks in the Orange, a campus bar, with hundred-dollar bills.

Next began a series of moves from one Syracuse apartment to another. Skyline Apartments on James Street, his first address, was elegant. His successive new lodgings were not. Sometimes he did not leave campus for his apartment at all, but spent the night on a sofa in the basement of the Hall of Languages. Then abruptly, in January 1966, he left the city and the university for the last time. He gave no notice, despite the English Department's having supported unanimously his recommendation for tenure at the end of the previous year. When he departed, Schwartz left behind all the books and manuscripts he had accumulated. They later appeared one day at the Syracuse University Library. No one knows who boxed and delivered them—a landlord, a woman friend, a colleague? The cartons also contained many unpaid bills and dozens of uncorrected examination papers by Schwartz's students. How students ever received grades for his courses is not known. (These effects—bills, examination papers, and all—have since joined the Delmore Schwartz Papers at the Beinecke Library, Yale University.)

Schwartz returned to Manhattan and registered at the Hotel Dixie, now the Hotel Carter, on West 42nd Street. He began the life of a virtual recluse. Some friends who glimpsed him preferred to maintain their distance. These included Saul Bellow, who later wrote in *Humboldt's Gift* (1975) of his Schwartz-like protagonist: "I knew that Humboldt would soon die because I had seen him on the street two months before and he had death all over him. He didn't see me. He was gray stout sick dusty, he had bought a pretzel stick and was eating it. His lunch. Concealed by a parked car, I watched. I didn't approach him. I felt it was impossible. . . ."[6]

Others who tried to be sociable were turned away, including Lou Reed, now a rock star, who had been a protégé of Schwartz's at Syracuse and part of "the round table" at the Orange bar where Schwartz had held court most evenings. Erin Clermont, another former student also now living in Manhattan, agreed to meet Schwartz for drinks at the Dixie. She describes him as looking "really bad. He had on a black raincoat which looked like it was covered with toothpaste stains. He looked like he had been on 42nd Street."[7] His conversation that night was largely about his dislike for everyone at Syracuse, and how many of them had been spies.

William Barrett, the philosopher, recalls a final glimpse of Schwartz in a Greenwich Village restaurant: "For a while his conversation was normal and quiet, but then there burst forth a Delmore I'd never heard, not even in his most agitated moments. He started to rant and rave. I'd always been able to follow the acute zigs and zags of his talk without any effort, but this time I found him incoherent. . . ."[8]

In time Schwartz left—or was evicted from—the Hotel Dixie and took up residence at the Columbia Hotel, at 70 West 46th Street near Sixth Avenue. He spent days in the Reading Room of the New York Public Library or furiously typing in his room. Evenings were spent in bars such as Cavanaugh's in Chelsea, and he got through insomniac nights and early mornings by reading *Pilgrim's Progress*, the *Kāma-Sūtra*, the poems of Hölderlin, and "girlie" magazines. At about three o'clock in the morning of July 11, 1966, while taking out the garbage from his room, he suffered a heart attack in the hotel hallway. His life might have been saved. He lay in that hallway on the fourth floor for over an hour before a resident finally called the desk to report that a man was "making strange noises" outside his door. The police were called first. They in turn called an ambulance. On the way to Roosevelt Hospital, Delmore Schwartz died.

So out of touch had he been with friends and family, he was not missed for two days. A reporter, "routinely reading over the morgue lists," recognized his name, and three days later a two-column obituary and photograph appeared in *The New York Times*.[9] It stated that Schwartz had spent his last days "in his room typing, and he used to order food from a nearby delicatessen."[10]

Described by Elizabeth Pollet, who edited his notebooks and journals for publication, Schwartz's late entries are "indecipherable." A final notebook, found in the Columbia Hotel room by Dwight Macdonald, contains the following harrowing lines:

> The poisonous world flows into my mouth
> Like water into a drowning man's.[11]

NOTES

1. Atlas, *Delmore Schwartz*, p. 350.

2. Lawrance Thompson, *Robert Frost: A Biography* (New York: Holt, Rinehart & Winston, 1981), p. 513.

3. John Haffenden, *The Life of John Berryman* (Boston: Routledge & Kegan Paul, 1982), p. 319.

4. Quoted in "Wasted Genius" by Steven Blank, *Syracuse Herald American,* June 13, 1982, pp. 10–12.

5. Atlas, *Delmore Schwartz*, p. 372.

6. Saul Bellow, *Humboldt's Gift* (New York: Farrar, Straus & Giroux, 1975), p. 7.

7. Quoted in Blank, "Wasted Genius."

8. William Barrett, *The Truants: Adventures Among the Intellectuals* (Garden City, N.Y.: Anchor Press, Doubleday, 1982), pp. 239–40.

9. Atlas, *Delmore Schwartz*, p. 376.

10. "Delmore Schwartz Dies at 52; Poet Won 1959 Bollingen Prize," *The New York Times,* July 14, 1966, p. 35.

11. *Portrait of Delmore: Journals and Notes of Delmore Schwartz,* ed. Pollet, p. 648.

INDEX